THE

LONG

AND

SHORT

OF

IT

THE

LONG

AND

SHORT

OF

IT

▮ FROM APHORISM TO NOVEL ▮

GARY SAUL MORSON

STANFORD UNIVERSITY PRESS ▮ STANFORD, CALIFORNIA

Stanford University Press
Stanford, California

Printed in the United States of America on acid-free, archival-quality paper

Library of Congress Cataloging-in-Publication Data

Morson, Gary Saul, 1948– author.
The long and short of it : from aphorism to novel / Gary Saul Morson.
   pages cm
Includes bibliographical references and index.
ISBN 978-0-8047-8051-3 (cloth : alk. paper) — ISBN 978-0-8047-8169-5 (pbk. : alk. paper)
1. Aphorisms and apothegms—History and criticism. 2. Wit and humor—History and criticism.
3. Epigram. 4. Literary form. I. Title.
PN6269.A2M67 2012
818'.602—dc23

2011039934

Typeset by Bruce Lundquist in 10/14 Minion

FOR KATIE

They were arguing about something complex and important, and neither one of them could convince the other. They did not agree about anything, and that made their dispute all the more engaging and endless.

—*Mikhail Bulgakov, The Master and Margarita*

CONTENTS

ACKNOWLEDGMENTS

Some thirty years ago, my former teacher, the late Martin Price, commenting on my first book, remarked that my style tended to the aphoristic and suggested that I might someday examine the form systematically. Around that time, I attended classes and lectures given by the University of Pennsylvania's Department of Folklore and Folklife and learned a great deal from Dan Ben-Amos, Barbara Kirshenblatt-Gimblett, and the late Dell Hymes. Along with two other scholars associated with that department, Phyllis Gorfain and Joanne Mulcahy, they taught me to appreciate proverbs, jokes, and folktales as much more interesting and complex than we usually suppose. The work of the late Thomas M. Greene helped me to understand the complexities of quotations, aphorisms, and their place in Renaissance literature. Caryl Emerson convinced me, but not well enough, that, as aphorisms must not be too long, so they must not be too plentiful.

When I finally began writing this book in the mid-1990s, I discussed its key ideas with Robert Alter, Jonathan Brent, and Joseph Epstein. They remain the implicit addressees of many passages below. In my understanding of the great aphoristic philosophers, I benefited greatly from discussions and correspondence with Bracht Branham, Walter Jost, Kenneth Seeskin, Meredith Williams, and Michael Williams. Three times I co-taught a course with the late Stephen Toulmin, and my understanding of Wittgenstein developed under his guidance. Stephen's influence on my thinking will be apparent to anyone who knows our work. I changed no less, but in different ways, from the profound and unique conversation of the late Aron Katsenelinboigen and from the wise and warm words of Kenneth Mischel.

More recently, I had the pleasure of co-teaching a course using some ideas from this book with Morton Schapiro, who, in his role as president of Northwestern University, has fostered the spirit and atmosphere in which great research and teaching thrive. His responses to my ideas inspired some changes of which he is still unaware.

Perhaps Bud Bynack, Michael Denner, Dilip Gaonkar, Robert Hariman, Robert Louis Jackson, Richard Kieckhefer, Lawrence Lipking, Daniel Lowenstein, Kathe Marshall, Susan McReynolds-Oddo, Barbara Newman, Clara Claiborne Park, Janice Pavel, Helen Tartar, and Herbert Tucker are also not fully aware of all they contributed.

Even more than my colleagues, my students revive, at painful moments of doubt, my sense of dedication and purpose. I know I will regret omitting some names which will come to mind only after this book has gone to press, but, notwithstanding that risk, let me record my gratitude to Lindsay Sargent Berg, Wendy Cheng, Nava Cohen, Andrew Gruen, Robert Gurley, Omar Hassan, John Mafi, Lori Singer Meyer, Matthew Morrison, Karthik Sivashanker, Trish Suchy, Andrew Thompson, Ryan Vogt, Christina Walker, Cindy Wang, and Annabel We.

Robert Belknap and the late Wayne Booth not only taught me a good deal about aphorisms but also, and much more important, offered unselfish help and served as scholarly role models. When difficulties with this manuscript drove me to near despair, I knew I could count on Elizabeth Cheresh Allen, Henry Carrigan, Thomas Marullo, Robin Feuer Miller, William Mills Todd, and Andrew Wachtel. I cannot express enough gratitude for all they did and wanted to do.

Northwestern University offered a congenial environment in which to think and work. As I wrote this book, I was always mindful of the support of Dan Linzer, the late Lawrence Dumas, and Marilyn McCoy. Nava Cohen, Catherine Grimstead, and Mark Ratner helped in ways that mattered more than they know.

In his reading for Stanford University Press, and in subsequent correspondence, Frederick Crews showed me places where changes were needed. Thomas Pavel, in his reading and subsequent comments, suggested especially insightful ways to make those changes. The result, at least to my mind, is a better book. Emily-Jane Cohen's confidence in this project ensured its completion and appearance.

Steven Blumenkranz's commentaries and advice have been a guide for some six decades. No matter how often I try, I am always at a loss to express all I owe, in so many ways, to Frances Padorr Brent and Jonathan Brent.

Not a day goes by when I do not think of some conversation with Michael André Bernstein, who died while this book was in press. When I would forget important things about myself, he would remember. I know no one wiser. And I am always guided by his refrain that what really matters is "to keep the conversation going." As I worked on this manuscript over the past few years, I also learned to admire, and admire still more, all that Dalya Sachs-Bernstein does every day.

It is hard to imagine saying what I have learned from Shirley Morson. Even ninety-three million years would be insufficient to express my care for Alexander Morson and Emily Morson.

Could either brevity or length suffice to express what I owe to my wife, Katie Porter?

ABBREVIATIONS

1001D	*The 1001 Dumbest Things Ever Said*, ed. Steven D. Price (Guilford, CT: Lyons Press, 2004).
776S	Ross and Kathryn Petras, *The 776 Stupidest Things Ever Said* (New York: Broadway, 1993).
ABPE	*The Anchor Bible: Proverbs, Ecclesiastes*, ed. and trans. R. B. Y. Scott (Garden City, NY: Doubleday, 1981).
AE	*The Adages of Erasmus*, ed. William Barker (Toronto: University of Toronto Press, 2001). The volume contains one introduction by the editor (ix–xlvii) and one by Erasmus (3–28), which first appeared in the 1508 edition.
AIW	Lewis Carroll, *Alice in Wonderland: Authoritative Texts of "Alice's Adventures in Wonderland," "Through the Looking Glass," and "The Hunting of the Snark,"* ed. Donald J. Gray (New York: Norton, 1971).
AK	Leo Tolstoy, *Anna Karenina*, the Garnett translation revised by Leonard J. Kent and Nina Berberova (New York: Modern Library, 1965).
AWD1/AWD2	Fyodor Dostoevsky, *A Writer's Diary*, trans. Kenneth Lantz, vol. 1 (Evanston, IL: Northwestern University Press, 1993); vol. 2 (Evanston, IL: Northwestern University Press, 1994).
BBA	*Bartlett's Book of Anecdotes*, ed. Clifton Fadiman and André Bernard (Boston: Little, Brown, 2000).
BFQ15	John Bartlett, *Familiar Quotations: A Collection of Passages, Phrases, and Proverbs Traced to Their Sources in Ancient and Modern Literature*, 15th ed., ed. Emily Morison Beck (Boston: Little, Brown, 1980).

BK	Fyodor Dostoevsky, *The Brothers Karamazov*, trans. Constance Garnett (New York: Modern Library, 1994).
BOG	Gary Saul Morson, *The Boundaries of Genre: Dostoevsky's "Diary of a Writer" and the Traditions of Literary Utiopia* (Austin: University of Texas Press, 1981).
BOP	*The Book of Psalms: A Translation with Commentary*, ed. and trans. Robert Alter (New York: Norton, 2007).
BWA	*The Basic Works of Aristotle*, ed. Richard McKeon (New York: Random House, 1941).
C&P	Fyodor Dostoevsky, *Crime and Punishment* (New York: Modern Library, 1994).
CCAS	*Chinese Civilization: A Sourcebook*, 2nd ed., ed. Patricia Buckley Ebrey (New York: Free Press, 1993).
CEM	*The Complete Essays of Montaigne*, trans. Donald Frame (Stanford: Stanford University Press, 1965).
CHQ	*Cassell's Humourous Quotations*, ed. Nigel Rees (London: Cassell, 2003).
CWA2	*The Complete Works of Aristotle*, vol. 2, ed. Jonathan Barnes (Princeton, NJ: Princeton University Press, 1985).
DAF	Edward Gibbon, *The History of the Decline and Fall of the Roman Empire*, ed. J. B. Bury (New York: Heritage, 1946).
DD	Ambrose Bierce, *The Devil's Dictionary* (Garden City, NY: Doubleday, n.d.).
DI	M. M. Bakhtin, *The Dialogic Imagination: Four Essays*, ed. Michael Holquist, trans. Caryl Emerson and Michael Holquist (Austin: University of Texas Press, 1981).
DL1/DL2	Diogenes Laertius, *Lives of Eminent Philosophers*, trans. R. D. Hicks, vols. 1 and 2 (Cambridge, MA: Harvard University Press, 1995).
DPQ	*A Dictionary of Philosophical Quotations*, ed. A. J. Ayer and Jane O'Grady (Oxford: Blackwell, 1999).
DSQ	*A Dictionary of Scientific Quotations*, ed. Alan L. Mackay (Bristol, UK: Institute of Physics Publishing, 1991).

EPP	*English Prose and Poetry, 1660–1800: A Selection*, ed. Frank Brady and Martin Price (New York: Holt, Rinehart and Winston, 1961).
F&S	Ivan Turgenev, *Fathers and Sons*, ed. Ralph E. Matlaw (New York: Norton, 1966).
GSW	Leo Tolstoy, *Great Short Works*, trans. Louise and Aylmer Maude (New York: Harper and Row, 1967).
H	Herodotus, *The History*, trans. Henry Cary (Buffalo, NY: Prometheus, 1992).
HATH	Friedrich Nietzsche, *Human, All Too Human: A Book for Free Spirits*, trans. Marion Faber with Stephen Lehmann (Lincoln: University of Nebraska Press, 1984).
HBC	*Harper's Bible Commentary*, ed. James L. May et al. (San Francisco: HarperCollins, 1988).
HIQ	*History in Quotations*, ed. M. J. Cohen and John Major (London: Cassell, 2004).
I	Fyodor Dostoevsky, *The Idiot*, trans. Constance Garnett (New York: Modern Library, 1962).
IBE	Oscar Wilde, *The Importance of Being Earnest and Other Plays*, ed. Peter Raby (New York: Oxford University Press, 2008).
LaR	*The Maxims of La Rochefoucauld*, trans. Louis Kronenberger (New York: Random House, 1959). I have occasionally modified the translation according to the French version in François, duc de La Rochefoucauld, *Maximes et réflexions morales du duc de La Rochefoucauld* (Paris: Ménard et Desenne, fils, 1817; repr., Nabu Public Domain Reprints, n.d.).
LTSS	Leo Tolstoy, *Short Stories*, ed. Ernest J. Simmons (New York: Modern Library, 1964).
M&E	Karl Marx and Friedrich Engels, *Basic Writings on Politics and Philosophy*, ed. Lewis S. Feuer (Garden City, NY: Doubleday, 1959).
MBCP	Gary Saul Morson and Caryl Emerson, *Mikhail Bakhtin: Creation of a Prosaics* (Stanford: Stanford University Press, 1990).
MDQ	*The Macmillan Dictionary of Quotations*, ed. John Dainith et al. (Edison, NJ: Chartwell, 2000).

MM	George Eliot, *Middlemarch* (New York: Modern Library, 1984).
N&F	Gary Saul Morson, *Narrative and Freedom: The Shadows of Time* (New Haven, CT: Yale University Press, 1994).
NFU	Fyodor Dostoevsky, *"Notes from Underground" and "The Grand Inquisitor,"* ed. Ralph Matlaw (New York: Dutton, 1960).
OBA	*The Oxford Book of Aphorisms*, ed. John Gross (Oxford: Oxford University Press, 1987).
ODHQ	*The Oxford Dictionary of Humorous Quotations*, ed. Neil Sherrin (Oxford: Oxford University Press, 1995).
ODPQ	*The Oxford Dictionary of Political Quotations*, 2nd ed., ed. Anthony Jay (Oxford: Oxford University Press, 2001).
ODQ	*The Oxford Dictionary of Quotations*, 6th ed., ed. Elizabeth Knowles (Oxford: Oxford University Press, 2004).
ODSQ	*The Oxford Dictionary of Scientific Quotations*, ed. W. F. Bynum and Roy Porter (Oxford: Oxford University Press, 2005).
OTK	Sophocles, *Oedipus the King*, trans. Bernard Knox, in *Man and His Fictions: An Introduction to Fiction-Making, Its Forms and Uses*, ed. Alvin B. Kernan, Peter Brooks, and J. Michael Holquist (New York: Harcourt Brace, 1973), 355–86.
P	Blaise Pascal, *Pensées*, trans. A. J. Krailsheimer (Harmondsworth, UK: Penguin, 1987).
PDE	*The Penguin Dictionary of Epigrams*, ed. M. J. Cohen (New York: Penguin, 2001).
PDP	Mikhail Bakhtin, *Problems of Dostoevsky's Poetics*, ed. and trans. Caryl Emerson (Minneapolis: University of Minnesota Press, 1984).
PI	Ludwig Wittgenstein, *Philosophical Investigations*, 3rd ed., trans. G. E. M. Anscombe (New York: Macmillan, 1958).
PL	Plutarch, *The Lives of the Noble Grecians and Romans*, trans. John Dryden, rev. Arthur Hugh Clough (New York: Modern Library, n.d.).
PPC	*Products of the Perfected Civilization: Selected Writings of Chamfort*, trans. W. S. Merwin (New York: Macmillan, 1969).

PSS	L. N. Tolstoi, *Polnoe sobranie sochinenii* [Complete works], 90 vols., ed. V. G. Chertkov et al. (Moscow: Khudozhestvennaia literatura, 1929–58). Translations of Tolstoy's works have been amended by comparison with the Russian text in this standard edition. Where no translator is indicated, the translation is my own.
PSSVTT	F. M. Dostoevskii, *Polnoe sobranie sochinenii v tridtsati tomakh* [Complete works in thirty volumes] (Leningrad: Nauka, 1972–90). Where no translator is indicated, the translation is my own.
PU	*Platitudes Undone: A Facsimile Edition of "Platitudes in the Making: Precepts and Advice for Gentlefolk" by Holbrook Jackson with the Original Handwritten Responses of G. K. Chesterton* (San Francisco: Ignatius, 1997).
RAGP	*Readings in Ancient Greek Philosophy: From Thales to Plato*, ed. S. Marc Cohen, Patricia Curd, and C. D. C. Reeve (Indianapolis, IN: Hackett, 1995).
SCT	*Sources of Chinese Tradition*, 2nd ed., vol. 1, *From the Earliest Times to 1600*, comp. William Theodore de Bary and Irene Bloom (New York: Columbia University Press, 1999).
SJ	Samuel Johnson, *"Rasselas," Poems, and Selected Prose*, ed. Bertrand H. Bronson (New York: Holt, Rinehart and Winston, 1966).
SO	*The Stuffed Owl: An Anthology of Bad Verse*, ed. D. B. Wyndham Lewis and Charles Lee (New York: New York Review Books, 2009).
SSQ	*The Macmillan Book of Social Science Quotations*, ed. David L. Sills and Robert K. Merton (New York: Macmillan, 1991).
TC	Leo Tolstoy, *"A Confession," "The Gospel in Brief," and "What I Believe,"* trans. Aylmer Maude (London: Oxford University Press, 1971).
TI	Friedrich Nietzsche, *"Twilight of the Idols" and "The Anti-Christ,"* trans. R. J. Hollingdale (London: Penguin, 1990).
TLP	Ludwig Wittgenstein, *Tractatus Logico-Philosophicus*, trans. D. F. Pears and B. F. McGuinness (London: Routledge, 1977).
TRE	Leo Tolstoy, *Recollections and Essays*, trans. Aylmer Maude (London: Oxford University Press, 1961).

TTC	Lao Tzu, *Tao Te Ching*, trans. D. C. Lao (London: Penguin, 1963).
V	*The Portable Voltaire*, ed. Ben Ray Redman (New York: Viking, 1963).
VLR	Mardy Grothe, *Viva la Repartee* (New York: HarperCollins, 2005).
W&P	Leo Tolstoy, *War and Peace*, trans. Ann Dunnigan (New York: Signet, 1968).
WBS	*The Wisdom of Ben Sira*, trans. Patrick W. Skehan, ed. Alexander A. Di Lella, Anchor Bible, vol. 39 (New York: Doubleday, 1987).
WGS	*The World's Great Speeches*, 3rd ed., ed. Lewis Copeland and Lawrence W. Lamm (New York: Dover, 1973).
WIA	Leo N. Tolstoy, *What Is Art?*, trans. Aylmer Maude (New York: Bobbs-Merrill, 1960).
YB	Yogi Berra, *The Yogi Book: "I Really Didn't Say Everything I Said"* (New York: Workman, 1998).
YBQ	*The Yale Book of Quotations*, ed. Fred R. Shapiro (New Haven, CT: Yale University Press, 2006).

Translations have occasionally been modified for accuracy.

When no translation for a Biblical quotation is given, the source is the King James Version. I use "KJV" for the King James Version only when citing more than one translation.

THE
LONG
AND
SHORT
OF
IT

The Long and Short of It

"All happy families resemble each other; each unhappy family is unhappy in its own way."

Tolstoy's famous aphorism has long led a double life. Those who have read *Anna Karenina* remember it as the opening sentence of a great novel about love and families. But many who could not locate its source still recognize the line.

We all know countless aphorisms or famous short expressions of various sorts: ringing pronouncements, dark sayings, witticisms, maxims, proverbs, and many more. We browse anthologies and encyclopedias in search of them. We repeat witty responses made on the spur of the moment by Churchill, Shaw, or Dorothy Parker. Conservatives cite the wisdom of Burke and Hayek, liberals know inspiring lines of Franklin Delano Roosevelt and John F. Kennedy, and radicals can quote Marx and Engels. Graduate students in literature acquire famous sayings by Nietzsche, Freud, Derrida, and others, while philosophers learn to recognize the best-known aphorisms from Wittgenstein. People who rarely read long books, or even short stories, still appreciate the greatest examples of the shortest literary genres.

I have long been fascinated by these short genres. They seem to lie just where my heart is, somewhere between literature and philosophy. It may seem odd that someone could have written a book on *War and Peace* and yet be fascinated by the shortest literary genres, often no longer than a line. But both great philosophical novels and aphorisms work simultaneously as literature and philosophy, and each demands both literary and philosophical analysis to be properly understood. Tolstoy himself loved short forms, which, as we will see, he translated, combined into anthologies, and deployed strategically in his fiction. To be sure, some aphoristic genres seem to be more literary and others more philosophical, but, taken as a group, short genres may be viewed as lying on an implicit continuum between literature and philosophy.

"The aphorism, the apothegm, in which I am the first master among Germans, are the forms of eternity," proclaimed Nietzsche in *Twilight of the Idols.* "My ambition is to say in ten sentences what everyone else says in a book— what everyone else *does not* say in a book" (*TI*, 115). As Nietzsche well knew, numerous other philosophers, sages, and thinkers—from antiquity to the present, and from China to America—had exploited brevity. The thoughts of some wise men, like Greece's "Seven Sages," have survived as exemplary aphorisms and have attracted countless imitators. Other great thinkers included detachable aphorisms in longer works or made longer works from aphorisms in sequence. From the book of Lao Tzu to Wittgenstein's *Philosophical Investigations*, classic philosophical works have developed the possibilities of the aphorism.

So have philosophically inclined literary works. Alexander Pope explicitly constructed his *Essay on Man* and *Essay on Criticism* so as to be both readable as a whole and detachable for separate aphoristic couplets. Much the same can be said of Samuel Johnson's great philosophical meditation, "The Vanity of Human Wishes." Johnson's novel, *Rasselas*, uses a story concerning the quest for the best way to live as a vehicle for one famous aphorism after another. An aphoristic sensibility shapes the very essence of these masterpieces.

The lives of such writers often seem like a series of opportunities for aphorisms. Boswell's *Life of Johnson* reveals the great man's character through his sardonic maxims, witticisms, and pithy comments. In antiquity, Diogenes Laertius's *Lives of Eminent Philosophers* and Plutarch's *Lives of the Noble Greeks and Romans* work in much the same way, and, indeed, it is through such biographies, especially Diogenes Laertius's, that the sayings of many great philosophers have been preserved.[1] As philosophers, they are aphorists, and as aphorists, philosophers.

From Herodotus and Thucydides to Gibbon, great histories that have survived as literary masterpieces have also relied on detachable aphorisms. If we are willing to include comments up to a paragraph long, then we can discover many remarkable ones in George Eliot and Dostoevsky as well as in Tolstoy. Philosophical novels, including those elucidating the complexities of psychology, offer wise sayings and maxims in the course of narrating particular characters' actions. That is why so many readers have been able to read Dostoevsky's works as narrative guides to the dark side of the soul. These novelists are often supremely aware of aphorisms as whole works, such as those of La Rochefoucauld, as well as of their use by earlier novelists and historians. George Eliot cited, and Tolstoy translated, masters of the short form. Some of Dostoevsky's characters live as if they believe that a life can be redeemed if it results in a single brilliant aphorism.

Many of the best-known short literary works belong to the category specialists have called "wisdom literature." The oldest Western book we have, *The Instructions of Ptah-hotep*, consists of maxims, and it is obvious why such brief sayings, originally preserved by spoken repetition, would be the first works preserved. The Bible contains examples of wise sayings counseling prudence and justice, many collected in the books of Proverbs and Psalms. It also contains counter-wisdom about the futility of all things, such as the most famous lines in Ecclesiastes. Whether in the form of proverbs or pronouncements of great thinkers, wise sayings continue to be coined and still play an important part in our lives. As the first philosophy and the first literature, they seem never to go out of style.

Other short forms have a distinctly practical intent. In a moment of crisis, they summon us to action. These ringing lines demand we live up to our highest values. Like wise sayings, they eventually become part of the informal philosophy that makes a people what it is, or, rather, aspires to be. When repeated in later years, they become a central part of a people's literature.

■ ■ ■

Although aphorisms constitute the shortest literary genres, they rarely attract serious study. Universities give courses on the novel, epic, and lyric, while drama is often taught as a family of genres including comedy, tragedy, and melodrama. But I know of no course on the family of genres including proverbs, wise sayings, witticisms, and maxims. The explanation can hardly be the relative fame of the authors, because many aphorisms come from the very same well-known authors: Shakespeare, Pope, Voltaire, Jane Austen, and Tolstoy, for instance. Some authors best known for their pithy sayings or witticisms stand as true literary geniuses, such as Kraus, Chamfort, and La Rochefoucauld. The canon of great aphorists also includes La Bruyère, Lichtenberg, Nietzsche, Gracián, Vauvenargues, Joubert, Schopenhauer, Ambrose Bierce, Francis Bacon, and Samuel Johnson. As much as any author of epic poetry, these authors demonstrated keen awareness of writing in a tradition. Canetti observed that "the great writers of aphorisms read as if they had all known each other well" (*OBA*, 364).

The present study examines the aphorists' relationships with each other. If it succeeds, it will show why these short works repay serious study. The very fact that aphorisms figure so prominently in our speech and writing demonstrates the pleasure, however guilty, we take in them. It is as if we hid our taste for them under a bushel, instead of displaying unapologetic appreciation. If we did, we would see the many complex ways in which different genres of short literature work, the fascinating dialogues that have developed among them, and the inventive techniques by which longer masterpieces have included them. Above all, we would grasp the distinctive wisdom aphorisms offer.

■ ■ ■

Even the most cursory examination of the topic will convince us that there is no agreed-upon definition of terms such as "aphorism," "saying," "apothegm," or "maxim." Meanings vary even more than with such controversial designations as "novel" and "epic." Aphorisms sometimes include all short works, sometimes just those examples that have an author, and sometimes only a small subset that may be variously identified either by tone, form, or idea. One man's aphorism is another man's maxim. Etymology rarely helps, since the meanings of terms shift radically over ages and cultures. Hippocrates' aphorisms would not be called that today. They are closer to what we might call maxims, while the works La Rochefoucauld called maxims bear little resemblance to maxims as we usually think of them. If one struggles to arrive at the true meaning of these terms, one will surely be lost in an endless labyrinth.

I therefore prefer to classify the works themselves and then, merely for the sake of consistent usage, apply a term to each class—with the understanding that a different term could have been chosen and that I am not trying to regulate the proper use of terms. With this proviso, I will use the term "aphorism" to refer to the entire family of short genres, although others may prefer a different designation. But how shall the works themselves be classified?

Like arguments over terminology, classification debates may seem pointless, and yet, as thinkers from Aristotle to Linnaeus and Darwin have understood, one can often best understand a range of phenomena by first examining its types. If nomenclature proves less than helpful in doing so and the phenomena lend themselves to different groupings, one needs to reflect on *why* one is interested in the phenomena in the first place. Articulating the questions one hopes to answer also helps. Only by deciding on the sort of thing one is looking for can one hope to find it. There is no single correct way of classifying genres. Rather, principles of classification properly depend on the reasons for classifying. Different purposes demand different classifications.

Let me be clear: I do not aspire to be the Northrop Frye of short genres and offer the definitive classification to supplant or forestall all others. Because classification depends on purpose, I regard the idea of a single true system, irrespective of purpose, as intellectually muddled. Choose a different set of questions, and you will arrive at a different classification.

The purpose that guides this study resembles the one that has guided my earlier studies of great writers and works. I most often read literature as a source of wisdom and insight, and I have long been attracted to the shortest works for this reason. The best seem to capture important facts about experience, thought, and human nature. That is presumably why, in almost all cultures, the most widely represented, as well as the earliest, short genres consist of "wise sayings," essential truths meant to be passed on to subsequent generations. This form is far from my favorite, but not because I reject its aspiration to wisdom. Rather, I find still greater wisdom in other genres, some critical of the wise saying's assumptions.

Given my preferences, I decided to classify genres according to their worldviews, the distinct sense of human experience that each conveys. How does each genre imagine life, what does it value, to whom does it appeal and why? When genres dispute each other, what issues shape their disagreement? What kinds of arguments do they use and to what emotions do they appeal? What forms of expression does each genre find most suitable and most effective?

I largely share Mikhail Bakhtin's approach to genres as "form-shaping ideologies," that is, as worldviews seeking expression.[2] It is an approach admirably suited for genres lying on the continuum from literature to philosophy. So understood, formal features do not define a genre but follow from the sense of experience that does. Given certain beliefs and values, genres seek out appropriate forms of rhetoric. Over time, they develop sets of tacit but recognized conventions and assumptions. With short genres, these conventions and assumptions play an especially large role because brevity does not allow for much to be explicitly stated.

Brevity can have surprising consequences. We shall see that short genres typically presume a particular social setting, a distinct role for the reader or audience, and a specific attitude to the moment of uttering. Time, knowledge, and self-knowledge prove to be recurrent topics that each genre approaches in its own ways.

For every occasion there is a genre: a kind that laughs and a kind that despairs; a kind that voices public defiance and a kind that meditates alone; a kind that wonders and a kind that banishes wonder; a kind that is intensely personal and a kind summoning the whole people; a kind that displays remarkable quick-wittedness and a kind that exhibits epic stupidity; a kind that is amazed at the world beyond and a kind that is fascinated by the most prosaic, unhistoric acts of daily life.

We shall examine each of these short genres as well as the ways in which they interact. Like philosophers from diverse schools or theologians representing rival orthodoxies, aphoristic genres enter into dialogue, sometimes friendly and sometimes hostile. Those dialogues shape future works, which contribute to the ongoing conversation among worldviews. Aphorisms of one genre quote or allude to other genres in order to comment on them, and those others, aware of such commentary, respond.

World literature is a great symposium, and we are invited to the banquet. With short genres, it is a banquet of delicious morsels.

■ ■ ■

The first chapter of this study raises some general questions of literary classification and the ways in which genres interact. Then in the following chapters I consider pairs of genres related to each other in interesting ways, usually as opposites or dialogic antagonists.

I first consider the type of aphorism I call "apothegms" (in a special sense).[3] These intriguing works picture the world as fundamentally mysterious and so contrast with "dicta," which purport to have at last resolved all mystery. To illuminate these opposing genres, I also consider a number of related forms, such as the "riddle" and what I call the "hypothesis."

The next chapter considers the varieties of wit and witlessness. I begin with the philosophy conveyed by great witticisms, the kind of intelligence they value, and the view of life they implicitly or explicitly endorse. I contrast these gems with comments that have survived for the opposite reason, their remarkable stupidity or inarticulateness: like the sublime ineptness of Inspector Clouseau, these comments rise (or fall) to their own unexpected splendor. The Clouseau principle governs what I call the "witlessisms" of Sir Boyle Roche, Dan Quayle,

and many other negative paragons. Some witlessisms, such as those made famous by Yogi Berra and Sam Goldwyn, turn out to be readable as paradoxical
expressions of real wisdom. Although these paradoxes are unintentional, some
authors have fabricated them deliberately by assuming a witless persona who,
in sincere silliness, voices an important point. Mark Twain stands as the great
master of such inspired innocence.

The oldest and most commonly used aphoristic genre is the "wise saying":
the pronouncements of sages and the anonymous wisdom of past generations
that circulate as proverbs. As the biblical book of Proverbs repeatedly tells us,
nothing could be more important than "to know wisdom and instruction, to
perceive the words of understanding . . . [t]o understand a proverb, and the
interpretation; the words of the wise, and their dark sayings" (Proverbs 1:2–6).
Wise sayings typically view the world as providential, guaranteeing reward for
prudence and righteousness.

Such optimism provokes the ire or contempt of a more skeptical genre,
which questions the rationality of the world and stresses the numerous ways in
which the supposedly wise, no less than the rest of us, arrange to see only what
they want to see. In the Bible, the moral calculus of Proverbs, Psalms, and some
other books is answered in Ecclesiastes and debated in Job. La Rochefoucauld
counters the sages and moralists with masterful explorations of human vanity
and self-deception.

Borrowing the term used by La Rochefoucauld, I call these works "maxims"
(or occasionally, "sardonic maxims"). Maxims unmask vanity, self-deception,
and egoism disguised as virtue. Of course, one may unmask others' egoism to
feed one's own. Self-deception ambushes those who expose self-deception. The
best maximists avoid the trap of exempting themselves from the scrutiny they
direct at opponents. Nietzsche, Kraus, Guicciardini, Bierce, and others appeal
to the disillusioned psychologists among us, and their maxims seem to gain in
force as we age.

At times of crisis, when a group's survival is threatened, great orators and
heroes encourage the people with the sort of ringing words we all learn at
school. Later in life, these words may seem childish to some but even more
inspiring to others. If a new crisis arises, an orator may use earlier models to
formulate sayings encouraging the people. Reminding them of the best of their
tradition, or inventing that tradition under the guise of reminding them, the
orator summons the people to meet the challenge. The "summons," as I call
this form, was popular in antiquity and figures in more recent national his-

tories. Europeans know Pericles, and the genre he exemplifies includes great lines spoken, or occasionally written, by Thomas Paine, Napoleon, Admiral Nelson, the Duke of Wellington, Abraham Lincoln, and Winston Churchill. In the times that try men's souls, these orators may offer nothing but blood, sweat, and tears.

The summons constitutes one kind of literature of trial. The form of trial I call the "thought" could not differ more. While the summons tends to be perfectly polished and is pronounced before a public audience on a solemn occasion, the thought offers a private meditation, still incomplete and tentative, as it first occurred to the author. This trial—in the sense of a trying out—experiments as it goes along. Thoughts therefore tend to be rather diffuse and to test the criterion of brevity characterizing short genres as a group. They are barely memorizable or not memorizable at all, and yet, by their very testing of the norm, they affirm it. Anthologies of aphorisms, perhaps somewhat apologetically, often include them.

Thoughts fascinate by their capacity to reveal the very process of thinking and to show ideas when they could still be developed in many different ways. They are typically collected and published by others, or, if not, are written to resemble those that have been. Lichtenberg, Pascal, and Nietzsche have offered impressive thoughts that invite us to extend them in new directions. They call to mind *how* we think—or at least how we might hope to think—when meditating on a question that truly matters.

In the last chapter, I return to the form I call apothegms. Instead of contrasting apothegms as I have described them with an antithetical genre, I juxtapose them to apothegms of a different type. "Mystical apothegms," as I retrospectively rename the ones discussed in Chapter 2, regard the world as ultimately beyond our ken because it is based on principles transcending language and defying the very categories with which we think. By contrast, "prosaic apothegms" trace the inadequacy of mind not to otherworldly mystery but to thoroughly mundane complexity.

Montaigne, Guicciardini, Lichtenberg, George Eliot, and other masters of the prosaic apothegm (let us call them apothists) show how our minds tend to simplify the sheer multiplicity and variety of the world. At least when we are dealing with human beings, causes do not reduce to a few underlying laws. Everything shifts before our eyes in unpredictable ways. Inherently skeptical, prosaic apothegms teach us to suspect hasty generalizations and to perceive ever finer distinctions.

If a genre can be said to be a hero, then the hero of this book is the prosaic apothegm and the longer forms it generates, especially a particular type of realist fiction I call the prosaic novel. The reader will not be surprised to learn that the world's greatest prosaic novels include *War and Peace* and *Anna Karenina*.

▪ ▪ ▪

In the *Rhetoric,* Aristotle explains that truths not amenable to logical proof may be demonstrated more or less persuasively in two distinct ways: by a brief statement (or enthymeme) or by an extended example (or case study). The former appeals to the deductive, and the latter to the inductive, spirit.[4] It is also possible to combine the two methods. A long work may tell a story to illustrate an insight. The insight may demand such expansion not only to exemplify it but also to show its complex implications.

For much the same reasons, a short genre typically has a longer counterpart (often more than one). A given worldview may be developed aphoristically or at length. We can best understand each by considering the other. A longer work may explore the worldview of a shorter one and contain many examples of it. That is one reason so many aphorisms come from longer works.

Sometimes the relationship between short genre and longer work may be relatively simple, as Aesop's fables illustrate a moral and as Oscar Wilde's play *The Importance of Being Earnest* serves as a vehicle for witticisms. At other times the relationship turns out to be considerably more complex. Gibbon's *Decline and Fall of the Roman Empire* contains many brilliant sardonic maxims, but it does considerably more. Maxims themselves achieve a new richness as Gibbon's very long book deploys them. In *Middlemarch*, George Eliot formulates maxims worthy of La Rochefoucauld and apothegms as good as Samuel Johnson's. But the book could hardly be considered just an expansion of these.

The very fact that some long works contain examples of more than one short genre illustrates one way in which aphorisms can be developed. The author of a long work can take the side of one genre against another or create an unresolved dialogue among several of them. Many short genres play a role in *War and Peace.* Although this work respectfully explores the wisdom of proverbs, maxims, and apothegms, Tolstoy treats the summons with irony and the witticism with contempt. Tolstoy regarded the sense of life expressed by witticisms as supremely shallow for valuing mere cleverness above all else.

To illustrate how short genres relate to long ones, each chapter of the present study considers, along with a short form, its longer relatives. I hope that the discussion of each illuminates the other and that it will become clear why an understanding of short works opens new perspectives on longer ones.

■ ■ ■

I remember my surprise at discovering that the author of *War and Peace* was fascinated by literature's shortest forms. Three thick volumes of Tolstoy's complete works contain his published and unpublished anthologies of aphorisms. He translated La Rochefoucauld, La Bruyère, Lao Tzu (from a French version), and many other masters of short forms. In his *Circle of Reading*, an anthology with aphorisms for each day of the year, he also included weekly short stories to develop the insights of short sayings.

Some of Tolstoy's later tales explicitly develop the implications of well-known sayings, which they take as titles. Those tales include some of his greatest, such as "God Sees the Truth, but Waits to Tell," which I discuss in the chapter on wise sayings. We have seen that *Anna Karenina* exemplifies an aphorism by following it with a lengthy narrative, which in turn contains examples of many short forms. Tolstoy grasped the relations of short genres to long ones better than any writer I know, and so, in my discussions of that topic, his works appear especially frequently.

The present volume therefore has three goals. It offers a discussion of several fascinating short genres, the worldviews they express, and the forms with which they express them. It also explores the relation of each genre's sense of the world to other genres or long works developing that sense. Finally, those interested in Tolstoy will discover the relation of his pithy sayings to his longer works and a new way of understanding his masterpieces. If we indulge a taste for paradox, we might say that *War and Peace* is the longest apothegm in the world.

■ ■ ■

It may seem odd to find so many types of works consisting of only a few sentences or less. In fact, aphorisms come in many more kinds than I have had the space to discuss. Short genres evidently can display considerable variety. Concision itself offers opportunities as well as constraints.

All short genres are brief, but each short genre is brief in its own way.

GENRE AND BREVITY

Genres and Species

Like anything else, literary works may be classified in many ways. It is not difficult to discover a large number of sensible orderings of works by genre.

Consider the analogy of species. By the eighteenth century, it was clear that any classification system assigning a single, agreed-upon name to a given group of organisms was better than no system at all. Researchers could then be sure that their terms had the same referent. The same logic applied to groups of species, and to groups of groups of species, in an ascending hierarchy. Systems also recommended themselves by ease of use.

These two criteria—consistency of terms and ease of use—allow for an indefinitely large number of classification schemes. But it was also felt that classification ought somehow to conform to nature itself. Presumably, this third criterion could single out a best system.

Linneaus hoped to develop a nonarbitrary classification system for plants and animals. He wanted not only to give each species an unambiguous designation but also to discover the order genuinely present. Such a "natural" system would reflect the way species are arranged in the mind of God. What exactly that meant was not especially clear.

Reflecting on the history of classification, Darwin remarked, in the first edition of *The Origin of Species*, on the vagueness of the ideal of a natural system:

> From the first dawn of life, all organic beings are found to resemble each other
> in descending degrees, so that they may be classed in groups under groups. This

classification is evidently not arbitrary like the grouping of stars in constella-
tions. . . . Naturalists try to arrange the species, genera, and families in each
class, on what is called the Natural System: But what is meant by this system?
. . . [M]any naturalists think . . . that it reveals the plan of the Creator; but unless
it be specified whether order in time or space, or what else is meant by the plan
of the Creator, it seems to me that nothing is added to our knowledge.[1]

Evidently the Creator, too, could have classified his creations in different ways
depending on the principle he chose. Unless we know that principle, nothing is
gained by appealing to His mind.

Resemblance by itself is not an adequate principle, since organisms resembling each other in some features differ in others. Mere counting of common
features will not do inasmuch as some features seem much more important
than others.

Nature loves to hide.

Darwin argued that there actually is a natural classification system and that
Linneaus, by instinct and experience, came pretty close to it. The "natural system," Darwin argues, is "genealogical" and so "community of descent is the hidden bond which naturalists have been unconsciously seeking" (Darwin, 420). In
referring to species as "related," Linneaus thought he was speaking metaphorically, but he needed to take the metaphor literally. Today if someone should ask,
why is the chosen system better than any other?—what purpose does it serve
better than the alternatives?—an answer is ready: it illuminates the structure,
habits, and distribution of organisms by tracing their history.

Genres Differ from Species

No biologist today would use any other system. But there is no equivalent natural system of literary genres, nor is it likely there ever could be. Unlike organisms, significant literary works rarely, if ever, display a single line of descent.
Parentage is multiple.

No animal descends from sheep, trout, and sparrow, but it is not hard to
find compositions that descend from epic, romance, and novel. Fielding famously called *Tom Jones* a comic epic in prose. The subtitle of Gogol's *Dead
Souls* is "Poema" (a poem), but the narrator also calls it (or alludes to it as) a
satire, a romance, a novel, and a comedy modeled on Dante.

When species die out, they are extinct forever, but extinct genres rise again.

In a way that has no biological analog, the names of genres may shape their
development. Animals do not evolve depending on our nomenclature, but a

period's definition of epic may shape the "epics" it produces. Classifiers shape facts for later classifiers to arrange.

Most important, no single overriding purpose, such as the one Darwin discovered, guides our efforts. We approach products of culture in different ways for different reasons. No one has ever found, nor will anyone ever find, the natural classification system for cultural objects.

Some literary classification systems rely on one or another principle (in most cases, formal) used consistently. Others seem entirely ad hoc, with apparently different criteria used genre by genre. As a rule, logical or structural ways of thinking favor consistency of criteria while historical approaches, which trace the actual rise and fall of genres, necessarily reflect the contingencies and inconsistencies that govern developing cultural practices. Epics were once long poems in dactylic hexameters (and so Lucretius's versified treatise *On the Nature of Things* was for the ancients an epic), but as time went on, many thematic criteria, often inconsistent with each other, came to seem at least as important. Works as diverse as *Don Quixote, Moby-Dick, War and Peace,* Byron's *Don Juan,* and the *Cantos* of Ezra Pound have been plausibly classified as epics. Unplanned systems do not fit a geometrical grid, and the boundaries of literary genres grow asymmetrically.

Despite these difficulties, critics frequently find it useful to approach a given work as a representative of its genre. But how should they do so if classification is arbitrary?

Purpose

The question, what is the correct classification system to use?, cannot be answered because it is incomplete. It is something akin to demanding a solution to a single equation with two unknowns. Another piece of information is needed for a solution to be possible.

That missing piece of information is purpose. As you cannot hand someone the "right" tool until you know what is to be accomplished, you must first identify the problem a genre theory is to illuminate before the most appropriate one can be selected.

For all their impressive symmetry, structural approaches do not offer much help in describing, let us say, the rise of the realist novel in the English eighteenth century. By contrast, something more closely resembling the structuralist's favorite metaphor, Mendeleev's table of the elements, might illuminate *logical* possibilities. Tzvetan Todorov's famous distinction of "the fantastic" from "the uncanny" and "the marvelous"—each resolves a narrative's suggestion of super-natural causation differently—depends on no particular historical situation.[2]

Depending on one's purposes, different combinations of structural or historical, formal or semantic, and cultural or cross-cultural considerations might be suitable.

Classification by Worldview

Much of the appeal of aphorisms derives from the wisdom they contain. We may learn from them or marvel at what others have found worth learning. For thousands of years, proverbs have been collected in treasuries of wisdom, along with the sayings of sages and the dicta of philosophers or lawgivers. In a rather different spirit, people have delighted in witticisms, epigrams, or sardonic maxims for their sly insights into human nature. Mystical apothegms lure us into the ineffable.

Aphorisms fascinate me, as they have fascinated others, as repositories of wisdom. Different kinds of aphorisms convey specific views of life and experience. If we are to understand these diverse views, it makes sense to classify them accordingly. Approached in this way, each genre suggests a distinct sense of life as a whole. The world of the prophet differs from that of the wit. Given this purpose—to recover distinct kinds of wisdom and senses of experience—I classify aphorisms in terms of worldviews.

That was the approach to genres adopted by the Russian theorist Mikhail Bakhtin. Bakhtin worked as both a literary critic and a philosopher, and he accordingly developed a method to grasp each literary genre as an implicit philosophy, or what he called a "form-shaping ideology."[3] He meant that each genre proceeds from a particular worldview ("ideology") generating appropriate forms of expression. For his opponents, the Russian Formalists, forms *define* genres, but for Bakhtin they instead *result from* a defining ideology or sense of experience.

Bakhtin cautions that even "ideology," or the various synonyms I have used, does not quite capture what he means. A genre resembles an entity less than it does an energy, an impulse to apply a certain way of seeing to surprising circumstances with which it interacts and, as a result, changes. Genres are restless, some more so than others.

Moreover, a genre's take on life cannot be reduced to a set of philosophical premises. For one thing, any reasonably complex genre's sense of experience is ultimately inexpressible. It may be partly "transcribed" as a set of propositions, but such transcriptions will always prove too simple. For another, the genre always contains potentials for development in more directions than are apparent. Until the genre dies, its wisdom is never complete, and if resurrected, it can develop still further.

A genre is a moving target.

As a genre seeks out forms, it also discovers appropriate occasions, which, like forms, reflect its worldview.

Transcribed Wisdom

Although the transcribed wisdom of genres does not match the genre itself in richness, it often contains enough insight to stimulate thought. For Bakhtin, criticism, properly performed, gives us these transcriptions. So understood, criticism contributes to the development of thought.

Bakhtin's understanding of literary criticism reflects its role in nineteenth-century Russia, where speculation about philosophical, social, and psychological questions often took the form of essays explicating great works. If you wanted to advance a theory of motivation, you might publish on Dostoevsky; skeptical approaches to knowledge might arise in a discussion of Tolstoy.

In Bakhtin's view, great literature does not sugarcoat philosophy. On the contrary, it develops ideas that subsequent philosophy or social science transcribes. The eighteenth-century novel of education as Bakhtin understood it pioneered the ideas about temporality that obsessed nineteenth-century thinkers. Far from exhausting pioneering literature, such philosophy represents the mere "sclerotic deposit" of the genre's energy.

Intergeneric Dialogue

Great writers change the genres they use. Genres also evolve in response to changing social experience. And they interact with other genres in dialogues that alter participants. Genres argue, parody each other, and parody opposing parodies.

Among longer forms, utopias, which claim to know the true answer to all social problems, mock and are mocked by skeptical realist novels. In much the same way, the wise sayings of sages and the dicta of philosophers have faced the skepticism of sardonic maxims (such as those of La Rochefoucauld). Proverbs and witticisms dispute the motives of human behavior.

It would probably be possible to narrate literary history as the story of such intergeneric dialogues. Sometimes genres explicitly mention or quote their antagonists, as *Don Quixote* constantly cites romances and proverbs. At other times, the alternative is merely suggested by signs that, though clear at the moment of authorship, may eventually fade.

Works of one genre may include heroes typical of another. Utopias depict skeptics who appreciate novels and novels depict utopian ideologues, each with hostile intent. *War and Peace* respectfully argues with the epic worldview as its hero, Prince Andrei, gradually learns that real heroism does not lie in glorious exploits. In much the same way, the prologue to *Middlemarch* establishes the book's heroine as an expatriate from a saint's life. Wisdom argues with wisdom as genre disputes genre.

Intergeneric dialogues typically focus on a given aspect of life understood by each genre in its own way. Love in romance differs from love in realist novels, as Anna Karenina learns; the goodness of a saint, a prophet, or a utopian preacher does not resemble the goodness of ordinary people in Dickens, George Eliot, or Trollope. Reading such works requires our understanding of the opposing genres they evoke.

Short genres also evoke their antagonists to express their values.

Doubling

When a writer chooses a genre, he or she creates an encounter between its vision and his or her own. This encounter generates its own special form of dialogue. The genre "remembers" its history, and the author adapts what he or she finds for his or her own purposes.[4] Richness derives from a process of negotiation that readers can sense.

At any point, many different authors have contributed to a genre's resources of thought and expression. Particular masterpieces may therefore be interesting in two distinct ways: in their own right and as exemplars of the genre. We may read the fiction of Turgenev and Trollope as individual works or as representatives of the realist novel. There is Milton's *Paradise Lost* and epic's *Paradise Lost*. It is as if George Eliot wrote one *Middlemarch* and the genre of the realist novel wrote a double. The two works, though verbally identical, may differ in meaning. Sometimes this difference may itself be part of an author's plan. Short genres display the same kind of doubling.

Changing Forms and Occasions

Because a genre's wisdom evolves, the forms that express it may also change over time and across cultures. So may the occasions in which it is characteristically set.

Depending on period or culture, the witticism may favor the salon, the gallows, or the hustings. For obvious reasons, deflating comments addressed to political orators occur more often in England than in Russia, which specializes in the political joke told in private settings. The power of such jokes depends on the risk of telling and hearing them, and their forms convey a shared sense of danger.

The summons to courage usually seeks the battlefield just before combat or the graveyard where the hallowed dead now lie. But as the sense of heroism changes, it may abandon combat altogether for scenes of temptation or martyrdom. Not just Achilles but also Saint Anthony may define the heroic and, in a later age, so may Florence Nightingale or even Dorothea Brooke. In Tolstoy, we encounter heroines of the nursery.

Depending on age or culture, wise sayings may reflect the labor of the scholar, the adroitness of the thinker, or the inspiration of the poet. One culture may ascribe them to a ruler (Solomon or Solon), another to a philosopher (Socrates or Epictetus), a third to a scientist (Galileo or Einstein). Paintings of sages, such as Raphael's "School of Athens," Jacques-Louis David's "Death of Socrates," or Murillo's portrait of Galileo in his cell, may depict the circumstances giving rise to their sayings. Such art offers a setting to inspire future sayings of a similar sort.

Ascribing Antithetical Genres

Sometimes readers can plausibly ascribe a work to more than one genre. Each ascription may suggest a different meaning. If some readers take a work as an epic and others as a mock epic, their interpretations may contradict each other. Disputes over genre may also create less dramatic differences. Sometimes works switch genres from age to age and from culture to culture depending on the other masterpieces with which they are grouped.

Depending on the genre readers ascribe to a work, they may interpret it according to different conventions. Our assumption that a work belongs to a given genre often shapes our understanding from the outset. That is one reason authors often seek to preclude misunderstanding by indicating genre in the title, subtitle, or other material that appears before the text. Nevertheless, the genre of works, whether long or short, is frequently uncertain.

When we are dealing with works from distant times or unfamiliar cultures, it is especially easy to miss or impose signs of parody. Some cultures accept ideas or praise rhetoric we regard as absurd, while others ridicule what we regard with reverence. Bakhtin observes that there are doubtless many works we have come to regard as serious that are in fact parodies, and vice versa. Even in our own time, some readers have taken *Anna Karenina* as a romance and others as a parody of romance.

The very same *text* can be two opposite *works*. Text must not be confused with work, because a work's genre decisively shapes meaning but is not itself a textual feature.

If long works can be classified and interpreted so differently, what about very short works, where there is little room to indicate genre?

Ambiguity without Incompatibility

Works may become generically ambivalent not only through the accidents of time but also by the design of the author. Like the famous duck-rabbit drawing, the work may depend on double perspective. Whether or not a work was designed to be generically ambiguous, the two genres to which it can be assigned may or may not be incompatible. Often enough, the vision of one genre overlaps with that of another. Sardonic maxims can easily be reread as apothegms and witticisms as sardonic maxims.

Authors may exploit generic ambiguity as a source of richness. In such cases, we may be prompted to take the work each way in turn. If we are not sure whether the ambiguity is deliberate, we may want to say: if we take it one way, it suggests one meaning, but regarded differently, it suggests another.

Short works exhibit generic ambiguity more frequently than long ones precisely because they are so short. That is one reason for the special difficulty in classifying them. Apothegms, dicta, witticisms, and other genres of aphorism do not typically have separate titles or subtitles; by the time their first sentence has been uttered, they may be over. Short forms often must signal their genre and state their point simultaneously. No one would begin a witticism by warning that it is one. If we misidentify tone in a long work, subsequent passages usually enable us to correct ourselves, but short forms by definition lack such continuations.

Epics have room to evoke each other and novels to discuss each other, while wise sayings and maxims require greater economy. Allusions do occur, and carry special weight, but it is easier to miss them. I will therefore pay special attention to instances when works of one genre suggest another genre.

Constraints and Opportunities

Aphorisms are necessarily brief, and each genre of aphorism, whatever its sense of experience, must operate within very narrow limits.

To be sure, as every wit knows, brevity offers compensating advantages. Constraints also provide opportunities, which different genres exploit in various ways.

Short works or their anthologizers may signal genre by providing the occasion. A conventional title ("Gettysburg Address") or a note indicating the occasion of uttering may offer a clue. One voices a summons before the people or Parliament, not in a salon, and eulogies do not lend themselves to witticisms. Sometimes the source of the aphorism, which anthologies often indicate, may be telling: we expect the proverbial or sententious from *Poor Richard's Almanac* or *Pilgrim's Progress*, even if we might discover irony in the very same words attributed to Jane Austen or Mark Twain.

Regardless of the source, the location in which we discover an aphorism may also signal how we are to take it. Place anything on a Celestial Seasonings box and it becomes a sappy saying. "Sappification" is as much a feature of placing as ironization. Posters and greeting cards, especially if sold in expensive craft shops, sappify or treaclify anything. We all cherish the enthusiasms of our youth, but if the words of Buckminster Fuller are offered as wise, what is foolish?[5]

When an anthology classifies an aphorism as "repartee," we may guess how it is to be understood. With short works, much more than with long, anthologies play a significant role in indicating genre. They often set up an aphorism or append a comment after it. Commentary can also ruin an aphorism. The quality of an anthology often depends on its tact.

For reasons we shall discuss, long works often contain numerous extractable short ones, and each gains by interacting with the other. In such cases, context in the longer work may suggest whether we are to take the short work one way or another—or both ways.

Because life is so complex, no single genre could ever be adequate.

2

APOTHEGMS

❚ APOTHEGM AND DICTUM ❚

But the mystery was solved long before the evening, and the solution also . . .
took the form of a new and agonizing mystery.   —Dostoevsky, *The Idiot*

The short works I call apothegms appeal to those who find the world to be
fundamentally mysterious. No matter how deeply we probe, we uncover still
greater enigmas. Apothegms contrast with dicta, which not only regard all significant questions as answerable but also claim to have finally answered them.
For dicta, the world is a riddle that has been solved, while for apothegms it is a
mystery leading to ever deeper mysteries.

All genres of aphorism considered in the present study could be given other
names. My concern here, as in the chapters to come, is not to regulate the use of
terms but to describe a distinct group of short masterpieces and the fascinating
sense of experience they convey.

Nature Loves to Hide

Let us examine a model apothegm:

The Lord whose oracle is at Delphi neither speaks nor conceals, but gives a sign.
                                                        —Heraclitus (*RAGP*, 28)

Apollo, the Lord at Delphi, responds to a question not with a solution but
with a sign, which must itself be deciphered. He answers one enigma with

another. Question begets question, sign points to sign, and mystery engenders mystery.

Like this very apothegm, signs given by Apollo prove anything but transparent. Countless Greek stories relate disputes about an oracle's meaning or the consequences of a tempting but mistaken guess. The very brevity of these signs encourages multiple interpretations and interpretations of interpretations. The sign opens a door to a potentially endless maze.

For the apothegm, truth is always postponed. Anyone who regards its meaning as clear not only misreads it but also mistakes its very nature. One cannot simply solve an apothegm, like a puzzle, and those who think they can meet disaster. Mistaken for a puzzle, the sign becomes a trap.

Apothegms teach that reason can go only so far. The world was not made so that we could comprehend it, and we have no guarantee things make sense. Nothing could be further from this sense of mystery than modern confidence in the intelligibility of things, the quest for a "theory of everything." No one can read the mind of God.

Tragedy dramatizes this kind of wisdom and so contains many apothegmic lines. Five plays of Euripides end with the chorus voicing this thought:

> The shapes of divinity are many,
> And the gods fulfill many things surprisingly.
> What was expected has not been accomplished,
> And for the unexpected god found a way.
> That is how his affair turned out.[1]

The variant in *Medea* reads:

> Zeus in Olympus is the overseer
> Of many doings. Many things the gods
> Achieve beyond our judgment. What we thought
> Is not confirmed and what we thought not god
> Contrives. And so it happens in this story.[2]

"And so it happens in this story": the play's events illustrate the apothegm with which it concludes. The gods' designs lie beyond our judgment, and our most confident expectations are overturned. The shapes of divinity are many.

Because modern Western culture typically presumes to have grasped a world amenable to rational and scientific investigation, tragedy retains special power to shock. It reminds us that there is no more reason to presume that the

universe fits human reason than to regard the Earth as its center. Behind ratio-
nalism lies an unnoticed anthropomorphism.

Tragedy narrates how, despite our supreme confidence, our predictions
prove mistaken. What we never imagined takes place. Surprise will always persist, not because we are temporarily ignorant of its laws but because the universe is essentially surprising.

Heraclitus: "Nature loves to hide" (*RAGP*, 28). Pascal: "God wished to hide
himself" (*P*, 103). Lao Tzu: "The way is forever nameless" (*TTC*, 37).

Into a Space Unseen

Much speech leads inevitably to silence.

Better to hold fast to the void.   —Lao Tzu (*TTC*, 9)

The view of life as mystery solvable only by more mystery may provoke despair,
as if, like Sisyphus, we were condemned to endless, futile effort. It may also
inspire a wise, if sorrowful, acceptance of the nature of things. In *Oedipus at
Colonus*, Antigone speaks to the chorus about Oedipus's death:

> Now the finish
> Comes, and we know only
> In all that we have seen and done
> Bewildering mystery. . . .
> It was not war
> Nor the deep sea that overtook him,
> But something invisible and strange
> Caught him up—or down—
> Into a space unseen.[3]

The chorus concludes the play:

> Now let the weeping cease;
> Let no one mourn again.
> These things are in the hands of God.   (*Sophocles I*, 155)

Sometimes joy, or even exhilaration, may result from appreciating mystery.
It promises the numinous feeling of enigmas too wondrous to be exhausted.
Far from futile, the endless process of inquiry achieves wisdom. Although each
answer supplies a new question, each step leaves us more discerning. The jour-
ney progresses even if the horizon always recedes.

At the end of the nineteenth century, physicists commonly thought that the world had already given itself away. As Albert Michaelson observed, "Physical discoveries in the future are a matter of the sixth decimal place" (*DSQ*, 172). It is a prediction now famous precisely because it proved so rapidly and so spectacularly mistaken. Pascal understood: "The incredulous are the most credulous" (*P*, 100). For the apothegm, the world does not give itself away. Wisdom begins when we recognize that we do not even know what we do not know.

Apothegms teach: there are always more doors to open. In attaining knowledge, as in probing an apothegm, each step begets another. Much as counting never reaches a highest integer, so knowledge increases without coming any closer to completion.

Oedipus and the Riddle

Oedipus: There's no felicity in speaking
Of hidden things.   —*Oedipus at Colonus* (*Sophocles I*, 108)

Teiresias: Aren't you the best man alive at guessing riddles?
                                                     —*Oedipus the King* (*OTK*, 365)

The *riddle* differs from the apothegm because the riddle has a solution. In Judges 14:5–18 Samson wagers that the Philistines cannot answer his riddle and is tricked into divulging the solution. The very existence of such a wager presumes that a definite answer exists. So does the widespread institution of the riddling contest.

The answer to a riddle leaves nothing unexplained. By contrast, any good answer to an apothegm only deepens its mystery. To regard the world as a riddle is to presume a complete solution. To regard it apothegmically is to anticipate that solutions always pose new questions.

In *Oedipus the King*, Oedipus is a riddler, while Teiresias speaks in apothegms. The play dramatizes the conflict between these two genres and their views of the world. The vision of tragedy that shapes the story speaks within the play through the seer's apothegms.

The greatest riddle solver who has ever lived, Oedipus has defeated the Sphinx by solving the riddle that perplexed all others. If he can solve this riddle, he reasons, then surely he can solve anything. With royal power to serve his great intelligence, Oedipus seeks the cause of the plague with confidence. As the play opens, the priest implores Oedipus to save the city again:

You came to us once and liberated our city, you freed us from the tribute which
we paid that cruel singer, the Sphinx. You did this with no extra knowledge you

got from us, you had no training for the task. . . . You are a man of experience, the kind whose plans result in effective action. (*OTK*, 357)

Oedipus rules by puzzle-solving reason and expresses contempt for the sense of mystery, as does Jocasta. Prophecy notwithstanding, Laius was murdered not by his son, but by a stranger, and so, she concludes, "there is no human being born that is endowed with prophetic power" (370).

For Jocasta, as for Oedipus, the very vagueness of mysterious sayings casts doubt upon them: "If God seeks or needs anything, he will make it clear to us himself" (370). She insists as well that the world is governed rationally. Oedipus takes pride that his gifts—intelligence and will, mind and courage—correspond to the world's intelligible order. That is why his plans "result in effective action." "I came, know-nothing Oedipus, I stopped the Sphinx, I answered the riddle with my own intelligence—the birds had nothing to teach me" (364). "The birds" symbolize mysterious revelation.

It is not only what Teiresias says that irritates Oedipus, but also how he says it. Obscurities and vague sayings suggest a world in which irrational prophecy must be taken into account.

> Teiresias: This present day will give you life and death.
> Oedipus: Everything you say is the same—riddles, obscurities.
> Teiresias: Aren't you the best man alive at guessing riddles?
> Oedipus: Insult me, go on—but that, you will find, is what makes me great.
> Teiresias: Yet that good fortune was your destruction. (365)

The plot turns on the irony that solving the riddle of Laius's murderer reveals a world of unfathomable mysteries. The riddle-solver destroys himself, and the riddle's solution shows the limitation of riddle solving. The essence of things transcends human reason, purpose, and justice.[4]

As in other Greek tragedies, the chorus concludes with an apothegm, in this case a version of a particularly famous one. "Therefore we must call no man happy while he waits to see his last day, not until he has passed the border of life without suffering pain" (386). An obvious paradox pertains to this truth, for it seems to suggest that no one could ever call himself happy. Aristotle commented:

> Must no one at all, then, be called happy while he lives; must we, as Solon says [in enunciating this apothegm], see the end? Even if we are to lay down this doctrine, is it also the case that a man *is* happy when he is *dead*? Or is this not quite absurd, especially for us who say that happiness is an activity?[5]

A man cannot be happy when alive, for he has not yet seen his last day; but he cannot be happy when dead, for happiness demands activity and life. The very condition of human life precludes the most important knowledge, and so the claim to possess it must always be hubris.

The same logic applies to a related Greek apothegm, that the greatest blessing is not to have been born at all. In *Oedipus at Colonus* the chorus declares: "Not to be born surpasses thought and speech. / The second best is to have seen the light / And then go back quickly whence we came" (*Sophocles I*, 134). But how can one be fortunate—or rather, who is it that is fortunate?—by never having existed?

Two paradoxes govern *Oedipus the King*: reason reasons its way to truths beyond the grasp of reason, and action for a purpose defeats the purpose. The second paradox occurs repeatedly. In trying to avoid the prophecy, Laius and Jocasta have ensured its fulfillment. By escaping from Corinth to avoid murdering his father, Oedipus meets and kills him. The play's countless other ironies, like Oedipus's curse of the killer who turns out to be himself, flow from these two. As the play begins with the priest's plea to Oedipus to solve a problem, its final words point to mysteries we can never fully solve. If even Oedipus cannot solve them, then no one can.

Oedipus the King orchestrates a dialogue of genres. Its hero is a riddle solver, its seer voices apothegms. The play culminates in an apothegm because it is *about* the difference between apothegm and riddle.

Tragedy is a long form conveying and deepening the wisdom of a short one.

Dramatizing the Riddle

As tragedies create narratives from apothegms, so detective stories add plot to riddles. The detective discovers the solution to a real-life puzzle.

First, clues lead to mistaken solutions, or there would be no story to tell. When the detective at last finds the correct solution, convention dictates a scene in which he explains how he arrived at it. The explanation is necessary because the detective story is about the process of answering. It celebrates method. We know in advance *that* the detective will find the criminal; the suspense pertains to *how*. As readers try to anticipate his answer, the story tests their own mastery of the method.

Unlike apothegms and tragedies, detective stories presume that a rational method exists. The genre believes in social *science*. It embodies the same set of assumptions that have led so many thinkers since the seventeenth century to assume that what Newton accomplished in astronomy will soon be accomplished with human beings. Governed by natural laws no less than any star or planet, we must be as knowable to rational investigators. "Moral Newtonianism," as Elie Halévy famously called this assumption, is above all the belief in method guaranteeing answers.[6]

Anthologies typically include these famous lines from Conan Doyle:

"You know my methods, Watson."
                                    —"The Adventure of the Crooked Man" (*YBQ*, 215)

"How often have I said to you that when you have eliminated the impossible, whatever remains, *however improbable*, must be the truth?"
                                    —"The Sign of the Four" (*YBQ*, 214)

Like all Holmes's reasoning the thing seemed simplicity itself when it was once explained.   —"The Stock-Broker's Clerk" (*YBQ*, 215)

"Detection is, or ought to be, an exact science, and should be treated in the same cold and unemotional manner. You have attempted to tinge it with romanticism, which produces much the same effect as if you worked a love-story or an elopement into the fifth proposition of Euclid."
                                    —"The Sign of the Four" (*YBQ*, 214)

The method, once grasped, should be "simplicity itself"—should seem "commonplace" and "elementary" as other famous aphorisms from the Holmes stories have it—because all exact sciences presumably rely on laws as simple as Newton's and on theorems as indubitable as Euclid's. Some day everyone will be a Holmes, just as schoolboys now can solve problems in physics that would have baffled Aristotle and Copernicus. Freud evidently chose to present case histories as a kind of detective story because they cast him as the Holmes of a new science of detection.

Apothegms and Inverse Detectives

The general case, the case for which all legal forms and rules are intended, for which they are all calculated and laid down in books, does not exist at all, for the reason that every case, every crime for instance, so soon as it actually occurs, at once becomes a thoroughly special case unlike any that has gone before.
                —Porfiry Petrovich in *Crime and Punishment* (*C&P*, 332–33)

Those who have denied the possibility of an entirely rational method have, understandably enough, sometimes composed a kind of *inverse detective story*.

Their stories convey the apothegmic, opposing truth, that the world is not a riddle but a mystery. Human beings above all are best understood by an apothegmic consciousness.

Inverse detective stories suggest that behind the crime is a mystery. Only by appreciating the mystery can the crime be solved, if it can be solved at all. And so G. K. Chesterton's Father Brown leads us not to social scientific method but to faith.

The key story, "The Secret of Father Brown," self-consciously reflects on the detective story as a genre and its assumption of a scientific method. One Grandison Chace of Boston questions Father Brown to find out what his *method* is. We are all well acquainted, Chace explains, with how Dupin, Lecoq, Holmes, and Carter solve crimes, but no one has yet discovered your "strictly tabulated scientific method":[7]

> "Edgar Poe throws off several little essays in a conversational form, explaining Dupin's method, with its fine links of logic. Dr. Watson had to listen to some pretty exact expositions of Holmes's method, with its observation of material details. But nobody seems to have got on to any full account of your method, Father Brown." (Chesterton, 425)

At last the priest explains that he engages in a "religious exercise" irreducible to a method. It reflects the Christian understanding that we are all capable of crime, "that no man's really any good till he knows how bad he is" (427). By recognizing his original sinfulness, the investigator empathizes with the criminal. Father Brown considers from within "how a man might come to be like that, until I realized that I really was like that, in everything except the actual final consent to the action. . . . And when I was quite sure that I felt exactly like the murderer myself, of course, I knew who he was" (426).

The American holds to his belief in the "science of detection," but Father Brown denies the possibility of science in moral matters. Empathy is not applied psychology:

> "Science is a grand thing when you can have it. . . . But what do these men mean, nine times out of ten, when they use it nowadays. . . . They mean getting *outside* a man and studying him as if he were a giant insect; in what they would call a dry impartial light. . . . When the scientist talks about a type, he never means himself, but always his neighbor." (426–27)

The reference to the "dry impartial light" alludes to Holmes's adherence to a "cold and unemotional manner." For Father Brown, science falls short because of its ambition to identify general laws, which means viewing others as one cannot view oneself. It is always *other* people's beliefs that reflect not evidence but their psychic needs.

Our essential humanness comes from what cannot be seen from an outside perspective. The inexplicability of one's own consciousness, which each person senses as different from all other phenomena, must somehow be extended to grasp the mystery of other selves. For Father Brown, that's not a method—it's Christian faith.

The Dictum

To clarify the nature of the apothegm, let us consider a philosophically antithetical short genre, the dictum. The dictum, as I shall use the term, offers itself as the solution to a supremely important riddle that has long perplexed humanity.

Consider some representative dicta. Jeremy Bentham imagined that he had discovered the one principle behind all human behavior:

(a)   Nature has placed mankind under the governance of two sovereign masters, *pain* and *pleasure*. It is for them alone to point out what to do, as well as to determine what we shall do. On the one hand the standard of right and wrong, on the other the chain of causes and effects, are fastened to their throne. They govern us in all we do, in all we say, in all we think: every effort we make to throw off their subjection, will serve but to demonstrate and confirm it. In words a man may pretend to abjure their empire: but in reality he will remain subject to it all the while. The *principle of utility* recognizes this subjection, and assumes it for the foundation of that system, the object of which is to rear the fabric of human felicity by the hands of reason and law. Systems which attempt to question it, deal in sounds instead of sense, in caprice instead of reason, in darkness instead of light.

> —Jeremy Bentham, *An Introduction to the*
> *Principles of Morals and Legislation*[8]

(b)   The greatest happiness of the greatest number is the foundation of morals and legislation.   —Bentham (342)

Marx and his followers were equally certain of an entirely different principle explaining human history:

(c)   The history of all hitherto existing society is the history of class struggles.

> —Marx and Engels, *The Communist Manifesto* (*M&E*, 7)

(d)   It is not the consciousness of men that determines their existence, but on the
contrary it is their social existence which determines their consciousness.
—Marx, *Critique of Political Economy* (*BFQ15*, 562)

(e)   Capitalist production begets, with the inexorability of a law of nature, its own
negation.   —Marx, *Capital* (*BFQ15*, 562)

Freud's dicta locate the underlying principle within the mechanisms of the
mind, which he elucidates scientifically, for the first time:

(f)   I named the process *repression*; it was a novelty, and nothing like it had ever
before been recognized in mental life.
—Freud, *An Autobiographical Study* (*SSQ*, 70)

(g)   The poets and philosophers before me discovered the unconscious. . . . What
I discovered was the scientific method by which the unconscious could be
studied.   —Freud, on his seventieth birthday (*SSQ*, 70)

Closer to our own time, many have fallen under the utopian spell of behavior-
ist dicta:

(h)   The one fact that I would cry from every housetop is this: the Good Life is waiting for us—here and now! . . . At this very moment we have the necessary techniques, both material and psychological, to create a full and satisfying life for
everyone. . . . We want a government based upon a science of human behavior.
—B. F. Skinner, *Walden Two*[9]

Among Lenin's dicta, we find one expressed as a rhetorical question. All history
can be seen as the application of brute force:

(i)   Who Whom?   —Lenin

As the Russian original suggests more clearly, all that matters is power, who can
dominate whom.

      The great seventeenth-century rationalist philosophers—Descartes, Leib-
niz, Spinoza, and others—sought, and imagined they had found, secure foundations for knowledge. Their dicta assert the unshakability of these foundations
and the certainty of conclusions drawn in Euclidean fashion from them:

(j)   Even though there may be a deceiver of some sort, very powerful and very
tricky, who bends all his efforts to keep me perpetually deceived, there can
be no slightest doubt that I exist, since he deceives me; and let him deceive

me as much as he will, he can never make me nothing as long as I think that I am thinking. Thus, after having thought well on this matter, and after examining all things with care, I must finally conclude and maintain that this proposition: *I am, I exist*, is necessarily true every time I pronounce it or conceive it in my mind.   —Descartes, *Meditations*[10]

(k)   Finally, as the same precepts which we have when awake may come to us when asleep without their being true, I decided to suppose that nothing that had ever entered my mind was more real than the illusions of my dreams. But I soon noticed that while I thus wished to think everything false, it was necessarily true that I who thought so was something. Since this truth, *I think, therefore I am*, was so firm and assured that the most extravagant suppositions of the skeptics were unable to shake it, I judged I could safely accept it as the first principle of the philosophy I was seeking.

—Descartes, *Discourse on Method* (Descartes, 24)

(l)   Nothing happens without a reason why it should be so rather than otherwise.
—Leibniz, second letter to Clarke[11]

(m)   Just as the individual concept of each person includes once for all everything which can ever happen to him, it can be seen, a priori, the evidences or reasons for the reality of each event, and why one happened sooner rather than later.   —Leibniz, *Discourse on Metaphysics*[12]

(m)   God does nothing which is not orderly, and it is not even possible to conceive of events which are not regular.   —Leibniz, *Discourse on Metaphysics* (10)

For the scientists of this period, a rebirth of Pythagoreanism led to dicta affirming that the true solution must be mathematical:

(o)   Where there is matter, there is geometry.   —Kepler (*DSQ*, 139)

(p)   Philosophy is written in that great book which ever lies before our gaze—I mean the universe—but we cannot understand it if we do not learn first the language and grasp the symbols in which it is written. The book is written in the mathematical language, and the symbols are triangles, circles, and other geometrical figures, without the help of which it is impossible to conceive a single word of it, and without which one wanders in vain through a labyrinth.   —Galileo (*DSQ*, 98–99)

Of course, religious catechisms contain dicta of a quite different kind:

(q)   The desire for God is written in the human heart, because man is created
      by God and for God; and God never ceases to draw man to himself. Only in
      God will he find the truth and happiness he never stops searching for.
                              —*Catechism of the Catholic Church*[13]

Each of these comments expresses supreme confidence in a truth long
sought and now attained. Dicta appear particularly frequently in eras imagining they have dispelled darkness (the seventeenth-century rationalists) and in
disciplines claiming to have at last achieved scientific status (the social sciences).

Apothegms induce wonder at a world of mystery, while dicta presume to
decipher the text of nature or society. What long appeared dauntingly complex
has turned out to be quite simple; what seemed cloudy or labyrinthine proved
clear and straight. One must only see matters in the right light, find the correct
starting point, and then use the proper method. We have discovered the algo-
rithm of being. Much may be unknown, but nothing significant is unknowable.

People have always sought the fundamental principles of human behavior and have offered explanations of dizzying complexity and mind-numbing
vagueness, but the answer can be easily stated: (a).

Since antiquity, people have looked for the best way to organize society, and
now we know it: (b).

The fundamental laws explaining economic, social, cultural, and intellectual
history have hitherto defied investigation, but they can now be succinctly stated.
We now know the principle for effective action: (c), (d), (e), (h), (i).

Nothing has seemed more complex and bewildering than the human
psyche, but we have at last discovered the key to its workings: (f), (g), (h), and
again (a).

Philosophers have striven to base human knowledge on an absolutely firm
foundation, which skepticism could not shake, and we have at last done so: (j),
(k), (l), (m), (n).

It is absolutely clear that rational principles are adequate to understanding
the world: (n). It is inconceivable that things could be other than they are: (l).

God (or Nature) seemed to speak in a language we could barely understand,
but we have now deciphered the divine (or natural) script: (o), (p).

We know the best way to organize society: (b), (h). What once seemed a
matter only for poets now belongs to science: (g). We have discovered the key
fact about ourselves: (f). The secret of happiness has been revealed: (a), (q).

Rhetoric of the Dictum: Totality

The rhetoric of dicta tends to totality. Bentham's opening paragraph assures us that pleasure and pain "govern us in all we do, in all we say, in all we think: every effort we can make to throw off their subjection, will serve but to demonstrate and confirm it." Every, all, without exception, each time: these categorical words typify dicta. Sometimes the very absence of qualification indicates that none is possible. We are as far as possible from the phrase Aristotle loved to use, "on the whole and for the most part."

One would have radically changed these dicta to say, for instance: "Generally speaking, nothing happens without a reason why it should be so rather than otherwise"; "Where there is matter, there is usually geometry"; or "The history of most hitherto existing society is more or less the history of class struggles." Often enough, followers embarrassed by overstatement add such qualifications, but in so doing they alter the very spirit of the originals, which cease to be dicta and become mere rules of thumb.

For Bentham and his intellectual descendants up to the present, not only actions but also thoughts and desires obey the principle of utility.[14] For Marxism to be scientific, rather than just another form of socialism, it must have discerned the iron laws of history. Capitalism must not tend to result in disorder but must beget "with the inexorability of a law of nature, its own negation."

We have not solved just *a* riddle, but *the* riddle, the one providing the key to all others. Not just the key itself but also the claim to have it confers immense power. Dicta attract followers more readily than qualified suggestions. They promise rewards, the most important of which is the banishment of doubt. There must be no exceptions.

The possibility of exceptions became the central issue in Leibniz's correspondence with Clarke, who represented Newton. Unable to prove the stability of the solar system, Newton had suggested that God might occasionally intervene to set things right. For Leibniz, one intervention was as bad as a thousand. Either God made the universe perfectly at the outset, or He was nothing but an "inferior watchmaker." God had a *sufficient reason* that everything must be exactly as it is. To understand something is to see why it could not be otherwise.

Opinion

Because dicta convey absolute certainty and demand unlimited confidence in their veracity, they allow no legitimate disagreement. Much as one cannot grasp a proof in Euclidean geometry without assenting to it, so the dictum offers itself as beyond coherent challenge.

Dicta remove us from the realm of opinion. Anyone who disagrees is, if not venal, then insane. Regarding the principles of Marxism-Leninism as on a par with the laws of physics, the Soviet government imprisoned dissidents in insane asylums not out of sadism but out of a genuine conviction that they were mad. Masses are attracted to each other by a force inversely proportional to the square of the distance between them, and capitalism will perish through its own internal contradictions. On such issues there can be no opinions.

In Skinner's *Walden Two*, Cole objects to the rule forbidding anyone publically to question the Code. Such a rule, he reasons, violates "simple democracy," which entails open discussion. The answer is plain: "'You won't find very much "simple democracy" here,' said Frazier casually, and he resumed his discussion as if he had referred to the absence of white flour in the Walden Two bread" (Skinner, 164). Science is not a matter of democracy because democracy demands respect for different opinions.

Bentham's dictum makes its status as no mere opinion explicit. "Systems that question it [the principle of utility], deal in sounds instead of sense, in caprice instead of reason, in darkness instead of light." In many cases, the dictum is indubitable, not, as we might suppose, because other views do not fit the facts or have been refuted but because one cannot even formulate a coherent alternative. As Leibniz argues, "it is not even possible to conceive of events which are not regular." For Descartes, it is impossible even to imagine doubting one's own existence.

In a related rhetorical move, the author of a dictum maintains that any attempt to refute it actually confirms it. Bentham explains that "every effort we can make to throw off our subjection" to the rule of those two sovereign masters, pleasure and pain "will serve but to confirm it. In words a man may pretend to abjure their empire; but in reality he will remain subject to it all the while." Doubt refutes itself.

Skeptics object that such reasoning often relies on alternating between two meanings of a key term. When a significant claim is to be advanced, one uses the terms "utility" and "pleasure and pain" so as to predict one choice rather than another. But when the wolf is at the door, one defends the proposition tautologically, so that any choice must maximize "utility" precisely because it was chosen.

Metaphor, Imagination, Purge, Self-Reference

As the examples above illustrate, dicta eschew metaphor, which, if used at all, is restricted to mere illustration and kept under strict control. One may speak of a principle as "governing an empire" or as illuminating darkness; or one may say that without it one "wanders in a labyrinth." But such metaphors are almost entirely dead and easily dispensed with.

To read a dictum's key terms metaphorically would be to change it decisively. By "class struggle" Marx and Engels mean precisely the struggle of (carefully defined) social classes; they are not speaking metaphorically of inner psychic conflict or ethnic hostility or the war of orthodoxy with heresy. Indeed, authors of dicta often try to imitate the absolutely clear language of mathematics (as Spinoza did). Leibniz proposed to construct a language free of all ambiguity so that philosophical reasoning would resemble algebra.

Dicta typically offer themselves as axiomatic. Begin here, and all will follow; the right starting point and the right method together guarantee progress. Bentham offers the "foundation" for morals and legislation, Descartes the first principle for philosophy, Freud and Marx firm beginnings for psychology and sociology. From now on, change will not be mere alteration of beliefs but genuine advancement.

Consider the following dicta of Spinoza:

Nothing in the universe is contingent, but all things are conditioned to exist and operate in a particular manner by the necessity of the divine nature.[15]

He who has a true idea, simultaneously knows that he has a true idea, and cannot doubt of the truth of the thing perceived. . . . No one, who has a true idea, is ignorant that a true idea involves the highest certainty. . . . Even as light displays both itself and darkness, so is truth a standard both of itself and falsity. . . . [T]ruth is its own standard. (Spinoza, 115)

Before all things a method must be thought out of healing the understanding and purifying it at the beginning, that it may with the greatest success understand things correctly. From this everyone will be able to see that I wish to direct all sciences in one direction to one end, namely, to attain the greatest possible human perfection.[16]

Nothing could be anything but what it is, knowledge precludes the very possibility of doubt, and—above all—truth is its own standard. Truth can never be told so as to be understood and not to be believed.

For Spinoza, the idea of *self-verifying truth*—truth as its own standard—is indispensable because without it justification faces an infinite regress. For knowledge to be indubitable, some point must exist where proof is no longer required. As Stuart Hampshire paraphrases Spinoza's point, "[I]t is the mark of an adequate idea that, as soon as presented, it conveys certainty; for it represents something which, in the logically necessary constitution of the universe, could not be otherwise" (Hampshire, 73).

But if truth verifies itself, and is recognized as soon as understood, why have earlier thinkers made so many mistakes? Authors of dicta often follow Spinoza's answer: careless thinkers have allowed imagination and prejudice to affect their conclusions. Therefore, part of the project of knowledge must be to "cleanse and purify" the mind itself, "that it may with the greatest success understand things correctly."

The theory explains why it is not accepted. Imagination blocks reason, repression obscures insight, false consciousness creates mistaken ideology. "Ideology is a process accomplished by the so-called thinker consciously, it is true, but with a false consciousness" (Engels, *SSQ*, 60).

In response, skeptics ask how the authors of dicta know that their own understanding does not suffer from false consciousness, has not repressed counterevidence, or is not distorted by irrational imaginings. But to pose such questions is already to leave the world of dicta. They cannot be coherently formulated within that world, because dicta, unlike apothegms, assiduously avoid this kind of self-reference. Bentham does not fear that he accepts his beliefs only because it is pleasant to do so. The sociology of knowledge is almost always the sociology of other people's knowledge.

Dictum and Utopia

The end of our foundation is the knowledge of causes, and secret motions of things; and the enlarging of the bounds of human Empire, to the effecting of all things possible.   —Francis Bacon, *The New Atlantis* (*YBQ*, 39)

Utopias may be regarded as dramatized dicta. The two genres express essentially the same worldview, and utopias typically contain dicta for readers to memorize and repeat.

Bentham, Marx, and Skinner imagine that their discoveries ensure the greatest possible human happiness, while Spinoza believes that his ideas will achieve "the greatest possible human perfection." Bacon promises "the effecting of all things possible." Like dicta, utopias banish doubt. They promise to solve every problem once and for all.

Utopias resemble detective stories because both derive from an unlimited faith in reason. Both dramatize the riddle to create a story about finding the answer. One shows the solution to a crime and the other the solution to Crime.[17]

Utopias typically tell the story about how a skeptic *arrives at* the truth and so take the form of a voyage through space or time. In an opening section, a hero from the reader's own society witnesses social conflict, which everyone assumes to be inevitable because of "human nature" or some other unchangeable factor. The hero then falls asleep and wakes to, or journeys to and discovers, another world that has solved apparently unsolvable social riddles by methods that have come to seem obvious. Like dicta, utopias seek to advance a method (for utopias, usually some form of socialism).

From this point on, utopias resemble tour guides. A representative of the new world leads the visitor, and so the reader whom he represents, from one perfect institution to another. Without a hint of doubt, this representative outlines the simple solution to all the errors of the visitor's world. There are no unanswered riddles.

It turns out that the master solution has changed human nature itself. The answer to all questions is the same: the institutions your society deemed impossible govern here because now no one wants to do anything antisocial. So tedious does this answer become that utopias face the problem of boring their readers or evoking unintended laughter. They anticipate such responses by denouncing them as the symptoms of the old world's corruption.

In the classic American utopia, Edward Bellamy's *Looking Backward, 2007–1887*, we repeatedly encounter questions-and-answers like the following:

> "Who does your housework, then?" I asked.
>
> "There is none to do. . . . Our washing is all done at public laundries at excessively cheap rates, and our cooking at public kitchens."[18]

> "Your courts must have an easy time of it," I observed. "With no private property to speak of. . . ."
>
> "We do without lawyers, certainly," was Doctor Leete's reply. . . .
>
> "But who defends the accused?"
>
> "If he is a criminal he needs no defense, for he pleads guilty. . . . The plea of the accused is not a mere formality with us, as with you. . . ."
>
> "That is the most astounding thing you have yet told me," I exclaimed. "If

lying has gone out of fashion, this is indeed the 'new heaven and the new earth wherein dwelleth righteousness,' which the prophet foretold." (Bellamy, 140–41)

The folly of men, not their hard-heartedness, was the great cause of the world's poverty. It was not the crime of man, nor of any class of men, that made the race so miserable, but a hideous, ghastly mistake, a colossal world-darkening blunder. (Bellamy, 216)

The last example became one of Bellamy's signature lines. Of course, some utopians reverse the last statement to say that not mere folly but some "class of men" was the problem. Whichever cause of human ill is chosen, the cure is simple.

Tense and Turning Point

The dictum senses itself as a historical turning point. Before, all was darkness; from now on, all is light. Engels reminds us: "Just as Darwin discovered the law of development of organic nature, so Marx discovered the law of development of human history: the simple fact hitherto concealed by an overgrowth of ideology" (*SSQ*, 59).

"Hitherto concealed": truth became visible at a recent moment and everything changed. Socialism ceased to be utopian and became scientific, the workings of the unconscious were brought to light, scholastic disputes gave way to a firm basis for philosophy, the principle of utility was at last revealed as the basis of morals and legislation: this is the rhetoric of the dictum.

As in the Christian view of history, time is split in two. Once truth is discovered, earlier thinkers become predecessors and earlier doctrines "types" or foreshadowings.

The sense of the dictum is: The master has merely discovered the truth, but it does not depend on him, his word, or his personality. We do not take Euclid's word for it. Spinoza tried entirely to efface himself "as individual and author, being no more than the mouthpiece of pure Reason" (Hampshire, 21).

To be sure, Marxists and Freudians have sometimes treated the founder as a quasi-divine being. "Marx was a genius, we others were at best talented," Engels declared (*SSQ*, 60). They have taken the founder's words as "gospel" and wielded their words as proofs. Nevertheless, so long as we inhabit the world of the dictum, rhetoric likes Engels's means: anything the master said warrants careful consideration, but it is not automatically true because he said it. Insofar as followers do take the founder's word on faith, they have replaced the dictum with divine revelation. They betray their professed beliefs with what the Marxists call "a cult of personality." The dictum's attitude to itself makes this transition an easy one.

The dictum stands on its own. It requires nothing beyond itself. We do not need to know the story of its discovery or circumstances of its uttering. Unlike some other genres we shall consider, it is tied to no occasion. What Bentham, Descartes, Marx, and Freud said would be just as true if said by someone else on a different occasion and in a different culture, much as the Pythagorean theorem can be used without considering Pythagoras.

If one returns to the examples above, one notices that the truth dicta express is typically given in the *present tense*. This present is what linguists call "unmarked": its sense is not "now" but "at no particular time." "Twice two equals four" does not leave open the possibility that long ago it might have equaled five. The same is true of the principle of utility or the yearning of humanity for God.

Dictated by the Holy Ghost

To be sure, dicta do not offer themselves as *entirely* without precedent. Freud allows the poets awareness of the unconscious before he gave it scientific formulation, and he refers to "forerunners" of psychoanalysis, "above all the great thinker Schopenhauer."[19] Hegel and utopian socialism looked forward to Marx. But the change is still qualitatively different from all previous ones.

Dicta therefore often convey a sense of a spectacular discovery. Freud famously identified three great scientific theories that have delivered "severe blows" to "the universal narcissism of men": Copernican heliocentrism, Darwinian evolution, and, of course, psychoanalysis (Freud, 139). And "the third blow"—delivered by Freud himself—"is probably the most wounding" (141). Wounded ego explains resistance to a theory so plainly true: "No wonder, then, that the ego does not look favourably upon psycho-analysis and obstinately refuses to believe in it" (143).

"Obstinately refuses to believe it": this is how the dicta represent nonbelievers. In much the same spirit, Freud's beloved Schopenhauer wrote of his key idea:

> [M]y philosophy is the real solution of the enigma of the world. . . . [I]n the fourth book there are even some paragraphs which may be considered to be dictated by the Holy Ghost.[20]

An avowed atheist, Schopenhauer evidently means that his solution represents the secular equivalent of divine revelation. Kepler's assessment of his discovery is perhaps the most remarkable:

> See, I cast the die and I write the book. Whether it is to be read by the people of the present or of the future makes no difference: let it await its reader for a hundred years, if God himself has stood ready for six thousand years for one to study him. (*ODSQ,* 340)

Darwin and the Hypothesis

No matter how important the discovery, nothing dictates a dictum.

The Origin of Species stands as one of the masterpieces of nineteenth-century English prose, and only its spectacular scientific significance masks its importance as a major work of English literature. Although Darwin's theory of natural selection rivals in importance any discovery of recent centuries, he assiduously avoided the language of dicta. With supreme mastery of tone, Darwin advances each key idea with the utmost caution. Only after supplying countless examples, offering possible qualifications, and considering reasonable objections does Darwin allow it to follow from the preponderance of available evidence. The book entirely avoids the language of certainty. It begins:

> When on board the H. M. S. "Beagle," as naturalist, I was much struck with certain facts in the distribution of the inhabitants of South America. . . . These facts seemed to me to throw some light on the origin of species—that mystery of mysteries, as it has been called by one of our greatest philosophers. On my return home, it occurred to me, in 1837, that something might be made out of this question by patiently consulting and reflecting on all sorts of facts, which could possibly have any bearing on it. After five years' work I allowed myself to speculate on the subject, and drew up some short notes; these I enlarged in 1844 into a sketch of the conclusions, which then seemed to me probable: from that period to the present day I have steadily pursued the same object. I hope I may be excused for entering on these personal details, as I give them to show that I have not been hasty in coming to a decision.[21]

The last chapter summarizes:

> As natural selection acts solely by accumulating slight, successive favourable variations, it can produce no great and sudden modification; it can only act by very short and slow steps. Hence the canon of "Natura non facit saltum" [Nature takes no leap], which every fresh addition to our knowledge tends to

make more strictly correct, is on this theory simply intelligible. We can plainly see why nature is prodigal in variety, though niggard in innovation. But why this should be a law of nature if each species has been independently created, no man can explain. (Darwin, 471)

Only after "patiently consulting" all facts that could possibly have any bearing on the topic does Darwin allow himself to speculate and, at last, arrive at conclusions that seem "probable." He summarizes them with confidence but not as indubitable.

Darwin writes in what we might call reluctant utterances. He has waited twenty-two years to publish this book, while always seeking more evidence that might challenge or refine his conclusions. He explains in the work's second paragraph that it was only Mr. Wallace's arriving at similar conclusions that led him to publish this volume on the urging of others, and he offers it as a mere "abstract" of a future more considered work. "This Abstract, which I now publish, must necessarily be imperfect" (Darwin, 2).

Darwin repeatedly presents counter-examples that long puzzled him and acknowledges that his answers to some objections must be tentative. Because he presents his most important theories in this hesitant way, anthologizers find it hard to extract quotable lines from the *Origin*. The ones that are extracted most frequently come with qualifications and sometimes require notes or paraphrase to stand on their own.

Everyone acknowledges Darwin's influence, but how many quotations from him are widely known? Nothing could be further from *The Communist Manifesto*, with its many ringing lines. We do have the phrases "natural selection" and "struggle for existence," but even "survival of the fittest" belongs not to Darwin but to Herbert Spencer. Darwin sounds not like a prophet but like a plodding physician, who has at last arrived at a tentative diagnosis.

Appropriately enough, Darwin presents his conclusions as the result of a slow *evolution*. Knowledge has been achieved, and should be achieved, the way species have evolved: by slow and small steps, to compromise solutions that lack guarantees of perfection. Nature, and Darwin, take no leaps. From the book's opening paragraph to its closing lines, *the origin of conclusions imitates the origin of species*. The book ends:

Thus, from the war of nature, from famine and death, the most exalted object which we are capable of conceiving, namely the production of the higher animals, directly follows. There is grandeur in this view of life, with its several powers, having been originally breathed into a few forms or into one; and that, whilst this planet has gone on cycling according to the fixed law of gravity, from so simple a beginning forms most beautiful and most wonderful have been, and are being, evolved. (490)

Slow changes, usually leading nowhere but sometimes to more complex and viable forms, have produced nature as we see it and the still imperfect theory just presented. There is grandeur in this view of life and knowledge, perhaps even more than in their alternatives, instantaneous creation and blinding discovery.

In contrast to the dictum, Darwinian formulations present themselves as still in process. Conclusions, like forms, "have been, *and are being*, evolved." Life and knowledge never reach the perfect conclusion.

Let us call such provisional lines as we may extract from Darwin "hypotheses." Precisely because they are tentative, cautious, and understated, hypotheses appear much more rarely in anthologies than dicta. They require too much context. Brevity seems contrary to their very purpose.

Return to the Apothegm

Let us now consider several representative apothegms. Lao Tzu's *Tao Te Ching*, and other classics of Taoism, exemplify the form, and Dostoevsky finds himself using similar rhetoric:

The way that can be spoken of
Is not the constant way.
The name that can be named
Is not the constant name. . . .
Mystery upon mystery
The gateway of the manifold secrets.   —Lao Tzu (*TTC*, 5)

What cannot be seen is called evanescent;
What cannot be heard is called rarefied;
What cannot be touched is called minute.
There three cannot be fathomed . . .
Dimly visible, it cannot be named
And returns to that which is without substance.
This is called the shape that has no shape.
The image that is without substance.
This is called indistinct and shadowy.   —Lao Tzu (*TTC*, 18)

Is it possible to perceive as an image that which has no image?

—Ippolit Teretiev, in Dostoevsky's *The Idiot* (*I*, 389)

The famous mystical conclusion to Wittgenstein's *Tractatus Logico-Philosophicus* baffled Bertrand Russell by replacing logically sure propositions with apothegms of the ineffable:

How things are in the world is a matter of complete indifference for what is higher. God does not reveal himself *in* the world.   —Wittgenstein (*TLP*, 73)

When the answer cannot be put into words, neither can the question be put into words.

The *riddle* does not exist.

If a question can be framed at all, it is also *possible* to answer it.

—Wittgenstein (*TLP*, 73)

There are, indeed, things that cannot be put into words. They *make themselves manifest*. They are what is mystical.   —Wittgenstein (*TLP*, 73)

In the age of the seventeenth-century rationalists, Pascal responded to dicta with classics of the apothegm:

The heart has its reasons, which reason knows nothing of. [Le coeur a ses raisons que la raison ne connait point.]   —Pascal, *Pensées* (*BFQ15*, 300)

To ridicule philosophy is to philosophize truly. [Se moquer de la philosophie, c'est vraiment philosopher.]   —Pascal, *Pensées* (*BFQ15*, 300)

We shall all die alone. [On mourra seul.]   —Pascal, *Pensées* (*BFQ15*, 300)

Because they point beyond themselves to the ineffable, apothegms have appealed to "negative theologians" who insist on the complete unknowability of God:

For this [negative way], I think, is more appropriate to the divine essence . . . we do not know its superessential, and inconceivable, and unutterable indefinability. If then, the negations respecting things Divine are true, but the affirmations are inharmonious, the revelation of things invisible, through dissimilar representations, is more appropriate to the hiddenness of things unutterable.

—Dionysius the Areopagite, *On the Heavenly Hierarchy* [22]

For that very reason Denis the Great [Dionysius the Areopagite] says that an understanding of God is not so much an approach toward something as toward nothing; and sacred ignorance teaches me that what seems nothing to the intellect is the incomprehensible Maximum.

—Nicholas of Cusa, *On Learned Ignorance* (Colie, 27)

Samuel Johnson's *Rasselas* offers paradoxical apothegms, which express with perfect clarity what cannot be said and inform us confidently of what he cannot know:

> What then is to be done? said Rasselas; the more we enquire, the less we can resolve. —Samuel Johnson, *Rasselas* (*SJ*, 560)

> It [the pyramid] seems to have been erected only in compliance with that hunger of imagination which preys incessantly upon life. . . . Those who have already all that they can enjoy, must enlarge their desires. He that has built for use, till use is supplied, must begin to build for vanity, and extend his plan to the utmost power of human performance, that he may not be soon reduced to form another wish.
>
> I consider this mighty structure as a monument to the insufficiency of human enjoyments. —Imlac, in *Rasselas* (*SJ*, 572–73)

These apothegms share a sense that what is most important lies beyond our reach. Some barrier occludes ultimate reality, the quiddity of things, the right way to live, and our truest self. What we can dimly see only invites us to look farther.

Mystery upon mystery, the gateway of the manifold secrets: language, reason, the mind, and introspection all fail, though not utterly. Each tells us just enough to demonstrate that there is more to know, much more important than what we already know. No system ever takes us far enough. We must probe, guess, and explore as best we can.

We know more surely than anything else our own ignorance.

> One will be the more learned, the more one knows one is ignorant. . . . So the intellect, which is not truth, never comprehends the truth so precisely but that it could always be comprehended with infinitely more precision. . . . Clearly, therefore, we know of the truth only that we know it cannot be comprehended precisely as it is. Truth is like the most absolute necessity, which can be neither more nor less than it is, while our intellect is like possibility. Therefore the quiddity of things, which is the truth of beings, is unattainable in its purity, and although it is pursued by all philosophers, none has found it as it is. The more profoundly learned we are in this ignorance, the more closely we draw near truth itself. —Nicholas of Cusa[23]

In the lines just before this example, Nicholas cites Socrates' belief that he knew nothing except his lack of knowledge, "Solomon's" declaration that the most important things are too difficult to be put into words, and Aristotle's comparison of our difficulty with that of a night owl looking at the sun (Nicholas, 88).

And yet we cannot *not* look. Kant famously, and apothegmically, begins *The Critique of Pure Reason*: "Human reason has this peculiar fate, that in one species of its knowledge it is burdened by questions which, as prescribed by the very nature of reason itself, it is not able to ignore, but which, as transcending all its powers, it is also not able to answer."[24] A "hunger of imagination preys incessantly on human life."

The Tale of the Converted Rationalist

Because apothegms so often deal with reason's failure, they appeal to disillusioned rationalists. These thinkers, led on by "the very nature of reason itself," have discovered the limits of reason. They glimpse the importance of what lies beyond.

Wittgenstein's *Tractatus* argues in the precise analytic way that his mentor, Bertrand Russell, hoped would provide foundational knowledge. But the book concludes in a quite different spirit, with a few pages of apothegms about the realm of the "mystical," where reason cannot go. Pascal turned to God only after making key contributions to science and mathematics. Before probing the Void, he worked on vacuums. He invented probability theory before approaching the incalculable.

For Pascal, no matter what other rationalists might say, the questions that really matter cannot be addressed by science, mathematics, or any other form of abstract rationality. Even the very axioms from which mathematicians begin are grasped intuitively, by the "heart," a term that Pascal uses to include not just feeling but also what we grasp but cannot prove.

The God of the rationalist philosophers—of the scholastics, the seventeenth-century rationalists, and the deists to come—has nothing to do with our most urgent questions. We require "the God of Abraham, the God of Isaac, the God of Jacob. Not the God of the philosophers and intellectuals," Pascal wrote in his famous "night of fire."[25]

Like some modern Oedipus, Tolstoy's Prince Andrei believes that intelligence and will, if combined with sufficient courage, can accomplish anything. With each disillusionment, he comes closer to realizing reason's impotence before the infinite. In *War and Peace*, Prince Andrei's greatest revelations are negative. They show us the mirage, the delusion, the nonexistent on which we falsely confer substance and significance:

> All is vanity, all is delusion, except those infinite heavens. There is nothing but that. And even that does not exist.
> —Prince Andrei, in *War and Peace* (*W&P*, 344)

This insight reveals itself to Andrei at Austerlitz when, wounded and thrown on his back, he literally changes his point of view. He turns from the chaos of war, which he imagines conforms to scientific law, to the infinite heavens, which make nonsense of human ambitions. All is vanity before those infinite heavens, and, paradoxically, even they do not exist. Tolstoy deeply admired Pascal and later translated Lao Tzu. Wittgenstein's *Tractatus*, in turn, owes much to Tolstoy's fiction.[26] Together they constitute a chain of unknowing.

Paradox

We grope endlessly through obscurities. The apothegm senses the world as dim but not entirely dark. Each tool we use to examine it distorts it, and so a kind of uncertainty principle reigns. We need language, but language fails; and yet in failing, it points beyond itself to what cannot be spoken of. The Way is "dimly visible, it cannot be named / And returns to that which is without substance." It is a "a shape that has no shape." Dostoevsky's *The Idiot* (whose title may allude to Nicholas of Cusa's *Idiota de mente*) repeatedly evokes paradoxes of wise folly, learned ignorance, and imageless images. In part 3 Ippolit asks: "Is it possible to perceive as an image that which has no image?"

By inviting us to conjure shapeless shape, visible darkness, the pregnant void, and speech about what cannot be spoken of, apothegms cultivate the language of paradox. Particularly common are paradoxes of Nothing treated as a sort of something, as we see in negative theology and Lao Tzu. In Zen, such paradoxes train the mind to think about what it cannot think about. Absence, Nonexistence, and Silence often become palpable examples of negative substances. Or, as in *Oedipus at Colonus*, the most fortunate people are those that have never existed.

Source and Speech Center

Apothegms by convention emerge from a distinctive speech center. They seem to come from outside the speaker, much as the Delphic oracles come not from, but through, the Pythoness. The god speaks obscurely through her.

Authors of dicta understand exactly what they are saying, but the speaker of an apothegm often does not quite grasp the significance of his words. Or he may grasp it as a mystery he has identified. More precisely, it has identified him. Teiresias speaks as if from beyond the play, and the light from beyond leaves him blind. He knows people cannot fathom divine justice.

And so the apothegm's speaker withholds full responsibility for what he says. He seems to warn: I do not say these words, I only cite them, and they may have meanings I do not suspect. Apothegms are not so much proclaimed as posed.

The source of an apothegm often seems to partake of its mystery. We know almost nothing of Lao Tzu (Old Master, a name that is not his true name). He may be identified with Lao Tan, a recluse whom, it is said, Confucius himself visited for instruction.[27] In his "night of fire" Pascal was seized by a truth beyond himself. Wittgenstein intimates that his basic ideas have come from outside rational discourse. They can be communicated only to someone who has already experienced them. The *Tractatus* begins: "Perhaps this book will be understood only by someone who has himself had the thoughts that are expressed in it" (*TLP*, 3). But then, why would one need the book? Or is it somehow possible to *learn* what one already knows?

For the authors of dicta, such questions do not arise. They know what they mean, convey a truth to all listeners, and take responsibility for uttering it. Bentham sounds nothing like Teiresias, nor does Marx resemble Lao Tzu. We may apply a dictum, or take it as the key to many things, but we do not go beyond it.

The dictum is a conclusion, the apothegm a beginning.

Fragments

Appropriately enough, apothegms often come as fragments. It is as if the full intelligence is not present, only hinted at.

Pascal left us only fragments, which could be, and have been, assembled in different ways. Each ordering shifts the meaning of passages by changing their context. The division of Lao Tzu's book into eighty-one parts (a mystical Chinese number) seems to be a later editorial decision. Even the succession of lines in a single "poem" sometimes reflects not a progression of thought but a stringing together of assertions on a given theme. Heraclitus apparently wrote a book, but the fragmentary quality of surviving lines has long seemed an essential part of them. They speak of the necessary incompleteness of the most important knowledge and, gesturing beyond themselves, almost make the white space following each fragment a part of it. Each apothegm becomes a flash extinguished before we have quite made out what it reveals.

We also sense it to be fitting that collections of such fragments should have been made by *others*. Pascal did not assemble the *Pensées*, nor Heraclitus his fragments, nor Lao Tzu the *Tao Te Ching*. It is as if the author were constantly engaged in interminable probing, lost in his mysteries, and so could not return for a complete statement, which therefore had to be assembled, with no great authority, by daunted followers. Dicta are complete in themselves, but apothegms seem to ask for an editor.

The dictum is spoken directly in the clear language of mathematics or science; the apothegm emerges indirectly from a dark god speaking in the obscure language of mystery; the hypothesis is spoken by a fallible human researcher in the language of intelligent guesswork.

Lao Tzu

Apothegms often seem to understand themselves as a way to approach an unreachable truth. In Lao Tzu, the ultimate principle lies beyond words, beyond mind, beyond the world. The Way (Tao) is not even nothing because it precedes the division into something and nothing. Prior to all the "myriad creatures," it escapes all attempts to name it. It stupefies silence as well as language, and all tools for grasping it fail since they belong to this world. They have been invented too late.

And yet, the *Tao Te Ching* nevertheless demonstrates a constant attempt to name the unnameable. No name for the Way can be the true name, but we must keep trying because knowledge of the Way is so valuable. The book of Lao Tzu therefore offers myriad names, all inadequate but all saying something: the Way is the uncarved block, the valley, the shapeless; it is the evanescent and the rarefied, the minute and the broad, the female and the baby; it acts out of emptiness, like a bellows, yet produces all things. It does all by doing nothing. But it is also not empty because emptiness came from it.

A. C. Graham reads the first chapter (or "poem") as a process. Each step is inadequate but the process as a whole is illuminating. After the first lines expressing the futility of naming, the poem continues:

> What has no name is the beginning of heaven and earth,
> What has a name is the mother of the myriad things,
> Therefore, by constantly having no desire, observe the sublime in it,
> By constantly having desire, observe where it tends.

(cited in Graham, 219)

Graham comments: "The trouble with words is not that they do not fit at all but that they always fit imperfectly; they can help us towards the Way, but only if each formulation in its inadequacy is balanced by the opposite which diverges in the other direction. 'Correct seeing is as though the wrong way round'" (Graham, 219–20). So the author constantly frames contraries, and many chapters proceed by trying out antithetical formulations. "The approach of Lao Tzu is to lay out couplets which, juxtaposed as parallel, imply both that there is and that there is not a constant Way with a constant name, and then try out the two alternatives in turn. Call the Way nameless and it is put back to the time before there were things distinguished by names; name it, and it becomes itself a thing out of which all other things have grown" (220).

Trying out antitheses, the sage is "tentative, as if fording a river in winter / Hesitant as if in fear of his neighbors" (*TTC*, 19). The book consists of one apparently definitive statement superseded by another, as the Way becomes clearer in its infinite indistinctness.

Although such apothegms resemble dicta in cultivating the language of direct assertion, they could not differ more. Dicta eschew metaphors, and Lao Tzu multiplies them; dicta trust language carefully used, while he constantly senses its inadequacy. Dicta cultivate clarity because they presume a world intelligible in the terms of human language. Apothegms are amazed when the mind's powers prove sufficient. They know how rarely human categories fit the world. "Hence the greatest cutting / Does not sever" (33).

Tractatus Logico-Philosophicus: Changing the World

In a letter to a prospective publisher, Wittgenstein wrote rather oddly: "My work consists of two parts, the one presented here plus all that I have *not* written. *And it is precisely this second part that is the important one.*"[28] The part that can be written is not the true part. It is hard to imagine such an avowal enticing a publisher.

The *Tractatus* as we have it consists of a long main section, which particularly impressed Bertrand Russell, and a concluding set of apothegms, which puzzled him. These apothegms concern what can and cannot be said. As has often been pointed out, both sections maintain that the most important things cannot be expressed in propositions (*gesagt*) but can only be shown (*gezeigt*).

First, Wittgenstein argues that propositions can picture reality but cannot picture how they picture it. "A proposition *shows* how things are *if* it is true" (*TLP*, 21). This relation must be seen. Then he maintains that the sense of life lies beyond propositions but can be seen. In the book's concluding section, propositions pointing to what they cannot say become apothegms.

Propositions describe what is *in* the world, but the meaning and the value of things lie *outside* the world:

> The sense of the world must lie outside the world. In the world everything is as it is, and everything happens as it does happen; *in* it no value exists—and if it did, it would have no value.
>
> If there is any value that does have value, it must lie outside the whole sphere of what happens and is the case. For all that happens and is the case is accidental.
>
> What makes it non-accidental cannot lie *within* the world, since if it did it would itself be accidental.
>
> It must lie outside the world. (71)

Both the good and the beautiful therefore lie outside what can be said:

> So too it is impossible for there to be propositions of ethics.
> Propositions can express nothing that is higher.
> It is clear that ethics cannot be put into words.
> Ethics is transcendental.
> (Ethics and aesthetics are one and the same.) (71)

Because propositions can express nothing that is higher, Wittgenstein turns to apothegms, which gesture toward the inexpressible. The propositions found in treatises on ethics and aesthetics must be mere babble because they confuse what is in the world and can be said with what is outside it and cannot. But apothegms neither affirm nor deny, they give a sign.

Apothegms point to what Wittgenstein calls "the mystical":

> When the answer cannot be put into words, neither can the question be put into words.
> The *riddle* does not exist.
> If a question can be framed at all, it is *possible* to answer it. (73)

The riddle does not exist: the world is not a riddle because a riddle has an answer, but the world does not allow for a coherent question. It is not a riddle but a mystery. One cannot arrive at the apothegmic truth by a chain of reasoning, but one may glimpse it. It may show itself.

No dicta will ever lead to value. They cannot touch the "problems of life."

When all scientific questions have been answered, when all statements about the world have been provided, "the problems of life remain completely untouched. Of course there are then no questions left, and this is itself the answer" (73). But what is an answer to no question? It is a changed sense of the world *as a whole*:

> The solution of the problem of life is seen in the vanishing of the problem.
>
> (Is this not the reason why those who have found after a long period of doubt that the sense of life became clear to them have been unable to say what constituted that sense?)
>
> There are indeed things that cannot be put into words. They *make themselves manifest*. They are what is mystical. (73)

When we sense the meaning of things it is not because we have found the answer to a riddle, but because what lies beyond has shown itself. What changes then is "only the limits of the world, not the facts—not what can be expressed by means of language. In short, the effect must be that it becomes an altogether different world. It must, so to speak, wax and wane as a whole. The world of the happy man is a different world from that of the unhappy man" (72). And these worlds belong to the apothegm.

Section 7 of the *Tractatus*, which is only one sentence long, remains its best-known apothegm: "What a man cannot speak about, he must pass over in silence" (74). Although this appears to be the shortest section, it is also its longest. We understand that not its words, but the silence following them, is the book's ending; and that silence does not cease.

The dictum must be complete or it is nothing. But we sense the emptiness around an apothegm as part of it. The dictum *says* Something. The apothegm *shows* Something Else.

❚ PARADOXES OF APOTHEGMS ❚

Apothegms typically address ultimate questions, which have no solution. They presume such questions are worth considering, for the insights offered both by each tentative answer and by the very process of inquiry. We train our minds to increase wisdom.

Questions about the mysteries of existence tend toward paradox. As the mind ventures beyond its proper domain, it encounters contradiction, infinite regress, and self-referential paradox. Aware of their predecessors, the great authors of apothegms contribute to old mysteries with new ones, which remain visible through each addition. Let us consider a few recurrent paradoxical themes.

Theme 1: The Pierre Paradox

Everything in nature is lyrical in its ideal essence, tragic in its fate, and comic in its existence.   —George Santayana[29]

The theme I call "the Pierre paradox" points to a mystery encountered by Pierre Bezukhov in *War and Peace*. Captured by the French and taken along during their hurried retreat, Pierre suffers extreme privation. Seated motionless by a campfire, he suddenly

> burst into such loud peals of exuberant, good-natured laughter that on every side men looked up in astonishment. . . .
>
> "Ha, ha, ha!" laughed Pierre. And he said aloud to himself: "The soldier did not let me pass. They took me and shut me up. They held me captive. Who is 'me'? . . . Me? Me—is my immortal soul! Ha, ha, ha! Ha, ha, ha! . . ." and he laughed till the tears came to his eyes.
>
> . . . Pierre stopped laughing . . . and looked around him.
>
> The vast, endless bivouac . . . had grown quiet. . . . High overhead in the luminous sky hung the full moon. Forests and fields . . . unseen before, were now visible in the distance. And farther still, beyond those fields and forests, was the bright shimmering horizon luring one on to infinity. Pierre contemplated the heavens, and the remote, receding, glimmering stars.
>
> "And all that is mine, all that is within me, and is *me*!" he thought. "And they caught all that and put it in a shed and barricaded it with planks!" (*W&P*, 1217)

Pierre encounters one of the ultimate mysteries fascinating apothists. How is it that mind is housed in matter, and thought, which can encompass the universe, happens at a particular place? This radical incommensurability defies comprehension. Yet we feel we must somehow come to terms with it. As Pierre looks into the distance, he sees farther and farther, into "the bright shimmering horizon luring on to infinity." The mystery he contemplates also draws him on, step by step, to questions without end.

Pierre recognizes the discrepancy between mind and its locale as *comic*: how absurd that you can lock infinity in a shed! Santayana shared this sense of comedy.

Existence is always here and now. It partakes of the accidental. But what Pierre calls "my immortal soul" is by its nature eternal. How can eternity be present, and why can it not escape? Each consciousness, contemplating the totality of time and place, senses itself as radically different from the world it knows. As Pascal writes, "[O]ut of all bodies together we could not succeed in creating one little thought. It is impossible and of a different order" (*P*, 125). And yet thought is somehow subject to the chain of material causes.

What Pierre finds comic can be profoundly disturbing. The contingency of existence lies at the heart of existentialist absurdity. "Everything is gratuitous," Sartre famously wrote. "When you suddenly realize it, it makes you feel sick and everything begins to drift. . . . [T]hat's nausea" (*YBQ*, 666). What evokes laughter in Pierre and nausea in Sartre produced terror in Pascal. In some of his most famous apothegms, he evokes the frightening powerlessness of consciousness aware of its absurd location at a point in space and time:

> When I consider the brief span of my life absorbed into eternity which comes before and after—*as the remembrance of a guest that tarried but a day* [John 21:16]—the small space I occupy and which I see swallowed up in the infinite immensity of spaces of which I know nothing and which know nothing of me, I take fright and am amazed to see myself here rather than there: there is no reason for me to be here rather than there, now rather than then. (*P*, 48)

> I see only eternity hemming me in like an atom or like the shadow of a fleeting instinct. (*P*, 158)

> The eternal silence of these infinite spaces fills me with dread. (*P*, 95)

What reason can there be for consciousness to be here rather than there, now rather than then? Pascal's universe terrifies because it is radically *alien*. His apothegms represent mystery as the source of cosmic loneliness.

The ultimate source of the universe's terrifying otherness is that I am conscious and it is not. Power and mind in opposition rule our mortal day. I think, but am infinitely weak; it is totally unconscious, but infinitely strong. And yet that very difference proves our nobility, as Pascal explains in his most famous apothegm:

> Man is but a reed, the most feeble thing in nature, but he is a thinking reed. The entire universe need not arm itself to crush him. A vapour, a drop of water, suffices to kill him. But if the universe were to crush him, man would still be more noble than that which killed him, because he knows that he dies and the advantage the universe has over him; the universe knows nothing of this.[30]

And elsewhere:

> All bodies, the firmament, the stars, the earth and its kingdoms are not worth the least of minds, for it knows them all and itself too, while bodies know nothing. (*P*, 125)

The Pierre Paradox: My Death

Because consciousness is embodied, it dies. Death is the ultimate mystery, mine for me and yours for you. Tolstoy's greatest novella, "The Death of Ivan Ilych," creates a story from another of Pascal's most famous apothegms, "We shall all die alone" (*P*, 80).

The self that dies is radically separate, not only from the material world but also from other selves. My consciousness is essentially *private*; I cannot directly experience the mind of another. I may know everything public about another conscious being, but I cannot experience being that other. Knowing from direct experience is one thing, and knowing *about*, from an outside perspective, is quite another.[31] Mortality therefore entails unspeakable loneliness.

Itself a narrativized apothegm, Tolstoy's novella contains several of his most-cited lines. Ivan Ilych has lived as if his public role exhausted his identity, but in his mortal illness he discovers the private self, inaccessible from the outside, that he has overlooked. He senses with horror that his role will go on but his "I" will die.

None of us can really grasp this fact, but for Ivan Ilych it is all the more terrible because he is losing the self just as he realizes he has it. He has thought of himself as his "place" (*mesto*), a word that means not only physical location but also job (position) and social role (place in society). He has assiduously avoided doing anything "inappropriate" (literally, out of place). But the self is not a place, and so he has missed it until, when dying, he recognizes that besides what is here and now, there is something *else*.

What Ivan Ilych takes to be the glory of his life, his amazing ability to "fit in" with others, depends on a "virtuoso" erasure of self. But as he will learn, nothing can be worse than success in such a venture. That is the meaning of the frequently cited apothegm that begins Chapter 2:

> Ivan Ilych's life was the most simple and most ordinary and therefore the most terrible. (*GSW*, 255)

The line contains a concealed syllogism: the simpler and more ordinary a life— the more it fits an expected pattern—the more terrible. As such, it prepares us for the novella's apothegmic center, the hero's reflections on a syllogism.

> The syllogism he had learnt from Kiesewetter's Logic: "Caius is a man, all men are mortal, therefore Caius is mortal," had always seemed correct to him as applied to Caius, but certainly not as applied to himself. That Caius—man in the abstract—was mortal, was perfectly correct, but he was not Caius, not an abstract man, but a creature quite, quite separate from all others. He had been little Vanya, with a mamma and a papa. . . . What did Caius know of the smell of that striped leather ball Vanya had been so fond of ? . . . "Caius really was mortal, and it was right for him to die; but for me, little Vanya, Ivan Ilych, with all my thoughts and emotions, it's altogether a different matter. It cannot be that I ought to die. That would be too terrible. . . . If I had to die like Caius I should have known it was so. An inner voice would have told me so, but there was nothing of the sort in me and I and all my friends felt that our case was quite different from that of Caius. And now here it is! . . . It can't be. It's impossible! But here it is. How is this? How is one to understand it?" (*GSW*, 280–81)

The phrase "Kiesewetter's Logic" has come to express this horrible sequence of thoughts. There is all the difference in the world between recognizing that because all men are mortal I will die and truly grasping one's own approaching death. It is the same difference as that between viewing oneself as a member of society and as a consciousness radically separate from everything else. For it is that consciousness that is to die.

What is true of Ivan Ilych is true of all his friends. "Peter Ivanovich felt reassured . . . as though death was an accident natural to Ivan Ilych but certainly not to himself" (*GSW*, 253). Reassuring himself the story is only fiction, each reader also excludes himself or herself. The story disturbs because it assaults the reader on the most sensitive point.

Theme 2: Self-Reference
and the Limits of Knowledge

The perplexity into which it [the mind] falls is not due to any fault of its own. . . .
[H]uman reason precipitates itself into darkness and contradictions, and while it
may indeed conjecture that these must be in some way due to concealed errors,
it is not in a position to detect them.   —Immanuel Kant (3)

To convey their sense of mystery, apothegms often develop paradoxes of
knowledge. The most valuable knowledge lies beyond our capacity, but we cannot cease searching for it. We seek illumination in a realm of "darkness and
contradictions."

We have already seen one common paradox: our minds seek a form of
knowledge that by their very nature they cannot attain. Our minds can no
more escape their own limits than a person could, like Baron Munchausen, lift
himself out of a swamp by his own hair.

No matter how certain a truth appears, we could be deceiving ourselves out
of a desire for certainty. Our wakefulness could be part of a dream. The second
classic of Taoism, the book of Chuang Tzu, contains a particularly well-known
apothegm about the dreamer's paradox:

> Once upon a time, Chuang Chou dreamed that he was a butterfly, a butterfly
> flitting and happily enjoying himself. He didn't know that he was Chou. Sud-
> denly he awoke and was palpably Chou. He didn't know whether he were Chou
> who had dreamed of being a butterfly, or a butterfly who was dreaming that he
> was Chou. (*YBQ*, 151)

Chou would have no way of knowing whether he is Chou or only dreaming he
is Chou because in both cases he would feel like Chou. Any test could itself be
part of the dream. One can dream one is pinching oneself.

There is no safe place to stand, no position not already implicated in the
question. Numerous apothegms concern the necessity but impossibility of occupying an external vantage point. "Can a man himself tell that he is going
mad?" asks Ivan Karamazov (*BK*, 730). In *War and Peace*, Prince Andrei "pic-
tured the world without himself," but his picture of that world includes his act
of watching it (*W&P*, 926).

Can one be objective in knowing oneself? In Erasmus's *Praise of Folly*, the
goddess Folly offers what she presents as a sober self-assessment, but isn't she
a fool to believe it? "You shall hear, then, an encomium, not of Hercules, nor of
Solon, but rather of myself—that is, of Folly."[32] A physician might heal himself,

or a lawyer defend himself, but a judge cannot judge himself. One cannot discern if one is insane because one might be discerning insanely. Fools and wise men both consider themselves wise.

Folly praises folly itself as wise, but that is what fools do. Or is this the folly of God? "Hath God not made foolish the wisdom of the world?" asks Saint Paul (1 Corinthians 1:20). How does one tell wise folly from foolish folly, and wise wisdom from foolish wisdom? And is it the wise or the fools who are best situated to do so? Erasmus's book answers each question with its own inversion. Folly's companion Philautia (Self-Love) tells her to praise herself, but does this self-reference create an analog to the Liar paradox: the Folly paradox?

Erasmus's book belongs to a literary genre expanding on the apothegm's paradoxical logic. The "rhetorical paradox" praises something conventionally unpraisable. Ancient works in this genre (some of which Folly mentions) include Lucian's praise of the fly and Ovid's of the nut. Humanist collections included encomia to the ant, the flea, the fly, the ass, bastardy, the pox, tyranny, imprisonment, drunkenness, and incontinence (Colie, 4). Logical paradox necessarily inheres in the rhetorical paradox because if something is unpraisable it cannot be, but evidently is, praised. By convention, the speaker of a rhetorical paradox both does and does not mean the praise parodically. When he does, he may also intend parody of parody. The genre creates a dizzying experience. It allows no vantage point. In so doing, it dramatizes the endless labyrinth of the apothegm. Many famous apothegms come from rhetorical paradoxes.

Erasmus sharpens the tradition's paradoxes by choosing, as the author of a rhetorical paradox in praise of folly, Folly herself. Folly explicitly, even pedantically, instructs us in the genre to which her discourse belongs. Seriously and parodically, foolishly and wisely, consciously and self-consciously, she praises her folly, her self-praise, and her unpraisability.

Dostoevsky invented the most famous rhetorical paradoxes. One need only remember that the narrator of *Notes from Underground* offers a self-referential encomium to the advantage of disadvantage. Dostoevsky's novella develops the apothegm in two ways—as a diatribe in part 1 and a narrative in part 2—each of which answers the dicta of Bentham and other utilitarians.

Apothegms about the impossibility of important knowledge may also rely on the need to express in language what goes beyond language, to approach transcendent reality with mundane tools, to describe infinity in finite terms, or to account for the irrational rationally. The way that can be spoken of is not the true way. To mock philosophy is to philosophize truly.

And how does one speak about "things that cannot be put into words" (*TLP*, 73)? With self-canceling paradoxes and propositions that use themselves up.

> My propositions serve as elucidations in the following way: anyone who un-derstands me eventually recognizes them as nonsensical, when he has used them—as steps—to climb up beyond them. (He must, so to speak, throw away the ladder after he has climbed up it.)
>
> He must transcend these propositions, and then he will see the world aright.
> (*TLP*, 74)

Whoever sees the world aright will be unable to say what makes it so. Apo-thegms often seek to transcend themselves.

Theme 3: The Futility of Knowledge, or Luxurious in Disaster

Some apothegms about knowledge concern not its impossibility but its futility. It can be worthless or even harmful, just another source of pain.

Greek literature often dramatizes the futility of knowledge. In the *Oedipus*, Teiresias remembers dark wisdom about wisdom itself:

> Wisdom is a dreadful thing when it brings no good to its possessor. I knew this well, but I forgot. Otherwise, I would not have come here. (*OTK*, 362)

In much the same way, foresight causes only misery to Cassandra in Aeschylus's *Agamemnon*. As Teiresias is symbolically blind, she is symbolically captive, un-able to act on what she knows. She can only suffer in advance. Cassandra voices the meaning of her story:

> What does it matter now if men believe or no?
> What is to come will come. . . .
> Why do I wear these mockeries upon my body,
> This staff of prophecy, these flowers at my throat?
> At least I will spoil you before I die. Out, down,
> Break, damn you! This for all you have done to me.
> Make someone else, not me, luxurious in disaster.[33]

Herodotus narrates several stories, each closing with an apothegm, con-cerning paradoxes of knowledge. Close to the end of his history, the Thebans invite fifty Persians and an equal number of Thebans to a feast in honor of Mardonius, the powerful Persian general in Greece. The Persian seated with

Thersander offers him a "memorial of my opinion," so that Thersander can see to his own interest. "Do you see these Persians feasting here, and the army that we left encamped by the river? Of these you will see, after the lapse of a small space of time, only some few surviving" (*H*, 550). The Persian voices one of Herodotus's favorite morals, the instability of fortune. Thersander asks why the Persian does not share this insight with Mardonius, so the disaster can be averted. The Persian replies that the disaster to come is unavoidable, since it is one of those mysterious dictates of fate. Advance knowledge does no good.

Indeed, it is a mark of fate's mysterious power that it can handicap itself by giving advance warning. Speaking his Greek wisdom in Greek, the Persian voices the point of the story:

> My friend, that which is fated by the deity to happen, it is impossible for man
> to avert, for no one will listen to those who say what is worthy of credit; and
> though many of the Persians are convinced of this, we follow, being bound by
> necessity. (550)

Fate mysteriously includes the fact that even when it is revealed, "no one will listen to those who say what is worthy of credit." Foresight is futile. If the gods sometimes disclose the nature of things, we still cannot fathom their reasons nor act to change their mysterious dictates. On the contrary, painful and worthless knowledge of fate may itself be part of fate's design. The Persian concludes with a characteristic apothegm: "The bitterest grief to which men are liable is this, when one knows much, to have no power to act" (550).

Theme 4: Belief and the Will to Believe

Lord, I believe; help thou mine unbelief.   —Mark 9:24

For here possibilities, not finished facts, are the realities with which we have
to deal.   —William James[34]

Some apothegms concern paradoxes of belief. They center on what William James called the "will to believe" and Dostoevsky the "urge to belief."

How can one will to believe? If one wills to believe something, then one does not believe it. It would therefore seem that the will to believe is the desire for self-deception. But to desire self-deception is to desire belief in what one knows to be false, which would not really be belief at all. After all, does not belief mean the conviction that something is true?

And yet, as the line from Mark illustrates and James's essay argues, the will to believe may indeed be a kind of belief. If the test of belief is action, and one consults a priest about overcoming one's disbelief, then is one a believer or not? Could it be that most belief is of this sort?

James points to cases in which, paradoxically, "*faith in a fact can help create the fact*" (James, 25). There are "faiths that verify themselves" (61). James's logic resembles what Robert Merton later called "the self-fulfilling prophecy," except that what Merton takes to be an unfortunate tendency to be corrected, James describes with approval.[35]

Whenever a community relies on cooperative action, James explains, it depends on each member's "precursive faith" that in acting for the community's benefit, he or she will not be acting alone (James, 24). For each person, trust in others verifies itself, and so would distrust. This logic applies more broadly.

James reasons: scientists would have us withhold assent to any proposition not supported by sufficient evidence. But they ignore certain sorts of issues with three defining characteristics: First, these issues are essentially matters of "possibility" or "maybes." Second, one cannot remain aloof from them because the choice not to act or believe is itself a choice with consequences. And third, whatever choice one makes will have a tendency to verify itself, like the trust that makes cooperative action possible.

For James, the most vital question of all—suicide—is of this sort. In a world of "maybe," one *must* choose for or against faith in meaningfulness, because to hold aloof has the same effect as choosing against. Whichever choice one makes will itself tend to make life meaningful or meaningless. We cannot avoid this "maybe."

> But "*may* be! *may* be!" one hears the positivist contemptuously exclaim; "what use can a scientific life have for maybes?" Well, I reply . . . human life at large has everything to do with them. So far as a man stands for anything, and is productive or originative at all, his entire vital function may be said to have to deal with maybes. . . . It is only by risking our persons from one hour to another that we may live at all. And often enough, our faith beforehand in an unverified result *is the only thing that makes it true.* (58–59)

Maybe, choice, risk: one can no more avoid them than one can take a "time out" from life to weigh how to live. Living includes the time in which we choose how (or whether) to live. And choices may shape the world they presume:

> Refuse to believe, and you shall indeed be right, for you shall irretrievably perish. But believe, and again you shall be right, for you shall save yourself. You

make one or the other of two possible universes true by your trust or mistrust—both universes having been only *maybes*. (James, 59)

God himself, in short, may draw vital strength and increase of very being from our fidelity. For my own part, I do not know what the sweat and blood and tragedy of this life mean, if they mean anything, short of this. If this be not a real fight, in which something is eternally gained for the universe by success, it is no better than a game of private theatricals . . . but it *feels* like a real fight. . . . For such a half-wild, half-saved universe our nature is adapted. (James, 61)

James cites Pascal's apothegms and follows the logic of Pascal's famous "wager." Understood apothegmically, and in a Jamesian way, Pascal's point is not that the laws of probability prove the necessity of belief, but that one cannot stand aloof. "You must wager. There is no choice; you are already committed" by virtue of being alive (*P*, 150). For James, morality, no less than meaningfulness, entails commitment in the face of uncertainty: "If I refuse to stop a murder because I am in doubt whether it be not justifiable homicide, I am virtually abetting the crime. . . . Skepticism in moral matters is an active ally of immorality. Who is not for is against. The universe will have no neutrals in these questions" (James, 109).

Apothegms of belief often represent faith not as the opposite of doubt but as containing doubt. From this perspective, mere dogmatic assertion is not faith at all. Faith dwells in the realm of possibility. "A possibility is a hint from God," writes Kierkegaard (*A*, 18).

For Pascal, it is essential that "God should be partly concealed and partly revealed" (*P*, 167). If He were completely concealed, we would not suspect Him, while if He were completely revealed, we would not be *choosing* to believe in him. God wanted a world in which free beings, not automatons or slaves, risk worshiping him. They choose belief, and choice demands uncertainty. For Kierkegaard:

Without risk there is no faith. Faith is precisely the contradiction between the infinite passion of the individual inwardness and the objective uncertainty. If I am capable of grasping God objectively, I do not believe, but precisely because I cannot do this I must believe. If I wish to preserve myself in faith I must constantly be intent upon holding fast to the objective uncertainty, so as to remain out upon the deep, over seventy thousand fathoms of water, still preserving my faith. (*DPQ*, 234)

"Life is doubt," wrote Unamuno, "and faith without doubt is nothing but death" (*MDQ*, 202).

Dostoevsky regarded faith and dogma in much the same way as Pascal. In *The Brothers Karamazov*, the Grand Inquisitor reproaches Jesus for leaving room for doubt. He should have accepted the devil's temptation to prove his divinity once and for all. "Thou wouldst not enslave man by a miracle, and didst crave faith freely given, not based on miracle. Thou didst crave for free love and not the base raptures of the slave before the might that has overawed him forever" (*BK*, 304).

On his way to Siberian imprisonment, Dostoevsky wrote what is probably the most quoted letter of Russian literature. It contains a famous apothegm about faith defined by doubt:

> About myself I must tell you that I am a child of the age, a child of unbelief, to this day and even (I know) to the edge of the grave. What terrible torments the thirst to believe has cost and still costs me, becoming all the greater in my soul for the arguments against it in my mind. . . . Even more: *if somebody proved to me that Christ is outside the truth, and if it were a fact that the truth excludes Christ, I would rather remain with Christ than with the truth.*[36]

What does it mean to accept (not merely to profess) as truth what one believes to be untrue? For Dostoevsky, such paradoxes arise from the mysteries of faith, which demands doubt, and of belief, which consists of the struggle to believe.

Theme 5: Paradoxes of Action and Nonaction

As knowledge may prove harmful, so action designed to achieve a goal may achieve the very opposite. Victories may actually turn out to be defeats. We call such disastrous triumphs "Pyrrhic victories" because Plutarch, in his life of the Macedonian conqueror Pyrrhus, reports that after one battle with the Romans, "Pyrrhus replied to one that gave him joy of his victory that one other such would utterly undo him" (*PL*, 483).

By the same token, defeat can turn out to be victory and weakness can be a strength. For obvious reasons, the religion of the crucified Christ cultivates such paradoxes. "For my strength is made perfect in weakness. . . . Therefore I take pleasure in infirmities, in reproaches, in necessities, in persecutions, in distresses, for Christ's sake: for when I am weak, then am I strong" (2 Corinthians 12:9–10). Lao Tzu advised that nonaction can be the most effective action.

Do that which consists in taking no action; pursue that which is not meddle-some; savour that which has no flavour. (*TTC*, 70)

Hence the sage says,

> I take no action and the people are transformed of themselves.
> I prefer stillness and the people are rectified of themselves.
> I am not meddlesome and the people prosper of themselves.
> I am free from desire and the people of themselves become simple like the
>   uncarved block. (*TTC*, 64)

Whoever does anything to it will ruin it; whoever lays hold of it will lose it. Therefore the sage, because he does nothing, never ruins anything; and, because he does not lay hold of anything, loses nothing. (*TTC*, 71)

> Therefore the sage desires not to desire
> And does not value goods which are hard to come by;
> Learns to be without learning . . .
> In order to help the myriad creatures . . . to refrain from daring to act.
>   (*TTC*, 71)

In his essay "Non-acting," which cites Lao Tzu, Tolstoy offers his own apo-thegms:[37] "If work be not actually a vice it can from no point of view be consid-ered a virtue. It can no more be considered a virtue than nutrition" (*TRE*, 153). "That men may organize their life in conformity with their consciences, they need expend no positive effort; they need only pause" (169).

Kutuzov offers much the same advice in *War and Peace*, which reads like an extended Taoist parable. Like Napoleon, most Russian and Austrian generals believe in aggressive action. Kutuzov wins by nonaction, or what he calls "pa-tience and time." The French attribute their defeat to the "ferocity of [Mayor] Rostopchin," and Russians "place the heroic torch in the hands of the people," but in Tolstoy's view Moscow burned down without anyone's action, because any city made of wood and abandoned by its inhabitants was bound to burn down (*W&P*, 1076). The ones responsible for the fire had no thought of setting one. They caused it to burn by what they did *not* do: contrary to Napoleon's expectations and Rostopchin's orders, they did not stay. "Moscow was burned by its inhabitants, it is true, but by those who abandoned her, not by those who stayed behind" (1076).

Taken as a whole, Plutarch's "Life of Pyrrhus" reads as a story about action taken because of a pointless love of action. Like Achilles, Pyrrhus "could not endure repose" and therefore caused all the horrors of war (*PL*, 475). Plutarch leaves it to Pyrrhus's chief diplomat and resident philosopher, Cineas, to point out the pointlessness of restless ambition. When Cineas asks what Pyrrhus will do after conquering Rome, Pyrrhus replies that he will go on to conquer all Italy, and when Cineas asks, what then?, Pyrrhus, "not yet discovering his intention," replies by identifying more and more conquests until all is under his sway. And what then? "Said Pyrrhus, '[W]e will live at our ease, my dear friend, and drink all day, and divert ourselves with pleasant conversation.'" Cineas answers memorably: "And what hinders us now, sir, if we have a mind to be merry?" (477).

Theme 6: The Process Paradox

Paradoxes of action and nonaction concern striving for a goal. Like paradoxes about the will to believe, they focus on means as more than mere means.

Dicta and utopias offer knowledge capable of perfecting life. Apothegms of process and anti-utopias suggest that, even if such goals could be achieved, their very realization would prove disastrous. Such apothegms point to a mystery at the heart of purpose itself.

If life were perfect, people would suffer boredom. If they had achieved all goals, they would be miserable until they invented more. Those who have already all that they can enjoy, must enlarge their desires. Somehow, humanness requires the process of striving itself.

Apothegms of process imagine boredom as a key force in life. Boredom is a nothing understood as a something, an ever present absence people would do almost anything to avoid. The most famous expression of this idea belongs to Pascal: "I have often said that the sole cause of man's unhappiness is that he does not know how to sit quietly in a room" (*P*, 67).

Give a man everything he desires, Pascal muses, and his "limp felicity" will soon make him wish for more wishes. Vacuity horrifies, both in itself and because of thoughts of "inescapable death and disease" to which it gives rise (67). Let us say a man gambles a small sum every day. "Give him every morning the money he might win that day, on condition that he does not gamble, and you will make him unhappy" (70). Fear of boredom therefore creates "the insatiable nature of cupidity" (69). "All our life passes in this way: we seek rest by struggling against certain obstacles, and once they are overcome, rest proves intolerable because of the boredom it produces" (69). "Telling a man to rest is the same as telling him to live happily. . . . It means not understanding his nature"

(68). Pascal reads Plutarch's story of Pyrrhus and Cineas in these terms: "Thus when Pyrrhus was advised to take the rest towards which he was so strenuously striving, he found it very hard to do so" (68).

For Pascal, life *is* process. We imagine we want goals, but in fact we want the process of achieving them. Pyrrhus already has the goal for which he ostensibly strives. People spend all day chasing a hare they would not want if given to them, because "the hare itself would not save us from thinking about death and the miseries distracting us, but hunting it does so" (68). Therefore, as another of Pascal's best-known apothegms reads, "we prefer the hunt to the capture" (68).

Pascal's paradox lends itself to anti-utopian narratives. We should reject utopian schemes not just because they fail (the third book of *Gulliver's Travels*), or because the attempt to realize them leads to endless bloodshed (novels about the French revolution), or because if utopians ever gained power their heaven would more closely resemble hell (*The Possessed, 1984*). Even if utopian schemes could create the heaven they imagine, that very heaven would create a hell of vacuity and boredom.

Anti-utopias often tell the story of escape from utopia. The hero leaves certain happiness to pursue misery—or, more accurately, the possibility of misery. The world must be uncertain if life is to have any meaning. Effort must matter. The eponymous hero of Dr. Johnson's *Rasselas* seeks to escape from the "happy valley," where "the blessings of nature were collected, and its evils extracted and excluded" (*SJ*, 506). The only vicissitudes allowed are "the soft vicissitudes of pleasure and repose" (508). Rasselas discovers "the wants of him that wants nothing" (510). "That I want nothing, said the prince, or that I know not what I want, is the cause of my complaint; if I had any known want, I should have a certain wish; that wish would excite endeavour" (511).

Candide flees Eldorado. When at last he and his companions achieve a respite from adventure and suffering, they cannot endure the stupefaction of inactivity.

> [W]hen they were not arguing, the boredom was so excessive that one day the old woman dared to say to them: "I should like to know which is worse, to be raped a hundred times . . . to have a buttock cut off, to run the gauntlet . . . to be whipped and flogged in an *auto-da-fé*, to be dissected . . . to endure all the miseries through which we have passed, or to remain here doing nothing?" "'Tis a great question," said Candide. (*V*, 324–25)

The wise Martin concludes that "man was born to live in the convulsions of distress or the lethargy of boredom" (325). In *Brave New World*, the Savage demands what people have always avoided: "I don't want comfort. I want God, I want poetry, I want real danger, I want freedom, I want goodness, I want sin. . . . I'm claiming the right to be unhappy."[38]

The Process Paradox: Dostoevsky

Without suffering what could be the pleasure of it [life]? It would be transformed into an endless church service; it would be holy, but tedious. . . . [T]he indispensable minus would disappear at once . . . and that, of course, would mean the end of everything, even of magazines and newspapers, for who would take them in?

—The devil, in *The Brothers Karamazov* (*BK*, 780–81, 787)

The psychology of Pascal's paradox fascinated Dostoevsky and inspired several of his best-known apothegms. In one anti-utopian sketch appearing in his *Writer's Diary*, he argues that people do not want what they want. Satisfy all human desires, as Russian socialists promise, and before a generation has passed, people would recognize that "there is no happiness in inactivity," that without striving life makes no sense, and that one cannot love without real sacrifice. If perfection were achieved, "people would be overcome by boredom and sickness of heart" simply because "*happiness lies not in happiness but only in the attempt to achieve it*" (*AWD1*, 335). A passage in *The Idiot* begins and ends with two of the best-known apothegms in Russian literature:

> Oh, you may be sure that Columbus was happy not when he had discovered America, but while he was discovering it. Take my word for it, the highest moment of his happiness was just three days before the discovery of the New World, when the mutinous crew were on the point of returning to Europe in despair. It wasn't the New World that mattered, even if it had fallen to pieces. . . . It's life that matters, nothing but life—the process of discovering, the everlasting and perpetual process, not the discovery at all. (*I*, 375)

The narrator of *Notes from Underground* ascribes the human instinct for destruction—what Freud was to call the death instinct—to our dimly perceived awareness that we must make sure not to achieve our goal. The Crystal Palace of the socialists resembles an "anthill," but, unlike the ant,

> man is a frivolous and incongruous creature, and perhaps, like a chessplayer, likes only the process of the game, not the end of it. And who knows . . . perhaps

the only goal on earth to which mankind is striving lies in this incessant process of attaining. . . . Anyway, man . . . likes the process of attaining, but does not quite like to have attained, and that of course, is terribly funny. In short, man is a comical creature; there seems to be a kind of pun in it all. (*NFU*, 30)

The "pun" arises from the logic that makes Pascal's paradox paradoxical. As soon as one discovers that it is the striving that matters and not the goal, the goal loses its value. But with no goal, one could not strive. The hare does not matter, but without the belief that it does there is no hunt. Process is the end that matters only by virtue of an end that does not.

Is there a goal to which Pascal's paradox would not apply? One for which we could still strive despite knowing that it is the striving that really matters? Such a goal would continually recede. The more we strove to reach it, the more valuable it would become, but it would still be just as far away.

The apothegm itself follows this very logic. Life well lived resembles not a puzzle finally solved but an apothegm endlessly probed.

3

WITTICISMS AND WITLESSISMS

❚ THE RESOURCEFULNESS OF WIT ❚

They are fond of fun and therefore witty, wit being well-bred insolence.

—Aristotle[1]

Presentness

Witticisms express the power of mind over circumstance, especially social cir-cumstance. To whatever surprise may arise from the insults of others, the chal-lenge of fellow wits, or the sheer power of the unexpected, the wit proves equal. Always capable of parrying thrusts with surprising deftness, the wit serves as a model of agility, style, and intelligence.

As we have seen, dicta also express the power of mind, but a quite different power. The truths enunciated in the dicta of Marx, Freud, Leibniz, and Spinoza apply always and everywhere. No contingent circumstance prompts them. Like the propositions and proofs of Euclid, dicta neither require nor depend on knowledge of who said them for what reason. They are tied to no occasion, and although they may have been formulated at an identifiable time, they are tethered to no moment. For Aristotle, the truths I call dicta must always be true, whereas other judgments, like those reflecting practical wisdom, are cor-rect only, as he likes to say, on the whole and for the most part. Practical judg-ments are timely, but the theorems of mathematics and the philosophical dicta resembling them are, or claim to be, timeless.

Unlike dicta, witticisms depend on timing. Miss the moment and the witticism misfires. The sort of intelligence displayed by a successful witticism testifies to the importance of *presentness*.

Without delay, the successful wit masters all the complexities of a set of social circumstances and formulates the apropos response that illuminates them. A surprising challenge seems to allow for no good response, but the wit instantly finds one. A heckler may ambush him. Or the wit may offer to improvise on any suggested topic. Or he may just seize the opportunity offered by someone's ill-worded comment. Whatever the provocation, the wit is ready.

Lord Sandwich at the Beef Steak Club (or, in other versions, a heckler at a rally) told liberal politician John Wilkes he would die either of a pox or on the gallows: "'My Lord,' replied Wilkes instantaneously, 'that will depend on whether I embrace your lordship's mistress or your lordship's principles'" (*BBA*, 576). Asked by a vicar what he would like his sermon to be about, the Duke of Wellington immediately replied: "about ten minutes" (*MDQ*, 481). To a lady who told James Whistler that "this landscape reminds me of your work," Whistler promptly answered, "Yes, madam, nature is creeping up" (*MDQ*, 481). Disraeli (in other versions Wilde) offered to "speak on any subject," and Gladstone suggested "the Queen." Disraeli's instantaneous reply is a classic: "The Queen is not a subject" (*VLR*, 40).

Instantly, instantaneously, without missing a beat, promptly: these words constantly recur in anecdotes about great witty responses. When a lady insulted Churchill, when the audience booed Shaw, when someone challenged Dorothy Parker—the wit's clever response had to come at once. We marvel at how she could seize the moment and say something so clever so quickly. Like rescues in an adventure story, witticisms come in the nick of time. The wit cannot go home, work on a response, and return to pronounce it the next day. She must deliver it "on the spot" in both senses of that term: right here and right now.

It would not do to describe how someone insulted Dorothy Parker and, after scratching her head and pausing a while, Dorothy tried out a few replies until at last she found a good one. The opportunity for an apt response is fleeting, so the more quickly the wit responds, the better she displays the adequacy of mind to circumstance. Conversely, the common lament "I shoulda said" testifies that afterthought cannot substitute for presentness. "I can always make excellent impromptu replies, if only I have a moment to think," wrote Rousseau, sounding like Groucho.[2] Diderot referred to the witty answers that occur to one a bit too late as "staircase wit" (*l'esprit de l'escalier*; *ODHQ*, 350).

The ideal is to respond with no discernible break between challenge and response. When most successful, the wit replies before the full import of the challenge even registers with the onlookers, so they grasp both at the same time.
"The true *bon-mot*," observed Joubert, "surprises him who makes it as much as
those who hear it."[3]

Speed matters not only in its own right but also as a sign of effortlessness. The
cleverness we so admire must seem to come as readily as shifting one's weight.
Wit demands what Castiglione called "sprezzatura" (nonchalance) and "disinvoltura" (ease). To the extent the witty reply seems labored, it fails, and delay
bespeaks labor. Successful wit is a sample of that "true art" which, as Castiglione
explains, "does not seem to be art; nor must one be more careful of anything
than of concealing it, because if it is discovered, this robs a man of all credit."[4]

Just as one demonstrates the most bodily grace when executing a difficult
dance step as if it were as easy as walking, so the witty reply demonstrates the
greatest power of mind when it seems to show how the wit thinks when not
even paying much attention. Then "it impresses upon the minds of the onlookers the opinion that he who performs well with so much facility must possess
even greater skill than this" (Castiglione, 46). If Wilde can be so clever without
trying, what could he do if he were?

Audience and Salon

Unlike other short genres, wit demands an audience. The dictum smells of the
study or the laboratory. We eavesdrop on Pascal's "thoughts" because they are
essentially private, between himself and God. But only a fool makes witticisms
when no one is around. Indeed, one could hardly discover a more effective way
to make a wit look ridiculous than to represent him trying so hard to be witty
that, even in private, he is always practicing. In *Anna Karenina*, Tolstoy exposes
Stiva Oblonsky in just this way. Humiliated as he is kept waiting two hours by a
wealthy Jew, Stiva tries to master the situation mentally by doing what he does
so well in society, make a witticism, if only for himself. But humiliation does
not comport with nonchalance, and we watch him trying "very hard to hide
from others [in the waiting room] and even from himself the feeling he was
experiencing." We also spy on him laboring at what purports to be spontaneous
and feeling even more uncomfortable "because he could not get his pun just
right" (*AK*, 752).

The proper locale for a witticism is the salon, a social place where a crowd
of the right people has gathered. The salon developed from the court as de-

scribed by Castiglione, and both presume the sort of values, behavior, and cultivation that encourage wit. Other locales, such as formal dinners or receptions, work insofar as they resemble the court and the salon. The converse is also true. A successful witticism transforms the locale in which it takes place into a sort of salon substitute. Or we may say: not only is the salon a favorable place for a witticism, its aura constitutes an essential part of the witticism, much as the funeral or commemoration constitutes an essential part of the eulogy.

Story and Anthology

Because witticisms respond to a situation, they demand a story. That is why the very same witticisms appear in anthologies of aphorisms and collections of anecdotes. In the anecdote, the witticism serves as the climax, the reason the anecdote is told. Anthologizers of aphorisms work at a disadvantage, because they must *explain* the line which either would make no sense or not be witty presented as other aphorisms are, on its own and without a story.

> Sparrowhawks, Ma'am.
>> —Duke of Wellington (1769–1852). British general and statesman.
>> Advice when asked by Queen Victoria how to remove sparrows
>> from the Crystal Palace. Attrib. (*MBQ,* 481)

> How do they know?
>> —Dorothy Parker, on being told that Calvin Coolidge had died (*ODQ,* 586)

Jokes don't work as well when the punchline comes first; they turn into momentary riddles. When the explanation is provided, readers must then reread the line so as to understand it as a response. *The Yale Book of Quotations* comes closer to the anecdote by providing the explanation (a sort of abbreviated anecdote) first. In the entry devoted to Dorothy Parker we find:

> [Upon being challenged to use the word horticulture in a sentence:] You can lead a whore to culture, but you can't make her think. (*YBQ,* 581)

> [Of Clare Booth Luce, who was said to be invariably kind to her inferiors:] Where does she find them? (*YBQ,* 580)

Longer Forms: The Anecdote

Today, the anecdote and the witticism seem to be two sides of the same coin, but that was not always the case. Conventional discussions of the form, which rely too much on the term "anecdote," trace it at least as far back as the sixth-century historian Procopius's scandalous work about the emperor Justinian and his wife Theodora that we know as the *Secret History*. Its Greek title is *Anekdota* (things not given out). In the Renaissance, it came to mean a form of condensed and artful gossip. Isaac D'Israeli (1766–1848) claims in his *Dissertation on Anecdotes* that the French extended the meaning of the term to mean "any interesting circumstance," and Dr. Johnson defined it as "a *biographical incident*; a minute passage of *private life*." By the nineteenth century, it was already clearly associated with wit, perhaps especially the wit of worldly older men, who (as the bon mot had it) could eventually fall into their "anecdotage."[5] Thus *Bartlett's Book of Anecdotes* senses in these short narratives "the atmosphere of the court, the great house, the capital . . . the club, the dinner party, the university, the theatre, the studio and gallery, the law courts, parliament and senates"—that is, the same locales in which we expect to find witticisms.

If we do not worry too much about the term, it becomes obvious that the genre we now call anecdotes extends, if often by other names, back to antiquity. The ancient Greeks and Romans loved pointed stories ending in a surprising display of wit. Diogenes Laertius's *Lives of Eminent Philosophers* reads like a compendium of philosophical witticisms, and stories culminating in witty remarks occur repeatedly in Plutarch. Ever since, biographies and, until quite recently, histories have served as a common source for collectors to mine.

One might think that when these collectors extract, shorten, and paraphrase stories from a much longer source, they would make the anecdotes and witticisms more effective. After all, brevity is the soul of wit, and no one wants to hear a shaggy dog anecdote. And yet, more often than not, the very opposite is the case. The extracted story, retold for a collection of such stories, comes to seem forced and not nearly so funny. Why should that happen?

A quick perusal of Bartlett's or similar anthologies provides ready answers. For one thing, witticisms work best when they come as a surprise, and the mere fact of appearing in an anthology makes surprise impossible. That is all the more so when they perforce occur one after another. No matter how much *sprezzatura* and *disinvoltura* the wit may have displayed, his collector's voice strains after effect. Anthologies of anecdotes, like joke books, convey the very opposite of what made the witticism funny in the first place. It's like telling someone to look elsewhere because one is sneaking up on him.

Moreover, many witticisms work by calling attention to details of a situation we may have vaguely noticed without grasping their significance. The wit shows us what we missed, why we missed it, and why it makes a difference, all in one remark. But once the anecdote mentions those details, as it must to set up the punchline, they move from the periphery to the center of our attention. It is virtually impossible to reproduce the surprise of showing that they were there. Imagine a detective story boiled down to a paragraph that had to contain the clues so easily overlooked in a novel.

Boswell and the Storyteller's Paradox

Once one understands how stories about anecdotes work, one may appreciate why Boswell, as well as Johnson, ranks as a master of wit.

Not just anyone can tell the story of a witticism. For example, the wit usually cannot tell it about himself. If he did, he risks demonstrating not presence of mind but an all-too-common pretense to it. That is why wits often attribute their own mots to another: "Someone once said . . ."; "As a wag once put it."[6]

As he well knew, Johnson required Boswell. A true artist of witty stories, Boswell also understood how a biography favored their telling. Biographies allow the storyteller to hide significant details in another context, so that readers, like people present at the witticism, have seen those details without appreciating their potential significance.

When anecdotalists provide key facts, they have no other context in which to disguise them. There is only one story, so nothing can belong first to one narrative and then acquire new significance in another. But a skillful biographer can place information pages distant. The first context gives it adequate meaning, so readers are surprised when another context reveals still more. That is just what Boswell repeatedly does.

Boswell knew that a long biography allows each anecdote to be short. The more we know about Johnson, the less we need be told what provokes him. To be sure, if later anecdotes too closely resembled earlier ones, they would lack the crucial element of surprise. But if they vary enough, the reader can appreciate not only the cleverness of each witticism but also the added surprise of yet another surprise. How amazing that Johnson can generate so many profound remarks all reflecting his personality yet differing from each other! Moreover, as witticisms accumulate, they can reflect how a personality gradually evolves. As the biography comes to the aid of each witticism, so the witticisms taken together help form the biography.

Sometimes, Boswell narrates how Johnson made a clever insult, as when he disparaged Lord Chesterfield: "This man I thought had been a lord among wits; but, I find, he is only a wit among lords" (*YBQ*, 402). But Boswell often plays a more complex role. As a spectator of an improvisation may also play a part in it, so Boswell not only relates the story but also becomes the disparaged character in it. He is both narrator and insultee.

> Boswell: I do indeed come from Scotland, but I cannot help it.
> Johnson: That, Sir, I find, is what a very great many of your countrymen cannot help. (*ODQ*, 428)

If Lord Chesterfield had been able to report Johnson's own insult so well, his report would have falsified it. Boswell here appears both foolish as the object of Johnson's remark and witty as he retells it.

Still more effectively, Boswell often plays a third role—the provocateur. He not only narrates to perfection his own diminishment, but has also had the wit to foresee exactly what would inspire Johnson to diminish him so wittily. Johnson demonstrates one kind of wit, Boswell another. As comic teams like Burns and Allen also show, both participants shape the humor. Only a fool fails to give the straight man credit. And only someone who does not appreciate wit undervalues the skill in preserving the sense of presence that has made the witticism so surprising.

Consider what we might call the anecdotalist's—or still more broadly, the storyteller's—paradox: the very fact that a story is being told conveys advance warning that something narratable happened, the sort of warning that people present at the event could not have had. After a certain age, children hearing a grown-up narrate a war story stop asking, "And did you survive?" In much the same way, few adults hearing an anecdote wonder if something witty will be reported. In such cases, the very fact that there is a narrative tends to frustrate its objectives. Whether suspense or humor is at stake, skill is required to overcome the storyteller's paradox. Perhaps few have displayed such skill more than Boswell. He makes the disadvantage an opportunity, and overcoming disadvantage is what wit is all about.

Verbal Duels and Instantaneous Games

Wit resembles other human activities that depend on presentness. A musical improviser, or a poet who accepts challenges to formulate verses on any suggested theme, must do so on the spot, or the whole point of the game is lost. For fans, sports events depend crucially on presentness, on *being there now*. That is why there is all the difference between attending a baseball game and watching a recording of it. Does it make sense to cheer for an event that is already over? Only by forgetting that the recording is a recording can one experience suspense. You might as well root for the English to win the Hundred Years War.[7]

Because wit, improvisations, and games all depend on presentness, it is easy to combine them. We refer to the sport of wit. The accomplished wit may issue a challenge to speak wittily on any theme, the way Disraeli succeeded in doing when someone suggested "the Queen" and Dorothy Parker did with "horticulture."

A different game of wit involves responding to an insult or earlier witticism, which serves as the challenge. This challenge is more difficult than the offer to discourse on a suggested topic because the insult has not been invited but comes as a surprise. It is designed to take its target off guard and leave him stammering for an adequate response. It's as if a baseball game could begin with a passed ball should a pitcher surprise a catcher while he was taking a shower. If he catches it, his unprepared dexterity impresses all the more.

Taken by surprise, the wit must, by a sort of mental judo, turn the energy of an unexpected attack to his or her advantage, and do so right then and there. Consider these famous examples:

> Clare Booth Luce meeting Dorothy Parker in a doorway, motioned her in and smirked: "Age before beauty." Parker walked right in, saying "Pearls before swine." (*MBQ*, 480)

> Lady Astor told Churchill that if she were his wife, she'd put poison in his coffee. "If you were my wife," he answered, "I'd drink it." (*MBQ*, 478)

> A descendant of the Athenian hero Harmodius reproached the general Iphicrates, the son of a cobbler, with his low birth. "The difference between us," Iphicrates replied, "is that my family begins with me, whereas yours ends with you." (*MBQ*, 479)

> George Gershwin to Oscar Levant: If you had it all over again, would you fall in love with yourself?
> Levant: Play us a medley of your hit. (*MBQ*, 480)

The last example works relatively simply. One insult matches another. Because the initiator of the exchange chooses the time, he has placed the other at a disadvantage. Therefore the responder wins the contest simply by doing as well as the challenger.

Iphicrates' response represents a particular subgenre of witty reply, the clever man's response when his low birth (or Jewish origin, or illegitimacy, or similar involuntary stigma) is insulted. Erasmus recounts this exchange:

> A young man, said to look strikingly like Augustus, was asked by the emperor if his mother had ever been to Rome. The young man replied: "My mother never, my father constantly." (*AE*, 9)

The responder does not contest the premise that birth matters more than brains. Rather, by turning the insult into a challenge, he demonstrates *why* brains matter. Iphicrates reminds Harmodius that noble families begin with an accomplished, but by definition less than nobly born, founder. A fool can be noble *only* by birth. The accomplished man of low birth therefore resembles the noble's ancestor, who is the very reason for his high birth, more closely than the noble himself does. Iphicrates also seems to suggest that Harmodius's descendant cannot father children.

The young man in Erasmus's story follows the logic of Augustus's suggestion but shows that it leads just as easily to the conclusion that it is Augustus's mother who is the whore. Such responses prove the superiority of mind over birth while demonstrating the wit's triumph over circumstance.

Churchill not only exhibits rapid agility and the readiness to use Lady Astor's premises, but also turns her very words against her. When she supposes that if she were Churchill's wife, she would poison him, she means that if she had the opportunity to kill him, she would. But Churchill discovers in this supposition not just opportunity but also the thought of marriage to such a woman. His insult uses her phrase and so produces all the satisfaction of poetic (or should we say anecdotal?) justice.

Dorothy Parker accomplishes an amazing number of clever things at once. We can see why she is far better known for her witticisms than for her work in other genres, light verse and short stories. She responds to Luce's insult with a worse one (as swinishness is worse than either age or lack of beauty); overcomes a disadvantage with her prompt reply; accepts the premise that the order of passing through the doorway determines the duel's winner; answers one famous line with another; imitates the verbal form of the original line; and plays on the key terms while doing so.

Though superficially similar as "noun before noun," the two phrases display different deep structures. "Age before beauty" condenses "Age should go before beauty," whereas "pearls before swine" abbreviates "Do not cast thy pearls before swine." In the first sentence, the initial noun is a subject, in the second a direct object; in the first, it is what is less desirable and in the second more. That is why the same (or apparently the same) wording can be imitated with opposite significance.

Because Parker strides in while delivering her riposte, she ensures that Luce, even if she could think of an answer, will not have a chance to make it. She thereby turns to her own advantage not only Luce's choice of words but also her sarcastic gesture. Caught unawares, Parker manages all this "without missing a beat": this presence of mind explains why her reply has come to define triumph in verbal dueling.

In such cases, the game is over almost as soon it has begun and before we have registered that it has begun. *Instantaneous games*, as we might call them, demonstrate all the more skill on the part of the fielder or wit.

Deathbed Wit

Because the best witticisms overcome the most formidable obstacles, sometimes the most favorable locale is the apparently least favorable one. Deathbed cleverness impresses because no place less resembles a salon, and so the ability to treat it as one demonstrates great presence. How can the wit be so clever even when breathing his or her last? Cleverness at the end constitutes another sort of instantaneous game, over as soon as it happens.

Although deathbed witticisms may excite admiration, they may also produce a contrary effect. They may call attention to the speaker's straining for effect. Still worse, they sometimes betray the wit's shallowness and, ultimately, the shallowness of wit itself. Or so it may seem when deathbed cleverness is viewed through the eyes of the apothegm and other short forms of greater seriousness.

Of course, not all famous last words are witticisms—some are heroic statements, others pull on the heartstrings, and still others evoke the apothegm's sense of mystery—but many witticisms are famous last words:

Bugger Bognor.
    —George V (1865–1936); his alleged last words, when his doctor promised
        him he would soon be well enough to visit Bognor Regis (*MDQ*, 316)

Thank you, sister. May you be the mother of a bishop!
    —Brendan Behan; said to a nun nursing him on his deathbed (*MDQ*, 315)

I have spent a lot of time searching through the Bible for loopholes.
    —W. C. Fields (*MDQ*, 315)

It is. But not as hard as farce.

> —Edmund Gwenn, British actor; on his deathbed,
> in reply to the comment, "It must be very hard" (*MDQ*, 316)

I owe much; I have nothing; the rest I leave to the poor.

> —Rabelais (*MDQ*, 316)

Here I am, dying of a hundred good symptoms.   —Pope (*MDQ*, 316)

I expect I shall have to die beyond my means.

> —Oscar Wilde, on accepting a glass of champagne
> on his deathbed (*MDQ*, 317)

Either that wall paper goes, or I do.   —Oscar Wilde (*MDQ*, 317)

One wonders at the capacity to retain the sense of irony, the feel for language, and the consciousness of an audience even to the very end. The body may be failing, but the mind never falters. Death is just another social challenge to cleverness. Perhaps this reduction of death explains why deathbed witticisms prove so appealing.

Gwenn and Wilde play by treating death as something one chooses, rather than something that happens to one. The king shows that his mastery of words lasts longer than his concern for things. Writers and actors treat the deathbed as a stage. Wilde might as well be in the salon, Fields still plays the character we know, Pope turns his phrase perfectly.

Of course, it is extremely unlikely that any of these last words were actually said. But even if they were, it is not hard to understand how empty they might appear from the perspective of another genre. Lytton Strachey's last words supposedly were "If this is dying, I don't think much of it" (*MDQ*, 317), to which one might imagine Pascal or Tolstoy adding: "If this is wit, I don't think much of it." The cleverer the last mot, the more trivial.

Or it might just be that, as Christians assert their most fundamental belief at the end, so wits reaffirm theirs: nothing in the world is worth anything except clever phrases and artful words. "There is no sin except stupidity."[8] "Art is the only serious thing in the world. And the artist is the only person who is never serious."[9]

Gallows Wit: Terror and Courage

If any place less resembles a salon than the deathbed, it is the scaffold, and so the place of execution has also become a conventional, because unconventional, locale for wit. What could be less amusing than hanging, guillotining, or roasting over a slow fire?[10] Even without torture, execution involves shame as well as death, and the condemned person faces not family and friends but an executioner and, often, hostile spectators.

Unlike the examples of wit on the deathbed just discussed, the most celebrated examples of wit on the gallows do not seem trivial at all. That is because torture and execution evoke terror. The situation to which the wit responds tests the limits of human endurance, and so any demonstration of presence of mind shows not only amazing self-control but also superhuman courage. Under such conditions, wit can demonstrate considerably more than cleverness. The mental presence required for wit serves a greater purpose.

Wit at the scaffold reveals its potential to express a philosophy quite different from Wilde's. The assertion of mental power achieves a peculiar form of stoicism. The wit shows utter contempt for what may be done to his body so long as he is master of his mind, soul, or will. Implicitly, he demonstrates a sense of life resembling that of Marcus Aurelius: "This Being of mine, whatever it really is, consists of a little flesh, a little breath, and the part that governs"; "The universe is change; our life is what our thoughts make it" (*BFQ15*, 124). Witticisms on the gallows demonstrate the rule of the part that still governs.

It is hardly surprising that many stories about the last words of a condemned man evoke terror. In part because he once faced execution and was pardoned at the last moment, Dostoevsky was fascinated by such stories.[11] In *The Idiot*, Lebedev relates:

> The Countess du Barry . . . rose from shame to a position like a queen. . . . [T]he way she died after such honors was that the hangman, Sampson, dragged this great lady, guiltless, to the guillotine for the diversion of the Parisian *poiss-ardes*, and she was in such terror she didn't know what was happening to her. She saw he was bending her neck down under the knife and kicking her, while the people laughed, and she fell to screaming, "*Encore un moment, monsieur le bour-reau, encore un moment!*", which means "Wait one little minute, Mr. *bourreau*, only one!" . . . When I read about the countess's cry for "one little minute," I felt as though my heart had been pinched with a pair of tongs. . . . And perhaps the reason I mentioned her was that, ever since the beginning of the world, probably no one has crossed himself for her sake, or even thought of doing so. (*I*, 186–87)

Dostoevsky argued that capital punishment was worse than murder because even a man attacked by brigands still hopes to escape—sometimes begging for mercy even *after* his throat his been cut!—whereas the man condemned knows he will die *for certain*. That certainty adds a whole new dimension of suffering and terror. Lebedev evokes as well the pain of mockery and public shame. Even reading such a story is awful.

Now consider that the evening before his execution during the Terror of 1793, the French astronomer John Sylvain Bally supposedly said: "It's time for me to enjoy another pinch of snuff. Tomorrow my hands will be bound, so as to make it impossible" (*MBQ*, 196). Treating execution as no more than an inconvenience preventing the use of snuff belongs to the province of the wit, who can be intimidated by no circumstance and so can always play. What would evoke terror in another provides the wit yet another opportunity for self-control. It is a challenge, but wit is all about challenges.

Like courage, wit demands mental presence when presence is most difficult. Not everyone can *make sport* of his or her own imminent dismemberment. Overwhelmed soldiers are, as we say, cut to pieces, but, as Herodotus narrates, when one Spartan hero at Thermopylae, Dieneces, is told that the Persians are so numerous that their arrows "obscure the sun by the multitude of their shafts," he replies: "All the better, for then we shall 'fight in the shade'" (*H*, 488). Herodotus recounts this story not to offer an example of verbal play but to show the calm courage that enabled a few hundred Spartans to resist several hundred thousand Persians.

From Witticism to Apothegm

We do not think of martyrdom as an occasion for play, but for the truly witty and courageous, it can become one. Such play is not mere play:

> Saint Lawrence, being burned alive on a gridiron, said at one moment that he might be turned over, since he was done enough on that side.[12]

> Thomas More, mounting the scaffold: I pray you, master Lieutenant, see me safe up, and [as for] my coming down let me shift for myself. (*ODQ*, 548)

> More, drawing his beard aside before placing his head on the block: This has not offended the king. (*YBQ*, 537)

Which of us, suffering the most extreme agony, would possess the presence of mind to think of one's own roasting alive as a scene of daily food preparation? In both of More's remarks, he speaks as if he were still the great counselor called upon to employ his mastery of words and subtle legal distinctions. He treats the execution scene not exactly as a salon but as another courtroom or cabinet meeting.

The double meaning behind More's pun on "shift" includes one activity requiring will ("to shift for" as to make do or improvise) and another describing what might happen to purely material objects, which, when subjected to a force, shift position. The pun thus calls attention to what he is now and what he will soon be, a difference that, for this religious martyr, expresses his belief in the separateness of immortal soul from mortal body.

So courageous is More, and so convinced of his salvation, that he can afford to jest at the last moment. That is obviously true of Saint Lawrence as well. The soul about to leave the body comments on it as if it were already outside it, looking on. More's second joke plays on the political, rather than religious, meaning of his death, his willingness to defy authority. More distinguishes his head, which offended the king and so must be cut off, from his beard, which is entirely innocent.

More and Saint Lawrence go beyond the witticism into the territory of the apothegm. Their remarks invoke an ultimate mystery, the housing of an immaterial mind and an immortal soul in a perishing, dismemberable body. Between the two meanings of "shift" lies the whole imponderability of consciousness. The body as the house of the soul is also the body as so much meat. And to treat the head as something no different from the beard, or the beard as if it, like the head, could choose to give offense, plays on this same mystery. The material head, unlike anything else material or any other part of the body, somehow contains, if only for a while, the mind that comprehends the difference.

Danton allegedly made three famous remarks before his execution:

> If I left my balls to Robespierre and my legs to Couthon, that would help the Committee of Public Safety for a while. [Robespierre was allegedly impotent and Couthon a cripple.][13]

> At least they can't stop our heads from kissing in the basket. (Danton to his fellow victim Hérault de Séchelles, after a guard had stopped them from giving each other a last embrace on the scaffold; *HIQ*, 525)

> Don't forget to show my head to the people. It's a pretty sight. (Danton to the executioner; *HIQ*, 525)

The first comment turns execution into a duel of insults. Robespierre and Couthon begin by condemning me to dismemberment; in response, I follow their logic by offering to replace their defective parts. The second demonstrates sufficient presence of mind to convict the executioner of a lapse in etiquette and so make the scaffold into a drawing room. About the third comment, the editors of *History in Quotations* observe: "Danton was an outstandingly ugly man, and such self-mockery, just seconds before his death, is breathtaking" (*HIQ*, 525). To be sure, but something else is involved. Like More, Danton alludes to the head as containing the mind. What makes a head valuable is *what is no longer there* after execution and can never be seen.

The ultimate mystery of dualism is the territory of the apothegm. At the same time, the triumph of mind over brute force belongs to the wit. The two may join. On the scaffold, witticisms may transcend themselves and *become* apothegms.

Two Kinds of Wit

Let us now distinguish two kinds of wit. They differ in their essential philosophy. Both display intelligence and timeliness, but for different reasons.

Some witticisms value nothing but quickness of mind. In a world perceived to lack real meaning, wits of this sort cling to the well-made artifice. Oscar Wilde repeatedly expressed this vision: "The first duty in life is to be as artificial as possible. What the second duty is no one has yet discovered."[14] Sometimes this kind of witticism hints at an existential void. At other times, it seems smugly content with itself.

The second type of witticism places cleverness at the service of higher values, such as stoic fortitude. The witticism then expresses the sense that, properly trained, mind triumphs over nature, over physical force, and over political power. It is not cleverness itself that is important but the capacity of the mind to transcend circumstances. Witticisms of this sort are "philosophical" in the way the ancients often used the term: they rise above everyday passions and concerns. They may or may not affirm a faith in immortality, as they did for More and Saint Lawrence. But whatever other higher value they assert, they demonstrate courage.

Unlike the wit of cleverness, the wit of courage affirms the world's meaningfulness. Such witticisms are *serious*. Most anthologies of witty sayings, put-downs, or "zingers" rely primarily on the wit of cleverness. Placed in this company, Dr. Johnson's best remarks would be trivialized. Wilde exemplifies the wit of cleverness, More the wit of courage.

Wit Outwitted

The classic anecdotes describing Alexander meeting Diogenes epitomize the second type of witticism, especially as it expresses a stoic understanding of life. The stoics, of course, claimed Diogenes as their predecessor. In two stories told by Diogenes Laertius and expanded by many others, the world-conquering general seeks out the Cynic:

> Alexander once came and stood opposite him and said, "I am Alexander the great king." "And I," said he, "am Diogenes the Cynic."[15]

> When Alexander the Great visited Corinth, Diogenes was living in a large earthenware tub in one of the city's suburbs. Alexander went to see the philosopher and found him sunning himself. The king politely asked if there was any way in which he could serve him. "Stand out of my sun," replied the surly Cynic. Alexander's courtiers began ridiculing Diogenes as a monster, but the king said: "If I were not Alexander, I should wish to be Diogenes." (*BBA*, 167; version in *DL2*, 39–41)

Diogenes Laertius explains that Diogenes "claimed that to fortune he could oppose courage" (*DL2*, 39–41), and that is what he does here. He resists the temptation to take advantage of the emperor's offer. Rather than improve his life, he transforms the encounter into a contest. To do so, he accepts the premise of Alexander's comment while rejecting its substance. Yes, Alexander has the power to reward and punish, but this power is of no significance. To the physical power of the emperor Diogenes opposes the superior power of the philosopher's mind.

And yet, Alexander has the last word. For unlike other anecdotes of this sort, this one allows a response to the wit. Alexander exhibits the intelligence to grasp Diogenes' point, to rise above insult, and to acknowledge that, indeed, mental power may be the only thing that can rival his political power. Rival, but not quite equal: for his answer indicates that wit, however impressive, is *only* a close second.

Alexander's victory is possible because his initial comment was not, like Claire Booth Luce's to Dorothy Parker, intended as a challenge to a duel. It is Diogenes who chose to take it that way. Alexander can therefore demonstrate his true superiority by *not* taking Diogenes' answer as an insult, but rather—as if he had the self-awareness to view his own defeat "philosophically"—to show his own presence of mind and rise above immediate circumstances.

Outwitting the wit, the emperor displays the courage to speak power to truth.

How to Discredit a Witticism

Once one understands how witticisms work, one readily grasps how they can be discredited, whether by other people or by opposing genres. Sometimes the point is to show that a celebrated wit is not as clever as all that. At other times, the intent is to expose wit itself as shallow. Such exposure is almost always directed at the first, Wildean, type of wit.

Wit depends on presentness. To discredit any sample of it, one need only show that the wit has actually prepared and rehearsed his comment in advance and waited for an occasion to voice it "spontaneously." In that case, the wit can hardly be responding to the unforeseen or showing exquisite sensitivity to the particulars of the situation. On the contrary, it is as if the wit had offered to speak on any subject and then had been discovered responding to an assistant planted in the audience.

Rehearsed spontaneity isn't spontaneous, and memorized improvisation is no improvisation at all. That, I take it, was the point of Whistler's famous retort to Oscar Wilde when they heard a clever comment:

> Wilde: I wish I had said that.
> Whistler: You will, Oscar, you will. (*MDQ*, 482)

Somewhere S. J. Perlman refers to a witticism prepared mendaciously in advance as a "prepigram."[16]

Where preliminary effort comes to light, there can be no *sprezzatura*. As Whistler's comment demonstrates, the exposure of such effort can produce a humor of its own. This is true of any act that depends for its power on spontaneity, like the love letters copied from a book or pattern in *The Charterhouse of Parma* and *War and Peace*. In *Anna Karenina*, the Countess Nordston wants to humiliate Levin so her friend Kitty will not consider marrying him. When she publically taunts him by exaggerating a remark he once made, Levin successfully parries: "'It's very flattering for me, Countess, that you remember my words so well,' responded Levin, who had succeeded in recovering his composure. . . . 'They must certainly make a great impression on you'" (*AK*, 54). But when a few moments later she exaggerates another of Levin's past comments, he finds himself replying in the very same way, "and suddenly conscious that he had just said the same thing before, he reddened" (56). He reddens because the repeated reply not only cannot succeed in answering the second remark but also retrospectively exposes its first use as an automatic response.

Wit cannot be automatic because it is supposed to show the power of *mind*. Neither can it be produced mechanically. To the extent one could build a machine or program a computer to make a remark, mind is not required.

The witticism as a genre presents mind as something resembling what Bergson meant by "soul" in its endless battle with "inertia": "The soul imparts a portion of its winged lightness to the body it animates; the immateriality which thus passes into matter is what is called gracefulness. Matter, however, is obstinate and resists. It draws to itself the ever-alert activity of this higher principle, would fain convert it to its own inertia and cause it to revert to mere automatism."[17] Bergson concluded not only that *bodily* movements are laughable "in exact proportion as the body reminds us of a mere machine" (Bergson, 79) but also that *mental* reflexes are laughable when they take place mechanically.

Mixed metaphors typically amuse because they betray mechanism disguised as thought. The example cited by George Orwell from a Communist pamphlet—"The Fascist octopus has sung its swan song"—demonstrates that its author was not thinking about his words but producing strings of them mechanically.[18]

It follows that if one could identify a formula by which the wit fabricated his or her remarks, one would have discredited them. A purportedly thoughtful and spontaneous response turns out to have been manufactured according to practiced rules. The hero of Turgenev's *Fathers and Children* refers to one such formula, which he calls "reverse commonplace": just take a platitude and say the opposite. "[T]o say that education is beneficial, for instance, that's a commonplace; but to say that education is injurious, that's a reverse commonplace. There's more style about it, so to say, but in reality it's one and the same" (*F&S*, 103).[19] At first the reversal sounds profound, but it is as shallow as the original. In his Father Brown stories, Chesterton makes much the same point: "When a man is told something that turns things upside-down, that the tail wags the dog; that the fish has caught the fisherman; that the earth goes around the moon; he takes some time before he even asks seriously if it is true. He is still content with the consciousness that it is the opposite of the obvious truth."[20]

Tolstoy takes the point one step further. In both *War and Peace* and *Anna Karenina* he introduces a character who utters reverse reverse commonplaces, that is, platitudes that achieve the status of witticisms because everybody is used to the cynical reversal of platitudes. "The sensation produced by Princess

Myakhaya's speeches was always unique, and the secret of the sensation was that ... she said simple things with some sense in them. In the society in which she lived, such statements produced the effect of the wittiest epigram. Princess Myakhaya could never see why it had that effect, but she knew it had, and took advantage of it" (*AK*, 143).

Wilde C++

He [Wilde] had nothing to say and he said it.

—Ambrose Bierce, attributed (*CHQ*, 778)

He [Wilde] left behind, as his essential contribution to literature, a large repertoire of jokes which survive because of their sheer neatness, and because of a certain intriguing uncertainty—which extends to Wilde himself—as to whether they really mean anything.   —George Orwell (*CHQ*, 778)

Some readers will disagree, but it feels to me that the more Wilde witticisms one reads, the more obvious their formulas and the more disappointing their shallowness. Anyone wanting to discredit witticisms as a genre would have a much easier time targeting Wilde than, let us say, Mark Twain or Samuel Johnson.

Sometimes it appears as if there were a computer program called "Wilde" (one could not call it "Pascal" ...). Consider the following famous witticisms from *The Importance of Being Earnest*, given in the order in which they appear in the play:

(1)   Really, if the lower orders don't set us a good example, what on earth is the use of them?

(2)   The amount of women in London who flirt with their own husbands is perfectly scandalous. It looks so bad. It is simply washing one's clean linen in public.

(3)   I haven't been there since her poor husband's death. I never saw a woman so altered; she looks twenty years younger.

(4)   The old-fashioned respect for the young is fast dying out.

(5)   I don't like novels that end happily. They depress me too much.

(6)   This suspense is terrible. I hope it will last.

(7)   I never change, except in my affections.[21]

These lines are all variations on the reverse commonplace. Take a hackneyed sentiment and replace a key word with its antonym: (1), (4). Find morality, not immorality, shocking: (2). Provide a situation and have someone react exactly contrary to usual expectations: (3), (5), (6). To see the formula behind (7), consider the following well-known Wilde lines: "I can resist everything but temptation"; "I can sympathize with everything, except suffering."[22]

As La Rochefoucauld observed, "No one can please for long with only one form of wit" (*LaR*, 109). Here are some more witticisms:

If one tells the truth one is sure, sooner or later, to be found out.

It is perfectly monstrous the way people go about, nowadays, saying things behind one's back that are absolutely and entirely true.

The subtlest form of deceit is sincerity.

Nothing is more substantial than illusion.

There is nothing more profound than surface.

We admit faults to triumph over them.

The most sincere form of flattery is self-praise. The most insincere form of flattery is self-praise.

In this world there are only two tragedies. One is not getting what one wants, and the other is getting it.

No crime is vulgar, but all vulgarity is crime.

When they can no longer set bad examples, people give good advice. Industry is the root of all evil.

A fool and his money are soon married.

Divorces are made in heaven.

Some of these belong to Wilde, some are by others and appear often in anthologies, and a few are made up on their pattern. Can the reader tell which? Wilde seeks to disarm the charge of shallowness by voicing it himself.

Jack. For heaven's sake, don't try to be cynical. It's perfectly easy to be cynical.
Algernon. My dear fellow, it isn't easy to be anything nowadays. There's such a
     lot of beastly competition about. (*IBE*, 259)

Algernon. All women become like their mothers. That is their tragedy. No man
  does. That is his.

Jack. Is that clever?

Algernon. It is perfectly phrased! And quite as true as any observation in civilized life should be. (*IBE*, 268)

Cecily (to Gwendolen). That certainly seems a satisfactory answer, does it not?

Gwendolen. Yes, dear, if you can believe him.

Cecily. I don't. But that does not affect the wonderful beauty of his answer.

Gwendolen. True. In matters of grave importance, style, not sincerity, is the
  vital thing. (*IBE*, 295)

One might object that *The Importance of Being Earnest*, at least, saves itself by
being *about* useless twits who have nothing better to do than sound like Wilde.
But that is itself the form of wit in which Wilde typically indulges. Applying an
accusation to oneself preemptively does not refute it, and if the charge is that
one values nothing but rhetorical cleverness, it may confirm it.

Though similar to sardonic maxims (as I shall call them) in form, Wilde's
lines differ from them in meaning. La Rochefoucauld, Swift, and other misanthropic thinkers may disparage human nature, but in their maxims they
try to speak the truth about it, whereas for Wilde truth is just another empty
moral category or another form of prudery. What matters is being "clever,"
formulating observations that are "perfectly phrased," and valuing above all
else "style."

Tolstoy's War on Wit

Tolstoy despised the wit of cleverness for much the same reason that he ridiculed the culture of salons.

War and Peace opens with a salon scene, where guests compete to amuse
each other with empty wit. The book's hero, Prince Andrei, easily bests them at
their own game while barely concealing his contempt for their shallowness. His
search for an alternative to the world of wit leads him to war.

At first, Andrei puts his faith in another kind of intelligence, sheer rationality, which, when combined with valor, supposedly guarantees victory in battle.
He eventually learns otherwise. The book's wisest figure, General Kutuzov,
despises rationality and intellect and regards the idea of a science of war as
absurd. He thinks apothegmically and wins, in a Taoist way, by a form of "non-
acting." To acquire Kutuzov's wisdom, the supremely intelligent Andrei must

overcome attachment to intelligence itself, whether expressed in the rational-
ism of dicta or the cleverness of witticisms.

When we first see Andrei in the army, he has been sent on a mission to the
Austrian emperor. He stays with an old friend, Bilibin, a diplomat of immense
verbal skill, social insight, and, above all, wit:

> Bilibin enjoyed conversation as he did work, only when it could be exquisitely
> witty. In society he was continually watching for an opportunity to say some-
> thing remarkable, and took part in a conversation only when he found this
> possible. His conversation was always sprinkled with original, witty, polished
> phrases of general interest. These locutions, prepared in his inner laboratory,
> were of a transmissible nature, as if designed to be easily remembered and
> carried from drawing room to drawing room. . . . And, indeed, Bilibin's *mots*,
> circulating through the salons of Vienna, often had an influence on so-called
> important matters. (*W&P*, 437–38)

In the references to Bilibin's premeditation, his "inner laboratory," and the
"so-called important matters" Bilibin's witticisms influence, we sense Tolstoy's
scorn for this kind of intelligence. Nevertheless, Tolstoy acknowledges wit as a
kind of intelligence and leaves no doubt about Bilibin's mental agility. Bilibin is
undeniably clever as he easily dispels the fog of self-justifications blinding others.

In so doing, he exemplifies a philosophy that we have come to call post-
modern. For Bilibin, nothing is true except from some point of view that is
disputable from other points of view. All perspectives are equally convincing to
those naïve enough to believe them and equally laughable to those who regard
them from outside. Thus, in the course of a sentence, Bilibin can switch from
French to Russian and German, and from the speech of generals to the language of propagandists and diplomats, as he orchestrates a dialogue of stand-
points. Each way of speaking, and the assumptions on which it depends, mocks
and is mocked by all the others.

Here is the philosophy of the wit of cleverness as Tolstoy understands it:
nothing matters except the dexterity to rise above all languages and perspectives with exquisitely polished phrases uttered at just the right moment. Andrei,
who still believes in heroism, respects Bilibin but returns from the salons to the
endangered army. He still hopes to be what Bilibin can only pronounce with
scorn, a hero. Without being told, Kutuzov understands the cynicism to which
Andrei has been exposed and, in place of a serious debriefing, questions Andrei
"with delicate irony . . . about the details of his interview with the [Austrian]

Emperor, about the comments he had heard at court concerning the Krems engagement, and about certain ladies of their acquaintance" (214).

Disappointed in military heroism, Andrei finds a hero in Speransky, the tsar's influential reformist minister. Speransky values nothing more than intellect, and his conversation consists almost entirely of witty remarks at the expense of more conservative or less thoughtful people. "Speransky told how at the Council that morning a deaf statesman, when asked his opinion, replied that he thought so too" (572).

In Speransky's circle, Andrei comes to appreciate how wit works by flattery and an implicit division of people into the clever and the dull. It seduces the right people "with that subtle form of flattery that goes hand in hand with self-conceit, and consists in a tacit assumption that one's companion is the only man besides oneself capable of understanding all the folly of the rest of the world, and the wisdom and profundity of one's own ideas. . . . [Speransky spoke] with an expression that seemed to say, 'We, you and I, understand what *they* are and who *we* are'" (523).

It does not take Andrei long to see Speransky as Kutuzov would. Arriving at one of Speransky's dinners, Andrei overhears the statesman's "precise" laugh—"a laugh such as one hears on the stage" (553). To Andrei, the dinnertime conversation now seems "to consist of the content of a jokebook." The gaiety of Speransky's inner circle "seemed forced and mirthless to Prince Andrei" and Speransky's "incessant laughter had a false ring that grated on him. . . . There was nothing wrong or out of place in what they said: it was witty and might even have been amusing, but it lacked something that is the salt of mirth, something they were not even aware existed" (562).

For Andrei, as for Tolstoy, the world is far more mysterious than we can ever know. If there is one attitude that is not warranted, it is smug self-confidence in one's mental superiority. "It was plain that it would never occur to him, as it did so naturally to Prince Andrei, that it is after all impossible to express all one thinks; nor had it ever occurred to him to doubt whether all he thought and believed might not be utter nonsense" (524). Andrei's reaction to Speransky traces the dialogue of the apothegm and the witticism.

Longer Forms: The Trickster

Both types of wit—the wit of cleverness and the wit of courage—have inspired a number of longer works and forms. Most obviously, the witty drama uses an amusing plot to showcase numerous witty remarks of the first type. Wilde's title

The Importance of Being Earnest captures the logic of both its plot and its most memorable lines. W. H. Auden observed that Wilde managed to "subordinate every other dramatic element to dialogue for its own sake and create a verbal universe in which the characters are determined by the kinds of things they say, and the plot is nothing but a succession of opportunities to say them."[23] Auden suggests that, however clever the lines may be, drama fails when it is little more than an excuse to say them. Such a play is no more than an anthology on stage, a stringing together of "the contents of a joke book."

Witticisms require narrative of some sort because they respond to the contingencies of a specific situation. As we have also seen, biographies, like those of Diogenes Laertius, Plutarch, and Boswell, can use wit—usually of the second type—to illustrate character. The reader encounters the wit bringing his philosophy to bear in an unexpected way when provoked by surprising contingencies. Humor goes hand in hand with a deeper sense of life.

Almost all parts of the world have given us what folklorists call "trickster" stories. They typically describe how the culture's favorite trickster overcomes brute force by cleverness, often, though not always, verbal cleverness. After Brer Fox outsmarts Brer Rabbit in "The Wonderful Tar-Baby Story," Brer Fox, "he rolled on de ground, en laughed en laughed twel he couldn't laugh no mo,"[24] but he is himself outsmarted by Brer Rabbit's tricky words in "How Mr. Rabbit Was Too Sharp for Mr. Fox" (Harris, 12). The North American Coyote stories work in much the same way. The trickster wins by cleverness, verbal dexterity, and the sort of psychological acumen that makes a good confidence man. Appropriately, he may be a shapeshifter. He is crafty (or inventive) in both senses of the word. The favorite trickster of North American folklore, Coyote, makes people, the earth, and the sun; he steals summer and fire. A Prometheus of cleverness, Coyote plays a role far more important than his European counterparts.[25]

As a trickster god, Hephaestus invents a strong but invisibly fine net to catch his wife Aphrodite in bed with Ares. When they are caught, he summons the gods to laugh at them. Trickster stories often end with laughter, a triumphant boast, or both.

Like the wit of cleverness, the trickster operates in a realm beyond good and evil. He steals and commits every possible sexual transgression. Fecundity of mind and body count more than any moral code.

We can discern the connection between such stories and witticisms if we regard both as examples of "using one's wits" under pressure. In well-known written literature, the essentially anecdotal nature of such stories easily leads to the picaresque, where one short adventure follows another (*Tom Sawyer*), or to the cycle of tales, like the many stories in the *Decameron* where the wages of wit is sex. Chaucer's "Miller's Tale" features a trickster who deceives a foolish husband and is himself tricked in turn. His "Pardoner's Tale" offers a more complex treatment of the subject. In a reversal not uncommon in such stories, the utterly loathsome trickster gets carried away by his own cleverness and is caught when, and because, he boasts of it.

Such reversals follow the pattern of insult duels. Clare Booth Luce's cleverness allows Dorothy Parker to be still cleverer. Brer Fox's inordinate laughter allows Brer Rabbit to turn the tables on him. Perhaps most famously, Odysseus, after outwitting the Cyclops, pays dearly for his boastful mockery.

Odysseus and Mêtis

The *Odyssey* probably represents the greatest story to develop the logic of wit. When the bard Demodocus performs at the court of Alcinous, he sings about a quarrel between Achilles and Odysseus, not, as in the *Iliad*, between Achilles and Agamemnon. We know from other sources that the two heroes argued whether Troy would be taken by the quality at which Achilles excels, *biê* (force), or *mêtis*, the quality embodied by Odysseus.[26] The word *mêtis* is variously rendered as wiliness, cunning, craftiness, or resourcefulness; and it includes the qualities we associate with wit: the ability to respond instantly to an unexpected challenge in a surprisingly apt way. It demands what Odysseus so evidently possesses, presence of mind and self-control as well as ingenuity and courage.

Odysseus responds to Demodocus's song by calling for the story of the wooden horse, his greatest stratagem. The opening of the *Odyssey* describes him as *polumêtis* (having much *mêtis*), or, in the Rouse translation, as "a man who was never at a loss."[27] Odysseus at last introduces himself to Alcinous and the Phaeacians: "I am Odysseus, great Laertes' son / Known for my cunning throughout the world" (Lombardo, 125).[28] The book shows his cunning in a variety of ways: the presence of mind with which, as a naked castaway, he addresses Nausicaa in just the right way, his "craftiness" in constructing the raft to leave Calypso's isle, the caginess in calling himself "noman" to Polyphemus, his mastery of disguise, his ability to outsmart Circe and even to outsmart himself with the Sirens.

But Odysseus is not *only* clever. He uses cunning in the service of higher values, especially loyalty to Penelope and home. And Penelope herself demonstrates not only proverbial loyalty, but also *mêtis*, as we see in the story of weaving and secretly unweaving the shroud for Laertes. She makes sure the visitor really is her husband by testing him with the secret of how the bed was made. Neither hero nor heroine is ever clever for the sake of cleverness, and both demonstrate seemingly endless courage.

Dostoevsky's Devil

The devil who appears to Ivan Karamazov, like Ivan himself, displays his mastery of wit. It was one of Dostoevsky's most striking ideas to make the avatar of evil not grand, fearsome, and satanic, but sociable, amusing, and witty. This devil attends soirees in the capital, tells charming anecdotes about the other world, and reveals secrets about the nature of life that are, like wit itself, trivial. Neither envious nor prideful, and preferring witty conversation to revenge, Ivan Karamazov's devil embodies complete cynicism and believes in absolutely nothing.

Ivan's devil is even, believe it or not, an agnostic. Descartes notwithstanding, he doubts his own existence, or at least offers clever arguments for doing so. He is quite well read and disputes earlier literary portraits of him as far too serious. As someone might say today, they demonize him. And yet precisely for all these reasons, Ivan's "petty demon" personifies evil, because what truly horrifies, what ultimately makes life a mockery, is sheer banality.

Wit leads this devil to unexpected insights about time, chance, and choice. Because wit must be unpredictable, a witty devil requires a world that is not completely determined in advance. There must be *surprisingness*, events that are truly eventful in the sense that they might well have turned out otherwise.[29] The devil's role, he maintains, is precisely to make time open. "I am X in an unsolvable equation," he declares, and though he would prefer complete annihilation, he must continue to exist. "No, live I am told, for there'd be nothing without you. If everything in the universe were sensible, nothing would happen. There would be no events without you" (*BK*, 780). He explains that if he were to embrace universal harmony and beauty— "you know how aesthetically impressionable I am"—"the indispensable minus would disappear at once. . . . And that, of course, would mean the end of everything, even magazines and newspapers, for who would take them in?" (787–88).

If there is wit, then the universe is indeterministic. Here then is an important reason that wit proves so appealing: it expresses and demonstrates human freedom.

Why Five-Year Plans Fail

In Bulgakov's masterpiece of wit, *The Master and Margarita*, a devil descended from the one in *Karamazov* plays practical jokes in Stalin's Moscow. His extremely clever escapades mock the complacency of those who, like Soviet Communists, claim the ability to understand and control events. In chapter 1, the mysterious "foreigner" asks Berlioz and Bezdomny, "Who controls the world if there is no God?" When these atheists reply that "man himself is in control," the stranger points out that control involves planning, "so how, may I ask, can man be in control if he can't even draw up a plan for a ridiculously short period of time, say, a thousand years?"[30] He laughs that Berlioz, who is so certain of his own plans, does not even foresee that his head will be cut off this very night. No wonder five-year plans fail!

When Berlioz's cousin—an economic planner, of course—tries to outwit the "foreigners" (actually the devil's retinue) occupying Berlioz's apartment, he is constantly surprised, while they know all his thoughts in advance. Bulgakov's fantasy transforms wit into a critique of social science, whether Marxist or any other. The trickster devil outwits the humorless by the sheer power of surprise.

The Improvised Wit of *Don Juan*

I don't know that there may be much ability
   Shown in this sort of desultory rhyme;
But there's a conversational facility,
   Which may round off an hour at a time;
Of this I'm sure at least, there's no servility
   In mine irregularity of chime,
Which rings what's uppermost of new or hoary
Just as I feel the "Improvvisatore."[31]

Because it demands presentness, wit is essentially *spoken*. Even when written, it transmits the aura of spokenness.

Without spokenness, how can there be presentness? All written examples must overcome the disadvantage of being already recorded, and therefore over and done with. As we have seen, anecdotalists face a "storyteller's paradox": on the one hand, a witticism's humor depends on its unexpectedness; on the other, the mere fact of narration warns the reader of the "surprise." Authors have found numerous ways around this contradiction. Byron even managed to turn it to his advantage.

As anyone who reads *Don Juan* will recognize, the poem both was and seems to have been written spontaneously. It re-creates the experience of a first draft, as if a professional improviser were making it up on the spot before an audience. As Bakhtin would say, it seems to take place in "the real present of the creative process."

No advance plan provides a plot for the whole poem. "You ask me for the plan of Donny Johnny: I *have* no plan—and I *had* no plan; but I had or have materials," Byron explained (Byron, vi). In this serialized work, each canto could be the last. No overall structure is being completed, and so the poem in principle could have only a stopping point, not an ending. Foreshadowing is out of the question.

Byron adapts this processual alternative to structure from Sterne's *Tristram Shandy,* which also creates humor through sheer improvisation and inventiveness with whatever material is already on the page. But Byron went one step further by writing his novel in verse. Like the poem as a whole, each stanza seems to begin with no clear idea of how it will end, as the writer devises concluding rhymes just in the nick of time. It is as if he records two pairs of A-B lines and then leaves it to the inspiration of the moment to come up with a third pair and an appropriate final couplet. Often enough, he succeeds with a solution so inventive, and yet so contrary to proper poetry, that "bad" rhymes become good:

> 'T is pity learned virgins ever wed
>> With persons of no sort of education,
> Or gentlemen, who though well born and bred,
>> Grow tired of scientific conversation:
> I don't choose to say much upon this head,
>> I'm a plain man, and in a single station,
> But—Oh! Ye lords of ladies intellectual,
> Inform us truly, have they not hen-pecked you all?   (canto 1, stanza xxii)

The sense of improvisation becomes all the stronger when the stanza itself comments on an inappropriate rhyme. The poem responds to its own ongoing composition:

> And if in the meantime her husband died,
>> But Heaven forbid that such a thought should cross
> Her brain, though in a dream! (and then she sighed)
>> Never could she survive that common loss;
> But just suppose that moment should betide.
>> I only say suppose it—*inter nos:*

(This should be *entre nous*, for Julia thought
In French, but then the rhyme would go for nought.)

(canto 1, stanza lxxxiv)

Sometimes the rhymes fail altogether: they are uninteresting, neither good nor especially bad. And yet they contribute to the poem's wittiness by strengthening the sense of improvisation in real time. They make the successes all the more impressive. If Byron could always succeed, either success would be too easy or else we would sense the improvisation as sham.

In wit, in sport, and in *Don Juan*, everything depends on presentness.

∎ STUPIDITY SHINES ∎

As presence of mind impresses us, so does absence. As professors know, absent-mindedness can be amusing. Zombies, as well as people of supreme vitality, excite interest.

As professors know, absent-mindedness can be amusing. The opposite of wit—stupidity, inarticulateness, folly, vapidity, emptiness—has generated its own canon of quotable lines, collected in volumes with titles such as *The 776 Stupidest Things Ever Said*, *1001 Dumbest Things Ever Said*, and *Don't Quote Me!: Things People Say Then Wish They Hadn't*. Let us call these samples of negative wit *witlessisms*.

Witlessisms come in at least four types. In each, we hear two voices, and humor arises from their discrepancy.

Witlessism Type 1: Quayle, the Bumbler

The worse, the better.   —Lenin

Verbal blunderers like Dan Quayle have provided notorious examples of the simplest type of wittlessism. Quaylisms (whether real or ascribed) impress by their extreme degree of witlessness. Normal inarticulateness or brainlessness will not do. Neither will pretentious mediocrity. Bumbling so common deserves little notice, but Quaylisms reach the sublime: they achieve Solomonic stupidity or Shakespearean inarticulateness.

Consider these classic comments ascribed to Sir Boyle Roche, the eighteenth-century politician who, in most anthologies, supplies the earliest examples of the form:

[Irish farmers are] living from hand to mouth like the birds of the air. (*776S*, 38)

Many thousands of them were destitute of even the goods they possessed. (*776S*, 38)

Half the lies our opponents tell about us are not true. (*776S*, 38)

In each case, we hear two utterances, the one Roche meant to say and the one he actually said. The greater the discrepancy between the two the more witless the utterance. Mixed metaphors, malapropisms, unintentional puns, unnoticed double entendres, translation howlers, instructions written for a product made abroad, warning labels composed to ward off lawsuits: all these have produced Quaylisms. Always in the public eye, politicians provide numerous classic examples:

It isn't pollution that's harming the environment. It's the impurities in our air and water that are doing it.   —Dan Quayle (*1001D*, 15)

The streets are safe in Philadelphia, it's only the people make them unsafe.

—Mayor Frank Rizzo (*776S*, 35)

Outside of the killings, [Washington, DC] has one of the lowest crime rates in the country.   —Mayor Marion Barry (*776S*, 45)

The more killing and homicides you have, the more havoc it prevents.

—Mayor Richard M. Daley (*776S*, 35)

We must rise to higher and higher platitudes together.

—Mayor Richard J. Daley (*1001D*, 48)

The presence of so many big-city mayors suggests why anthologies of the form appeal to intellectuals: they provide an opportunity to indulge educational snobbery. The gaffes of Daley, Barry, and Rizzo demonstrate that, unlike "us," they did not attend major universities. Those who condemn class prejudice in some forms easily slip into others.

When sports figures offer such comments, they become endearing because education is not part of an athlete's job description. Dizzy Dean, Danny Ozark, Phil Rizzuto, Jerry Coleman, and Casey Stengel were a sports reporter's delight. "A lot of people my age are dead at the present time," Stengel supposedly said (*1001D*, 59). And addressing his team, the Yankee manager ordered: "All right, everybody line up alphabetically according to your height" (*1001D*, 59).

The Stuffed Owl

Often enough, the supreme badness of a piece of prose or verse requires sophisticated taste. When Wordsworth stumbles, or when Johnson falls, / Not all, but us, the blackened page appalls. The appreciation of awfulness proves a mark of status, worthy only of the highly literate or the trained critic. The more refinement it takes to detect a sample of bad taste, the greater the status its detection confers.

Connoisseurs know *The Stuffed Owl: An Anthology of Bad Verse*, edited by Wyndham Lewis and Charles Lee and first published in 1930. As Lewis explains in his preface, the volume collects not what he calls "bad Bad Verse"—the endless efforts of poetasters who cannot master the craft—but the much rarer "good Bad Verse," which is innocent of faults of craftsmanship and yet obtains "an eerie, supernal beauty comparable in its accidents with the beauty of Good Verse" (*SO*, ix–x). It is no easier to say exactly what makes Bad Verse good than it is to say what makes Good Verse good. Neither can be produced by formula, or it would not be good at all. For this reason, Lewis explains, the greatest examples of Bad Verse are to be found in the works of the same poets who produce Good Verse or, at least, verse often taken to be good.

The Stuffed Owl contains egregious efforts by respected (often deservedly) poets from Cowley to Tennyson. It includes Dryden, Addison, Young, Smart, Goldsmith, Chatterton, Crabbe, Burns, Byron, Keats, and Emerson, as well as the easy targets, Cibber, Poe, Southey, and Bulwer-Lytton. The title and epigraph come from a Wordsworth poem about a lady, confined to her bed, who takes pleasure in inanimate objects: "Yet, helped by Genius—untired Comforter, / The presence even of a stuffed Owl for her / Can cheat the time . . ." (*SO*, epigraph and 151).

Well-known poets provide the best examples not only because they do not commit elementary errors in craftsmanship but also because "the more eminent the poet . . . the more shattering the bump below" (*SO*, xi). Moreover, the proximity of bad lines to good, and of terrible poems to successful ones, ensures a kind of alternate sublimity. When shallow, these poets are profoundly so: "There is often found in Bad Verse that windy splurging and bombinating which makes Victor Hugo's minor rhetoric so comic and so terrible. Other plain marks are all those connoted by poverty of the imagination, sentimentality, banality . . . inability to hold the key of inspiration, insufficiency of emotional content for metrical form" (*SO*, xiii).

Lee begins the anthology with his own poem about bad verse:

> Bad Verse I sing, and 'twere best, I deem,
> T' employ a style that suits my swelling theme,
> First, in my lines, some flatulence t' infuse,
> I thus invoke the Muddle-headed Muse.
> . . .
>
> Here batter'd tropes and similes abound
> And metaphors lie mix'd in many a mound,
> And oily rags of sentiment bestrew the ground.
> . . .
>
> So sing, the Master of Bathetic Verse.
> Follow their lead: do better, doing worse.
>
> —*SO*, xxii–xxiv

Negative Museums and Unwanted Prizes

Ah, think not, Mistress! More true Dulness lies
In Folly's Cap, than Wisdom's grave disguise.
. . .

For thee we dim the eyes, and stuff the head
With all such reading as was never read:
For thee explain a thing till all men doubt it,
And write about it, Goddess, and about it.   —Pope, *The Dunciad* [32]

The idea of a negative treasury, a museum of badness worth preserving, has occurred to many connoisseurs of awfulness. Boston's Museum of Bad Art collects paintings remarkable not for a lack of technical talent but for a singular combination of vulgarity, pretension, and shallowness. [33]

Applied to actions, such connoisseurship has also inspired the "Darwin Awards" given out, usually posthumously, to singularly stupid behavior ("honoring those who improve the species . . . by accidentally removing themselves from it"). [34]

Such prizes are not to be confused with those awarded for *deliberate* badness, such as the annual Bulwer-Lytton contest for the worst first line of a novel. [35] No one is embarrassed to win such a contest. As Billy Collins points out in his preface to the second edition of *The Stuffed Owl*, intentional badness of this sort is what distinguishes good *light* verse from good Bad Verse. The latter earnestly intends to be good, the former "when it's good—is good because it intends to be bad" (*SO*, iv).

To the great consternation of the winners and their admirers, Denis Dutton and the other editors of *Philosophy and Literature* established the "bad-writing contest" (1995–98) for literary theory. Winning entries were required to be not just bad but extraordinarily bad.

Winners earn shame, and so no one submits his or her own work. Rather, entries are submitted by amused readers. Dutton explains that "entries should be a sentence or two from an actual published scholarly book or journal article. No translations into English allowed, and the entries had to be nonironic: We could hardly admit parodies in a field where unintentional self-parody was so rampant." [36]

Prize-winning prose displays the characteristic failures of academic writing—jargon, vatic tone, obscurity, pretension—to a supreme degree. For Dutton, such writing constitutes "a kind of intellectual kitsch. . . . [T]hese kitsch

theorists mimic the effects of rigor and profundity without actually doing serious intellectual work." Just as *The Stuffed Owl* relies on established poets, so the
two winners of the *Philosophy and Literature* prize for 1998 were both highly
influential theorists, Judith Butler and Homi K. Bhabha.

> The move from a structuralist account in which capital is understood to struc-
> ture social relations in relatively homologous ways to a view of hegemony in
> which power relations are subject to repetition, convergence, and rearticulation
> brought the question of temporality into the thinking of structure, and marked
> a shift from a form of Althusserian theory that takes structural totalities as theo-
> retical objects to one in which the insights into the contingent possibility of
> structure inaugurate a renewed conception of hegemony as bound up with the
> contingent sites and strategies of the rearticulation of power.[37]

> If, for a while, the ruse of desire is calculable for the uses of discipline soon
> the repetition of guilt, justification, pseudo-scientific theories, superstition,
> spurious authorities, and classifications can be seen as the desperate effort to
> "normalize" *formally* the disturbance of a discourse of splitting that violates the
> rational, enlightened claims of its enunciatory modality.[38]

It should be obvious that not all literary scholars would find these passages
unintelligible. I don't, but the prize makes me wonder whether that is a bad
sign. Precisely because Butler and Bhabha inspire so many others, Dutton's
award constitutes a critique of current literary theory as a whole. That is often
the case with Quaylisms: the target supposedly *typifies*, or represents by exag-
geration of essential features, some larger group—such as Republicans, lawyers,
advertisers, or bureaucrats—found to be objectionable.

Negative prizes and anthologies run a risk that Lewis understood. They may
easily seem to compliment themselves and flatter their audience. Or as Lewis
puts the point, in revealing the follies of others, this volume seems to prove "by
implication what splendid fellows we are" (*SO*, xx). Does he successfully ward
off this criticism by making it himself?

Witlessism Type 2: Self-Betrayal

Like the Quaylism, a second type of witlessism unwittingly makes two statements when it means to make one. In this case, what is said unintentionally
reveals something that embarrasses the speaker. The humor arises from the
self-betrayal.

Freudian slips offer the most familiar examples. As Freud describes this kind of error, an element that the speaker has suppressed unexpectedly asserts itself. The speaker says precisely what he or she prefers not to know. The "suppressed element" often manages to be voiced at an embarrassing moment because, as Freud explains, although it "always strives to assert itself elsewhere, [it] is successful in this only when suitable conditions meet it half way."[39] One says "sex" instead of "sets," complains about one's wife instead of one's life, and refers not to another but to one's mother. Writers often let slip Freudian typos and, let us say, speak of "marital exercises" or "pubic affairs."

Or consider spoonerisms, the sort of utterance that—like the famous ones attributed to William Spooner—somehow switches the beginnings of words to produce a quite different sentence. Spooner supposedly offered a toast "to our queer old dean" and reprimanded one undergraduate: "You have tasted your worm, you have hissed my mystery lectures, and you must leave by the first town drain" (*YBQ*, 723). One wonders whether Spooner secretly entertained doubts about the dean and worried that students were disparaging his less than lucid lectures. And what was he thinking when he said he "searched every crook and nanny" (*1001D*, 215)?

Self-betrayals are not always Freudian. At least as often, the speaker knows the embarrassing second meaning quite well. He consciously tries to conceal the truth, but it slips out anyway. In Gogol's play *The Inspector General*, an official assuring the supposed government inspector how efficiently the local hospital is run tells him that patients are cured like flies. A government official in Turgenev's *Fathers and Children* describes how much he loves a summer day "when, in his own words, 'every little bee takes a little bribe from every little flower'" (*F&S*, 49).

Cheats and hypocrites, salesmen and quacks, unintentionally voice not something they have repressed but a thought all too much on their minds. When we watch the schemes of Basil Fawlty (John Cleese, in the BBC series *Fawlty Towers*), we wait for the critical moment when the poorly hidden truth comes out. One can admit a crime in the process of denying it, like the accused thief who, serving as his own lawyer, asked a witness: "Did you get a good look at my face when I took your purse?" (*776D*, 105).

Sometimes authorities betray their own lapses in the act of warning their subordinates against them. In his introduction to the *Oxford Dictionary of Humorous Quotations*, Ned Sherrin reports "the BBC *Women's Hour* directive to new presenters in the early 1990s: . . . 3. Do not be surprised that a woman has achieved something . . . 4. Do not be surprised that an older person has achieved something . . . 5. Do not be surprised that a black person has achieved something" (*ODHQ*, ix). And do not be surprised by what the propagators of this directive still find surprising.

Some comedy depends on the listener interpreting a perfectly clear sentence in a way that grammar permits but would occur to no one else. Endless examples of bad translations do this. In most cases, what the interpreter lacks is common sense. Computers follow rules to an absurd conclusion, as in the old joke about the automated physician that recommends a man suffering from migraines have his head amputated. Here there is no question of Freudian repression.

The master of this sort of humor was Gracie Allen. I recall one episode in which Gracie explains to her neighbor Blanche how she once had a house full of flowers. It seems that when Gracie's friend Clara Bagley was ill, George suggested, why don't you go down to the hospital and take her flowers?—"so when she wasn't looking, I did."

The Editor's Self-Betrayal

Interestingly enough, sometimes self-betrayal takes place by identifying someone else's comment as particularly stupid or inarticulate. In this way, anthologies of witlessisms unwittingly show their *editors'* intellectual limitations. Such editors often quote a political opinion with which they disagree as if it were obviously ridiculous, or cite a statement expressing another culture's values as patently absurd. In such instances, what the editors really show is not the stupidity of those they quote but their own inability to transcend their personal experience. Like so many op-ed writers, they cannot imagine anyone with a brain seeing the world differently.

Because it is more common to discover Quaylisms among Republicans than Democrats, one might imagine that the "editor's self-betrayal," as we might call this type of utterance, usually concerns those to the editor's right. Usually, but by no means always, it does. The editorial smugness of *The 776 Stupidest Things Ever Said* manages to go both ways, as we may see from these two entries appearing together (entry titles belong to the editors):

On Freedom:

Man has been given his freedom to a greater extent than ever and that's quite wrong.

—Martha Mitchell, wife of former attorney general John Mitchell (*776S*, 70)

On Freedom of Speech, Great Moments in:

Freedom of speech of the individual citizen must be based on the four basic principles of insisting on the socialist road, the dictatorship of the proletariat, the leadership of the party, and Marxism–Leninism–Mao Zedong thought. The citizen has only the freedom to support these principles and not the freedom to oppose them.

> —People's Republic of China prosecutor . . . [when] defendant Wei,
> a human rights champion, cited the Chinese constitution guaranteeing
> free speech in his defense. He lost. (*776S*, 70)

Martha Mitchell certainly had her Quaylish moments—I remember her magnificent confession that "World War II wreaked havoc with my social life"—but to regard as self-evidently absurd the idea that people can have too much freedom, and in America now do, is to demonstrate historical and cultural insularity of epic proportions. It is to assume, and assume one's readership assumes, that American liberalism constitutes the only intelligent position.

Whether we think of the European Middle Ages, Puritan England, contemporary Saudi Arabia and Iran, or the former Soviet Union, most societies have rejected freedom as we think of it. It is far from obvious that allowing people to do what harms themselves or to say what their culture regards as patently false must be considered a good thing. The Chinese prosecutor was certainly voicing a position that most Americans find abhorrent and defining "freedom" in a way that for us removes its essence, but from the perspective of twentieth-century Marxist-Leninist regimes—about eighteen of them that have ruled a third of humanity—the prosecutor expressed little more than common sense. It would certainly have been easy for the editors of *The 776 Stupidest Things Ever Said* to find 775 more such statements without much effort. The fact that they picked this one, as if it were exceptional, betrays their own narrowness.

It is also easy to find examples of academese, and so J. Hillis Miller and Paul de Man appear in this volume. Do the editors include them to express philosophical objections to what these critics stand for, as Dutton's contest does, or are they simply unable to imagine the need for language they cannot grasp?

An especially common form of editor's self-betrayal involves citing a prediction that turned out to be decisively mistaken. *Don't Quote Me*, edited by Don Atyeo and Jonathon Green, is entirely devoted to "false prophets" and "opinion-makers" whose "lovingly presented opinions prove disastrously incorrect."[40] *The 776 Stupidest Things Ever Said* includes economists who presumed that pre-Depression conditions would continue or, after 1929, predicted a rapid return to prosperity.

But it is so easy, after the fact, to laugh at someone else's error! The editors certainly do not risk much by identifying predictions already disproven. Besides, is a prediction that turns out wrong necessarily stupid? What if the odds strongly favored such a result even though it did not happen? What if what did happen resulted from the successful avoidance of a disaster we cannot now recognize as once likely?[41] To call these predictions stupid—still more, exceptionally stupid—is to suggest that most people, including the editors, would do better. They hardly offer any reason to think so.

A Digression on Headlines

Headlines offer opportunities to both the witty and the witless, and for much the same reason. Not only must headlines be brief, they also must not be *too* short, since they must fill a designated space. Conventions dictate special rules of tense and favor the language of action. Those who master these conventions can demonstrate their wit. Those who fail can produce sheer nonsense.

Newspapers embody presentness.[42] Published without advance preparation, they require headline writers to work in a hurry. It is easy to stumble and impressive to make the most of a fleeting opportunity. Because the author of an article rarely writes its headline, the headline offers the opportunity for a rapid response. In this way, editorial offices can function like a sort of salon.

Anthologies include classic (if apocryphal) examples of headline wit. On "the lack of enthusiasm for farm dramas among rural populations": "Sticks Nix Hick Pix" (*ODHQ*, 225). When Onassis thought of purchasing a home once owned by Buster Keaton: "Aristotle Contemplating the Home of Buster."[43] After Mia Farrow gave birth to twin boys: "Boy Oh Boy, Mamma Mia."[44]

The same factors allow for concise witlessness: "Police Begin Campaign to Run Down Jaywalkers"; "Prostitutes Appeal to Pope"; "British Left Waffles on Falkland Islands" (*1001D*, 158). Perhaps the best-known example, allegedly from a London newspaper, has come to exemplify insularity: "Storm over the Channel: Continent Isolated."[45]

Witlessism Type 3: Wise Folly, or, The Yogi Berraism

The doubleness of the third type of witlessism gives us stupidity and insight together. An apparent piece of nonsense proves, on reflection, to contain unexpected wisdom. It turns out to be not a contradiction but a paradox expressing an important truth. Crucially, these paradoxes arise unwittingly. We hear them first as hopelessly inarticulate or brainless and then, upon reflection, as surprisingly expressive and intelligent.

Today, the best-known examples belong to Yogi Berra. Berra's famous observation, "When you come to a fork in the road, take it," can be understood to mean that it is better to make *some* decision than to hesitate endlessly (*YBQ*, 58). "If the world were perfect, it wouldn't be" paraphrases the theme of countless anti-utopias (*YB*, 52). "Nobody goes there anymore, it's too crowded" captures the way in which we say "nobody" when we mean "nobody like us" (*YB*, 16). "It ain't over till it's over" does much the same with "over" (*YBQ*, 58). Omissions can be actions of a sort: "If the people don't want to come out to the park, nobody's gonna stop 'em" (*YBQ*, 58). A student of Wittgenstein might admire: "In theory there is no difference between theory and practice. In practice there is."[46]

Yogi seemed especially likely to touch on the mysteries of temporality. Philosophers have disputed whether the present is an illusion, and Yogi, when asked the time, replied: "[Y]ou mean now?" (*YBQ*, 58). "The future ain't what it used to be" is, after all, correct, because any moment of experience includes a sense of anticipated outcomes (*YB*, 118–19). And if ethics is based on *expected* reciprocity, one might well conclude: "[A]lways go to other people's funerals, or they won't go to yours" (*YB*, 73).

Is it moral to sacrifice the present generation to build a glorious future, as revolutionaries demand? Or do such demands fallaciously presume that the future somehow already exists? We could ask that question in the Yogi-like words of Sir Boyle Roche: "I don't see, Mr. Speaker, why we should put ourselves out of the way to serve posterity. What has posterity ever done for us?" (*776S*, 143).[47]

For Americans today, only Sam Goldwyn rivals Yogi. Goldwyn seemed to capture the logic of bureaucracy when, asked by his secretary if she could destroy some old files, answered: "Go ahead. But make copies of them first" (*776D*, 123). Much the same can be said of his warning that "a verbal contract isn't worth the paper it's written on" (*YBQ*, 317). "I'm giving you a definite maybe" precisely expresses an absolute commitment to being uncommitted (317). "Include me out" really is different from "exclude me" (317). "Let's have some new clichés" only seems contradictory (317). In fact, clichés arise all the time, and whoever can coin one that others adopt can profit handsomely. If psychiatrists cause more harm than good, as they may when a faddish diagnosis prevails, then it is true enough that "anybody who goes to a psychiatrist should have his head examined" (317).

Witlessism Type 4: Assumed Innocence

Mark Twain specialized in what might be called "pseudo-witlessisms," because the speaker he personifies, rather than Twain himself, proves witless. Twain typically plays a naïve or uneducated person commenting on high culture, proper opinion, or an assumed truth he does not really understand. He may explicate what we all know to others still less knowledgeable than he. Or he may convict himself of a lapse in taste, knowledge, or behavior in the very act of denying it.

In all these ways, the character Twain plays—let us call him "the innocent"— "bestranges" what educated readers take for granted by showing it as if it were some new truth. Faced with the innocent's incomprehension, we reflect on, rather than presume the correctness of, received opinion. The innocent thereby offers satiric insight without knowing it. The author's relation to this character can vary from near identification to considerable difference.

Consider the following classic examples:

> They spell it Vinci and pronounce it Vinchy; foreigners always spell better than they pronounce.   —*The Innocents Abroad* (*YBQ*, 774)

> Everybody talks about the weather, but nobody does anything about it.
>   —(attributed)

> Wagner's music is not as bad as it sounds.   —(attributed)

> The reports of my death have been greatly exaggerated.   —(attributed)[48]

Each of these comments make its point by missing the point. Twain's famous remark "It's very easy to stop smoking, I've done it a hundred times" tells us just what makes some "actions"—like breaking a habit—different from others. They are closer to significant nonactions, successful only if "performed" continually and forever.

Twain's first book, *The Innocents Abroad: The New Pilgrim's Progress* (1869), repeatedly offers its shrewd observations through a speaker who misunderstands. The line about Vinci derives its nonsensical conclusion from an assumption we have to reconstruct, that foreign languages are just English with different words but that everything else, including pronunciation, is the same. None of us would voice that thought, but we are only one step from it when, as I have often heard, we pronounce a foreign language we don't know as if it followed the rules of one we do, like French. The Russian Formalists coined the term usually transliterated as *siuzhet* for "plot" as they analyzed it, but I have heard American critics pronounce the "et"—which pronounced in Russian rhymes with English "yet"—as if it were "ay."

Twain's essay "The Awful German Language" depends on the same assumption about language, as does his less well-known sketch about French, "The Jumping Frog. In English. Then in French. Then clawed back into a civilized language once more by patient, unremunerated toil."[49] The sketch begins with Twain, in his persona as innocent, complaining about an article "in a French Magazine entitled, *Revue des Deux Mondes* (Review of Some Two Worlds), wherein the writer treats of 'Les Humoristes Americaines' (These Humorists Americans)" (Twain, *Sketches*, 261). It appears that the French critic, who provided a translation of Twain's most famous story, did not find it especially funny.

Twain objects that the problem lies in the translation, and to prove his point produces a reverse translation of the French back into English. This rendition of a rendition tacitly presumes, yet again, that foreign languages differ from English only in vocabulary, and so must employ the same grammar, syntax, and idioms. The story's title thus returns as "The Frog Jumping of the County of Calaveras" and the first paragraph contains formulations like "I no me recollect exactly" (for "je ne me rappelle pas exactement") as well as completely unintelligible nonsense (271).

But if Twain's assumption is obviously absurd, then why are translators still praised for imitating the syntax of the original language as if that were somehow more accurate and better preserved the author's style?[50]

Twain's famous "weather" comment fuses commonplaces to produce its nonsense. It does with sentences what mixed metaphors do with words. The speaker knows that the saying "everyone talks about the weather" means that everybody makes small talk in one of a few fixed ways. Even when phrased as statements and questions, such small talk is intended neither to convey nor elicit information. Presumably, the speaker has also heard the complaint that people all "talk about a problem but don't do anything about it." So he begins with the saying about weather and slides into the complaint about inaction, which is easy to do since both begin with the same words. The result creates absurdity for the obvious reason that, as a third commonplace has it, weather stands for something over which one has no control. We therefore have not two but three clichés combined. However we interpret this comment, it demonstrates how little thought goes into our usual indignation.

One can easily imagine an ill-educated person who knows he is supposed to like Wagner explaining to a still less-educated person that even though appreciating Wagner's music is hard, learning to do so repays the effort. Educated opinion vouches for that, after all. We also have the expression "is not as bad as it sounds," meaning that something is better than its *description* would make it appear. But when the two assertions are combined, the topic of music renders the word "sound" literal, so that we get the absurdity of music, which is sound, being better than it sounds.

In *What Is Art?* Tolstoy argues at length that Wagnerian opera is based on, and requires knowledge of, theories, which means that it pretends to be what it is not—better than it sounds. The appreciators of such art, Tolstoy observes, "are obliged to cling to some external criterion. And they find it in 'the judgments of the finest-nurtured,' as an English aesthetician has phrased it, that is, in the authority of the people who are considered educated not only in this, but also in a tradition of such authorities" (*WIA*, 112). Twain's innocent unwittingly makes the same point more concisely and much more tellingly.

The famous cablegram in response to reports that Twain had died abroad compresses more complexity than at first appears. It goes far beyond the familiar sort of humor that results from the assertion that one is not dead. To see why, imagine the cable's wording as: "I am not dead." That would be funny but not nearly as funny. Now consider in order these possible wordings:

The reports of my death are false.

The reports of my death are exaggerated.

The reports of my death have been greatly exaggerated.

The closer one comes to the final version, the funnier the comment gets, but why? The answer, I think, is that people call a statement about themselves "exaggerated" when it is, in fact, undeniably true and they are trying to escape the consequences. That is also why they refer to it as mere rumor or "report." But how could this report be true? Twain acts like a person accused of a crime who, in spite of all contrary evidence, tries unconvincingly to protest his innocence. "Greatly" exaggerated makes the denial still funnier because, as we know by experience, the more vehemently a criminal denies an accusation, the guiltier he is likely to be.

Without the persona Twain adopts, and without the dramatic situation it creates, the line would be only mildly amusing. As it is, the comment is not only hilarious but also quite profound. Death *can* seem like a transgression. In Tolstoy's novella *The Death of Ivan Ilych*, society regards dying as a sort of faux pas, like emitting an unpleasant odor or mentioning an inappropriate topic. A judge, Ivan Ilych now feels like a criminal in the dock. Could it be that all social life depends on denying the inescapable truth of mortality? Both Tolstoy's story and Twain's cablegram suggest as much.

Twain was not the only one to play the role of the innocently witless. One might almost say that this role defines American humor. Lincoln used a similar persona. The famous line attributed to him—"God must love the common people. He's made so many of 'em"—follows the logic of nonsense voicing paradoxical sense.[51] Marilyn Monroe could be all the more sultry when "uncomprehending." Asked whether she had once posed for a calendar with nothing on, she replied: "I had the radio on" (*YBQ*, 532).

Longer Witlessisms

The different types of witlessisms have inspired a variety of longer literary works. Quaylisms offer the simplest approach. As Oscar Wilde made comedies by stringing together opportunities for witty comments, so Sheridan's *The Rivals* does much the same with the sort of witlessisms to which its most memorable character, Mrs. Malaprop, gave her name. So odd are her substitutions that they can seem like daring metaphors. She berates one character for being "as headstrong as an allegory on the banks of the Nile."[52]

Mrs. Malaprop's famous lines follow the logic of the play's story. As two rivals in love turn out to be the same person, so two meanings compete for control of the same utterance. A few of these malapropisms intimate the paradoxical wisdom of Berraisms, particularly those concerned with time: "[W]e will not anticipate the past," Mrs. Malaprop declares, "our retrospection will be all to the future" (Sheridan, 60).

Several of Twain's longer works develop his specialty, the fourth type of witlessism. Their narrator, and sometimes their characters as well, utter a series of sage stupidities one after the other. *The Innocents Abroad* initiated a series of travel books in which tourism provides the opportunity to misunderstand, or understand all too well, culture after culture. *Dave Barry Does Japan* follows in Twain's footsteps.

Twain is probably best in his short stories, several of which develop the Twainian witlessism. In "How I Edited an Agricultural Paper," he explains how, with no knowledge of farming, he produced editorials that for some reason led the paper's readers to doubt his, or indeed their own, sanity. At last the former editor returns and complains to Twain: "You speak of a furrow and a harrow as being the same thing; you talk of the moulting season for cows; and you recommend the domestication of the pole-cat on account of its playfulness and its excellence as a ratter! Your remark that clams will lie quiet if music be played to them was superfluous—entirely superfluous. . . . Clams always lie quiet. . . . It makes me lose all patience every time I think of your discussing oyster-beds under the head of 'Landscape Gardening.'"[53] But Twain has an answer: supposed experts never know their field except theoretically. As we might say today, economists have never met a payroll. Educators who can't teach know the theories taught in schools of education. Or as Twain explains, journalists learn how to report and never know anything about their subject matter.

As someone who understands the newspaper business, Twain concludes self-righteously, "I tell you that the less a man knows the bigger a noise he makes and the higher salary he commands" (Twain, *Stories*, 50). There are always two ways to be an expert about an activity: to know the activity and to know how to be "an expert." The story's witless premise becomes a timeless warning.

Living Backwards

Two overlapping groups of great works develop the logic of the witlessism, the literature of defamiliarization and the literature of wise folly.

The literature of defamiliarization (or "bestrangement") allows us to examine customs, institutions, and beliefs we take for granted but which, if viewed from the perspective of an innocent or an outsider, make no sense. We must overcome the habits of seeing that impede real perception; we need to see what we are looking at as if it were still unfamiliar or strange. That is exactly the way the innocent views things, and so his perspective turns out to be, though utterly ignorant, illuminating.

The innocent may be a foreigner, a child, an animal, a provincial, an extraterrestrial, or, in Twain's case, an American. From antiquity to the present, authors have allowed the naïve to express the "natural" or "rational" point of view, while the civilized rely on scholastic dogma or artificial customs.

In antiquity, Diogenes, Menippus, and other heroes of menippean satire express witless wisdom. When Diogenes is reproached for masturbating in public, he points out how good it would be if rubbing could satisfy hunger as well. In Lucian's "Dialogues of the Dead," "Icaromenippus," and "Philosophies for Sale," the philosopher turns out to be the real idiot and the idiot the true philosopher. Thomas More translated Lucian, so it is not surprising that he names the hero of *Utopia* Raphael Hythlodaeus (Beloved-of-God Purveyor-of-Nonsense) and makes preposterous recommendations that, of course, may not be so preposterous after all. When Gulliver explains England to the Brobdingnagians or Diderot's priest explains Catholicism to the Tahitians, it is the ignorant foreigners who see clearly. Tolstoy's innocents include Natasha Rostova at the opera, the horse Strider explaining human institutions to the other horses, and, in one story, a tree.

The fool sees what the supposedly intelligent miss. "By his very uncomprehending presence, he [the fool] makes strange the world of social conventionality," as Bakhtin observes. "By representing stupidity, the novel teaches prosaic intelligence, prosaic wisdom . . . a sort of prosaic vision, the vision of a world confused by conventions of pathos [bombastic rhetoric] and by falsity."[54]

The literature of wise folly derives not only from this appreciation of stupidity that is not stupid, but also from the central Christian paradox of a messiah powerless in worldly terms. Paul stresses this paradox: "[F]or it is written, I will destroy the wisdom of the wise, and will bring to nothing the understanding of the prudent. . . . [H]ath God not made foolish the wisdom of this world? . . . But God hath chosen the foolish things of the world to confound the wise" (1 Corinthians 1:19–27). In Erasmus's *Praise of Folly*, the goddess Folly voices an endless stream of such paradoxes, praising folly as wise—or is it only a fool who says so?—and praising self-praise as well. From *Don Quixote* to *The Idiot*, the folly of the witless reveals wisdom overlooked by the wise.

A taste for witlessisms implies a taste for nonsense. Witlessisms transport us to wonderland, through the looking glass, into an inverted world that rigorously follows an alternative logic or proceeds by our logic from a preposterous premise. Such nonsense defamiliarizes not only logic but also social behavior, the laws of nature, and language itself, which is why commentators have been able to cite passages from the Alice books to illustrate concepts from physics to politics. You have to stand upside down, fall uphill, or experience cause after effect to see the world as it really is. "'That's the effect of living backwards,' the Queen said kindly [to Alice]; 'it always makes one a little giddy at first.'"[55]

WISDOM AND COUNTER-WISDOM

▌ WISE SAYINGS ▌

To understand a proverb, and the interpretation; the words of the wise, and their dark sayings.   —Proverbs 1:2–6

Collecting Wisdom

Not all cultures have collected witticisms and witlessisms, but every culture has treasured its wise sayings. The reason is obvious. Cultures sustain themselves by passing on their basic insights and values, and so, even before writing, they must have a way to do so. They must instruct the young in moral, practical, and spiritual truths, as the culture understands them. When writing begins, the words of the wise tend to be recorded first, because what could be more worth preserving?

The book sometime called the oldest book in the world, the Egyptian *Instructions of Ptah-hotep*, collects wise sayings that evidently date from much earlier.[1] So do the *Instructions for King Meri-ka-re* (c. 2100 BC) and the *Instruction of Amen-em-ope* (eleventh century BC). The Hebrew Bible boasts that "God gave Solomon wisdom and understanding exceeding much. . . . And Solomon's wisdom excelled the wisdom of all the children of the East country and all the wisdom of Egypt" (1 Kings 4:29–30). By "the east country" the Bible evidently refers to other wisdom literature long circulating throughout Mesopotamia, which includes the *Hymn to Shumash* and the *Counsels of Wisdom* (*ABPE*, li).

The book of Proverbs contains several distinct collections of proverbs, including two attributed to Solomon (Proverbs 10–22:16 and 25–29) and one described as "the words of the wise," or the thirty precepts of the sages (Proverbs 22:17–24:22). The precepts of the sages reflect the influence of *Amen-em-ope*. Proverbs also occur elsewhere in the Bible, where they are cited as ancient wisdom. Jeremiah and Ezekiel refer to the same received saying:

> In those days they shall say no more, The fathers have eaten a sour grape, and the children's teeth are set on edge.   —Jeremiah 31:29

> What mean ye, that ye use this proverb concerning the Land of Israel, saying, The Fathers have eaten sour grapes, and the children's teeth are set on edge? As I live, saith the Lord God, ye shall not have occasion any more to use this proverb in Israel.   —Ezekiel 18:2–3

The book of Tobit (1:22 and 14:10) mentions the Assyrian sage Ahiqar (*Words of Ahiqar*). It also contains two sets of precepts, uttered by Tobit (4:3–19) and by the angel Raphael (12:6–10).

The followers of Jesus collected his wise sayings, many of which never made it into the New Testament, and Muslims preserved the Sacred Hadith of Muhammad. The Hebrew *Pirke Aboth* (Sayings of the Fathers), the best known of the thirty-six tractates of the Mishnah, records the wisdom of some sixty rabbis from 300 BC to 200 AD, as well as anonymous sayings. Wise sayings appear in the Five Confucian Classics as well as in the work we call Confucius's *Analects* (more literally, *Conversations*).

The Greeks contributed the saying of the Seven Sages. Diogenes Laertius reports in his *Lives of Eminent Philosophers* that the seven are variously identified ("nor is there any agreement how the number is made up"). The number seven evidently carries the aura of sacred myth. The first sentence of the *Lives* concedes: "There are some who say that the study of philosophy had its beginning with the barbarians" (*DL1*, 3). Those who say so urge that the Persians had their Magi, the Babylonians their Chaldeans, the Indians their Gymnosophists, and the Celts their Druids, while the Egyptians trace philosophy to Hephaestus, who lived 48,863 years before Alexander. Zoroaster, these defenders of the barbarians continue, lived five thousand years before the fall of Troy. But Diogenes Laertius dismisses these claims because "these authors forget that the achievements which they attribute to the barbarians belong to the Greeks, with whom not merely philosophy but the human race itself began" (5). He questions whether one barbarian, Orpheus the Thracian, should be considered a philosopher at all, "for what are we to make of one who does not scruple to charge the gods with all human suffering?" (7).

The first book printed in England was *The dictes or sayengis of the philosophres,* published by William Caxton, whose interest in wise sayings reflected the same impulse that led Erasmus to compile his *Adages.* Of course, we have collections of proverbs from around the world. Interestingly enough, the *Yale Book of Quotations* includes a separate section on "Modern Proverbs" (apparently coined since 1900), many of which sound as if they are much older (*YBQ,* 526–29).

The Traditional Moral Calculus

Wisdom collections contain a variety of precepts and thoughts, but I should like to identify a core group that I shall refer to henceforth as "wise sayings." Wise sayings purport to contain wisdom beyond any individual's capacity. They draw on long human experience. Above all, they counsel behavior bound to be rewarded because it accords with the nature of things.

From the perspective of this genre, nature and human nature derive from an underlying, fundamentally moral order. Therefore the two broad counsels wise sayings offer—be righteous and be prudent—are ultimately the same. Evil is imprudent, and imprudence is evil. It is never prudent to steal from the widow, use false weights, or oppress one's subjects. And it is never truly righteous to indulge one's children, be incautious when making bargains, or grow angry and quarrelsome. Both sets of failings constitute wisdom's opposite, folly.

The wisdom of the ages teaches that providence governs. What is right is also in one's best interest. Prudence and righteousness are certain to be recompensed, usually in this world, but sometimes—it may be conceded—only in the next. In any case, we can be confident that the universe will ensure that good people are eventually rewarded and that the evil suffer. Foul deeds will rise, though all the earth o'erwhelm them, to men's eyes, or if not to men's eyes, then to God's, which see what people do in secret. As the Chinese proverb asserts, "Men's whispers sound like thunder in Heaven's ears; their secret thoughts flash like lightning before Heaven's eyes" (*CCAS,* 280).

Wise sayings insist: "Be not deceived; God is not mocked: for whatsoever a man soweth, that shall he also reap" (Galatians 6:7). We read in the *Sayings of the Fathers* that once Rabbi Hillel

> saw a skull floating on the surface of the water: he said to it, Because thou
> drownedst others, they have drowned thee; and at the last, they that drowned
> thee shall themselves be drowned.[2]

The *Sayings* reports that Rabbi Elazar advised us to know "who thy Employer is, who will pay thee the reward of thy labor" and then adds: "Rabbi Tarfon said, The day is short, and the work is great, and the labourers are sluggish, and the reward is much, and the Master is urgent" (*Sayings*, 43). Rabbi Elazar warned of judgment not just in this world but also the next: "[K]now also that everything is according to the reckoning and let not thy imagination give thee hope that the grave will be a place of refuge for thee. . . . [P]erforce thou wilt in the future have to give account and reckoning before the Supreme King of kings, the Holy One, blessed be he" (83).

In much the same spirit, the *Instructions for Meri-ka-re* counsel: "Do justice that you may live long upon the earth" (*BFQ15*, 4). The *Instructions* also extend recompense to the afterlife when the gods will judge the king: "[A]fter death . . . his deeds are placed beside him in heaps" while "for him who reaches it [the afterlife] without wrongdoing, he shall exist yonder like a god" (*ABPE*, xliii). The later Egyptian *Instructions of 'Onchsheshonqy* (fifth century BC) promises that "[t]here is no wise man who comes to grief; there is no fool who finds reward" (*ABPE*, xlv). "Heaven helps the good man," the Chinese proverb affirms. "Those who accord with Heaven are preserved; those who rebel against Heaven perish" (*CCAS*, 248).

Anyone who knows the book of Proverbs will recall that it contains countless sayings promising prosperity for the good and prudent while threatening destruction for the wicked and foolish. "Treasures of wickedness profit nothing: but righteousness delivereth from death. The Lord shall not suffer the soul of the righteous to perish; but he casteth away the substance of the wicked" (Proverbs 10:2–3). "Behold, the righteous shall be recompensed in the earth; much more the wicked and the sinner" (11:31). Several dozen verses in Proverbs assert such providential outcomes. In the deuterocanonical *Wisdom of Ben Sira*, Wisdom personified promises: "He who obeys of me will not be put to shame, / those who work with me will never fail" (*WBS*, 24:22).

Numerous "wisdom psalms" in the book of Psalms affirm what Robert Alter calls "the traditional moral calculus . . . that it pays to be good, whereas the wicked will be paid back for their evil."[3] Psalm 1, usually taken as an introduction to the whole, asserts this perspective:

> Blessed is the man that walketh not in the counsel of the ungodly, nor standeth in the way of sinners, nor sitteth in the seat of the scornful.
>
> But his delight is the law of the Lord; and his law doth he meditate day and night.

> And he shall be a tree planted by the rivers of water, that bringeth forth his fruit in due season; his leaf also shall not wither; and whatsoever he doeth shall prosper.
>
> The ungodly are not so: but are like the chaff which the wind driveth away.
>
> Therefore the ungodly shall not stand in the judgment, nor sinners in the congregation of the righteous.
>
> For the Lord knoweth the way of the righteous: but the way of the ungodly shall perish.

The Alter version gives the first words as "Happy the man," a phrase frequently used in Proverbs when evoking the calculus of recompense (*HBC*, 434). Alter's commentary stresses that in the Psalms the word the King James Version renders as "soul" means something closer to "life" and the word rendered as "salvation" means "rescue," but whether or not one reads the text to stress reward in this life or the next, it promises justice.[4]

Even in an age when the logic of providence seems hopelessly naïve, we say: "What goes around comes around." Or we refer vaguely to "karma." The American left and right have both insisted that foreign policy should be shaped by the awareness that justice ultimately pays. If we rescue those suffering under dictators, or reply to provocation with a good example rather than with force, we will serve our true national interest. When the Soviet Union collapsed, Francis Fukuyama famously discerned the final triumph of liberal democracy, vindicated by History—a later word for providence—itself.

Wisdom and the Mandate of Heaven

> Respect the gods, sir. We are your suppliants,
> And Zeus avenges strangers and suppliants,
> Zeus, god of strangers, who walks by our side.
>
> —Odysseus to Polyphemus, *Odyssey* (bk. 9, ll. 261–63)[5]

Sometimes the agent rewarding the good and prudent while punishing the wicked and foolish may be neither God nor the gods, but the very nature of things.

In the ancient Confucian classics, the "cosmic moral order" (*SCT*, 27) called Tian (Heaven) guides the world, and the wise man acts according to Heaven's dictates. We read in the *Classic of Documents* (*Shujing*): "Heaven, unseen, has given to humankind their constitution, aiding the harmonious development of it in their various conditions."[6] Confucius said: "The noble person has three objects of awe: he is in awe of the ordinances of Heaven (*tianming*); he is in awe

of the great man; and he is in awe of the words of the sage" (*SCT*, 61). When a
dynasty becomes unjust, it loses the "Mandate of Heaven" (as *tianming* is also
translated), which is given to another family. Chinese proverbs often invoke the
order and power of Heaven: "Heaven produces and Heaven destroys"; "Heaven
sets the price of fuel and rice" (*CCAS*, 248). Wisdom demands understanding
of Heaven's ways.

Wisdom so understood means more than the kind of insight to be found,
let us say, in Aristotle's *Nichomachean Ethics* or the *Meditations* of Marcus Aurelius. Aristotle's counsels make sense even if one understands the world as
entirely without meaning or moral value. But the truths of Wisdom, which
reflect the intelligence behind all things, are not merely empirical observations
but sacred invocations. Even if natural, Wisdom acts like a supernatural agent
and so is often personified as a goddess.

In Proverbs, Wisdom speaks directly not just about human life but also
about herself. She explains that she existed before creation as a sort of divine sibling or consort: "The Lord possessed me in the beginning of his way,
before his works of old. I was set up from everlasting, from the beginning,
or ever the earth was. . . . When he prepared the heavens, I was there; when
he set a compass upon the face of the earth. . . . Then I was by him, as one
brought up with him, and I was daily his delight, rejoicing always before him"
(Proverbs 8:22–30). Wisdom helped bring Being into being, and so "whoso
findeth me findeth life, and shall obtain favour of the Lord. But he that sin-
neth against me wrongeth his own soul: all they that hate me love death"
(Proverbs 9:35–36).

It is obvious how such a view can combine with Platonism, as it does in the
opening to the fourth gospel. In John, Wisdom is Logos, the Word that "was in
the beginning with God," by whom "all things were made," and in whom "was
life; and the life was the light of men" (John 1:2–4). The *Wisdom of Ben Sira*
begins by directly echoing Proverbs: "Wisdom sings her own praises, among
her own people she proclaims her glory; In the assembly of the Most High she
opens her mouth, in the presence of his host she declares her worth: From the
mouth of the most high I came forth" (*WBS*, 24:1–3).

Ben Sira offers a specifically Hebrew destiny for Wisdom. She seeks through
heaven and earth for an abode until God instructs: "In Jacob make your dwell-
ing, in Israel your inheritance . . . in Jerusalem is my domain" (24: 8–11). Wisdom now becomes identified with Torah, with the Law of Moses—"the book
of the Most High's covenant, the Law which Moses enjoined on us, as a heri-

tage for the community of Jacob" (24:23). Like the Logos in John, Torah, as the home of Wisdom, defines the plan of creation itself.

Wisdom remains active through history, and rewards those who obey her: "He who obeys me will not be put to shame, those who work with me will never fail" (24:22). Though always active, Wisdom and Torah are inexhaustible. Therefore, the more one eats of Wisdom the hungrier for her one becomes (24:21), and Torah overflows with understanding beyond human grasp. "The first human never knew wisdom fully, nor will the last succeed in fathoming her" (24:28). In the *Sayings of the Fathers*, Rabbi Akiba proclaims: "Blessed are Israel, for unto them was given the desirable instrument [Torah] . . . through which the world was created" (*Sayings*, 61).

The Value of Wisdom

Wisdom is the principal thing; therefore get wisdom.   —Proverbs 4:7

Because the literature of wisdom reflects the unfathomable nature of things— the ordinances of Heaven, Logos, Torah, God, the gods—its value exceeds all measure: "For wisdom is better than rubies; and all the things that may be desired are not to be compared with it" (Proverbs 8:11). When God offers Solomon whatever he desires, Solomon famously chooses wisdom, and God gives him "a wise and understanding heart; so that there was none like thee before thee, neither after thee shall any arise unto thee" (1 Kings 3:12).

Wisdom proves to be a gift like no other because, in choosing it over other goods, Solomon earns those other goods as well. God rewards the right choice: "And I have also given thee that which thou hast not asked, riches and honour: so that there shall not be any among the kings like unto thee all thy days" (1 Kings 13).

If Solomon knew enough to choose wisdom, he must have been wise to begin with. Symbolically, as well as actually, wisdom begets wisdom. Wisdom is both its own reward and the source of all others. Therefore what Wisdom counsels above all is the pursuit of wisdom, and what wise sayings recommend is the learning of wise sayings. "To know wisdom and instruction; to perceive the words of understanding. . . . A wise man will hear, and will increase learning, and a man of understanding will attain unto wise counsels. To understand a proverb, and the interpretation; the words of the wise, and their dark sayings" (Proverbs 1:2–6). Because Wisdom derives from the mind of the Creator, it begins with piety: "The fear of the Lord is the beginning of knowledge: but fools despise wisdom and instruction" (Proverbs 1:7).

The Source of Wisdom

By himself, no human being, no matter how intelligent, can attain wisdom. In fact, wisdom counsels against mere intelligence: "Trust in the Lord with all thine heart; and lean not upon thine own understanding" (Proverbs 3:5).

The source of wisdom cannot be a human being, because no reasoning is sufficiently powerful and no individual life sufficiently rich in experience. That is why proverbs are typically anonymous. They belong not to this person or that but to humanity, to the people, to the great mythic sages of remote times, to history, or to divine inspiration. If proverbs or other wise sayings do have an author, they contrive to lose him and so to "anonymize" themselves. Otherwise, they would represent but one person's opinion.

When wise sayings are ascribed to a single person, he becomes a mythic figure transcending normal human status. Solomon "spake three thousand proverbs" and is traditionally credited with the book of Proverbs (or with the two largest parts of it), but he has received his superhuman wisdom from God. Confucius, too, has enjoyed mythic status and, in any case, claims not to author but merely to pass on the wisdom of the ages: "I transmit but do not create" (*SCT*, 50). By "believing and loving the ancients" he can make their wisdom live in the present (50): "The Master said: 'One who reanimates the old so as to understand the new may become a teacher'" (47). Ben Sira speaks not from himself but affirms his status as a "rivulet fed by her [Wisdom's] stream." "Suddenly this rivulet of mine become a river" so that "I will pour out instruction like prophecy, and bequeath it to generations yet to come" (*WBS*, 24:30–33).

For Americans, the "founding fathers" have carried a quasi-mythic authority, and schoolchildren learn to treat the words of Washington and Lincoln as forming a sort of national Bible. We think of the phrase "a house divided" as Lincoln's, although he was citing Mark 3:25. As a mythic embodiment of ordinary people's wisdom, Lincoln has accumulated sayings of a special sort. Unlike Confucius, he has come to personify the democratic sage: "You can fool all of the people some of the time; you can fool some of the people all the time, but you can't fool all the people all the time" (*YBQ*, 465). His wry counsel, "Better to remain silent and be thought a fool than to speak and remove all doubt" (*YBQ*, 466), has become familiar to many who do not know its allusion to Proverbs 17:28: "Even a fool, when he holdeth his peace, is counted wise."

People can be "Lincolnized" or "Solomonized" this way: they become legends who, unlike the rest of us, can speak in proverbs. Typically, these Solomons acquire a semimythic biography, as Washington and Lincoln have. Lenin played a similar role in Russia, as did Mao in China. In antiquity, Socrates acquired a legendary biography and proverbial sayings: "I know nothing but the fact of my ignorance"; "How many things I can do without!"; "The rest of the world lives to eat, while I eat to live" (*YBQ*, 717). "These and the like were his words and deeds," reports Diogenes Laertius in his quasi-mythic biography, "to which the Pythian priestess bore testimony when she gave Chaerophon the famous response: 'Of all men living Socrates [is] most wise'" (*DL1*, 167–69).

Most people who use proverbs drawn from Pope remain unaware of their source. The nameless wisdom we invoke as true, / Would lose its force, if Pope received his due. His sayings circulate as if they came from the Bible or timeless tradition, and the *Oxford Book of Quotations* lists several of them, along with many anonymous lines, under the entry "Proverbs": "A little knowledge is a dangerous thing"; "To err is human, to forgive divine"; "Fools rush in where angels fear to tread"; "Hope springs eternal."[7] Of course, Pope offered these lines not as his own thoughts but as his memorable expression of received wisdom: "[W]hat oft was thought, but ne'er so well expressed."[8]

Just as a proverb can gain authority from anonymization, it can lose it when attributed. In *War and Peace* Pierre conveys to Andrei inspired wisdom he has learned, but Andrei replies dismissively: "Yes, that is Herder's theory" (*W&P*, 471). Andrei objects to any claim of wisdom that is more than one person's opinion. "You say . . . we will show you the purpose of life, man's destiny, and the laws that govern the universe. But who is this *we?*—Men. How is it you know everything? Why do I alone not see it? You see a reign of truth and goodness on earth, but I don't see it" (470–71). Wisdom of the sort you claim must come from a superhuman source, but you are all just people.

The Cry and the Scorners

Because wise sayings proceed from a superindividual, and perhaps superhuman, source, they exude confidence in their veracity. Wisdom *demands* our attention and obedience. Though she counsels humility, she is not humble: "Wisdom crieth without; she uttereth her voice in the streets: She crieth in the chief place of concourse, in the openings of the gates: in the city she utters her words" (Proverbs 1:20–21). Fools who fail to listen will learn too late the value of wisdom: "Then shall they call upon me, but I will not answer. . . . For that they hated knowledge, and did not choose the fear of the Lord" (Proverbs 1:28–29).

The fools and wicked who disregard wisdom often think of themselves as sophisticated. What we think of as modern skepticism evidently confronted pious believers in a moral order millennia ago. Believers in wisdom seem ever to be affirming that, in spite of the condescension of the worldly, the traditional calculus is still correct.

Wise sayings therefore teach us to beware: Folly flatters, and the evil look upon the good as naïve. Wise sayings presume as their opponent a "scorner" or "scoffer," whom we sense as their antagonist. They expect to be disregarded by most people, the fools and the wicked. "Reprove not a scorner, lest he hate thee: rebuke a wise man, and he will love thee" (Proverbs 9:8). But "surely he [God] scorneth the scorners" (Proverbs 3:34).

Numerous psalms consider the apparent triumph of the scorners. These psalms divide into three parts: the words of the scorners, their evil deeds leading to their apparent triumph, and a call for God's justice. Psalm 14 famously begins with the scorners: "The fool [Alter gives: the scoundrel] hath said in his heart, There is no God. They are corrupt, they have done abominable works, there is none that doeth good" (Psalms 14:1). But God Himself sees the scoundrels' scornful deeds: "The Lord looked down from heaven upon the children of men, to see if there were any that did understand, and seek God" (14:2). The psalm assures us that "God is in the generation of the righteous" and stands with the oppressed man, "because the Lord is his refuge" (14:5–6).

Psalm 10 begins with the apparent triumph of evil, phrased as a question: "Why standest thou afar off, O Lord? why hidest thou thyself in times of trouble?" (10:1). The scorner imagines himself immune from justice: "He hath said in his heart, God has forgotten: he hideth his face; he will never see it" (10:11). The psalmist calls upon God to restore justice and vindicate traditional wisdom: "Arise, O Lord; O God, lift up thine hand: forget not the humble" (10:12).

Just as Wisdom recognizes that many will not listen to her, she knows she abides among her enemies. All the same, her sayings assure us that justice will win out because, despite appearances, it is the will of God and accords with the nature of things. Indeed, part of justice will be the pleasure of seeing the scorners proven wrong and the righteous vindicated. It is a pleasure with which few others can compare. The famous twenty-third psalm includes the promise that "Thou preparest a table for me in the presence of mine enemies."[9]

Rhetoric and the Dialogue of Instruction

Because they serve to educate the young, numerous proverbs presume a dialogic situation of unequals: one person instructs, and the other learns. As we have seen, Egyptian proverbs presume a lesson ("instructions"), and the biblical book of Proverbs frequently addresses "my son": "My son, despise not the chastisements of the Lord; neither be weary of his correction: For whom the Lord loveth he correcteth; even as a father the son in whom he delighteth" (Proverbs 2:11–12). It is hardly surprising, then, that many proverbs advise the young to learn, to honor their teachers, and to regard reproof as a benefit.

The doubleness of many proverbs, where a second line repeats the first in other words, probably reflects this instructional setting. The teacher intones the first line, and the student responds with the second. "He becometh poor that dealeth with a slack hand: but the hand of the diligent makes rich" (10:4); "Riches profit not in the day of wrath: but righteousness delivereth from death" (11:4). Teachers and students recite wise sayings one after another, and so, although each saying stands on its own, they tend to accumulate into collections.

As these examples demonstrate, wise sayings typically use the present tense or an imperative that applies now and always ("therefore get thee wisdom"). The sense is that truths reflecting the nature of things must always be true. Proverbs seem to step out of the historical present, out of history altogether, to speak the eternal, the principles upon which the world was made. If they are in a foreign language—especially Latin—they carry the aura of endless time and universality of place: *carpe diem; de gustibus non est disputandum; homo sum, humani nil a me alienum puto*. But no matter how old they may be, or in what Scripture they may be recorded, wise sayings carry the sense of orality: they are *sayings*, what is said and what has been said, now and before the time of writing.

Wise sayings often contain an implicit part. In his discussion of "maxims" (which seem to include what we are calling "wise sayings"), Aristotle argues that formally they are incomplete rhetorical "enthymemes" (*BWA*, 1413).[10] It is as if their full form was: "If you would prosper, do [or do not] do X, because . . ." We hear the implicit beginning: *you will be well off if you remember*, neither a borrower nor a lender be, for loan oft loses both itself and friend. Thus, for Aristotle, "There is no man in all things prosperous" is a maxim, but if we add the explanation—"for all are slaves of money and chance"—we have a complete enthymeme (1414). Explanations are needed when the maxim is paradoxical or not obviously true, but best of all is when the maxim already includes its explanation: "O mortal man, nurse not immortal wrath" (1416).

Shrewd, If Not Wise, Use of Wise Sayings

Wise sayings offer considerable rhetorical advantage. In the preface to his *Adages*, Erasmus offers a number of reasons to master wise sayings, including their persuasive force. He points out that Aristotle classifies proverbs as a form of evidence that can lend crucial support to an argument. Erasmus recalls that Quintilian attributes the power of proverbs to the fact that "they have not been adapted to particular cases but have been said and done by minds exempt from hatred or partiality for no reason except their evident connection with honor or truth." He further recalls Quintilian's argument that proverbs "would not have lived forever if they did not seem true to everyone" (AE, 15).

But surely all power, including that of proverbs, can be abused? As it happens, Aristotle, describing their rhetorical uses, offers just the cynical advice that wise sayings typically deplore.[11] The orator can cite them when "working up feelings of horror and indignation" precisely because it is effective "to declare a thing to be universally true when it is not." Even hackneyed sayings can be useful: "[J]ust because they are commonplace, every one seems to agree with them, and therefore they are taken for truth" (BWA, 1415).

In Aristotle's view, maxims offer the orator a number of rhetorical advantages. One "is due to the want of intelligence in his hearers, who love to hear him succeed in expressing as a universal truth the opinions which they hold themselves about particular cases" (1416). Someone who wants to acquire popularity need only discover what views his hearers hold, and then "express, as general truths, these same views on these same subjects. This is one advantage of using maxims" (1417). By its very nature, a maxim "invests a speech with moral character" (1417). Used shrewdly, such sayings therefore "display the speaker as a man of sound moral character" (1417), or perhaps a well-trained demagogue who has read his Aristotle.

Variations: Anti-Sayings

The basic pattern of wise sayings allows for a number of variations. These variations may convey a different, and often antithetical, worldview. We may imagine the wise sayings we have discussed so far as a center around which we find concentric circles at lesser or greater distance.

Some proverbs, especially those used by the educated, counsel prudence apart from righteousness. They offer guidelines for entirely practical behavior: "If you want something done, ask a busy person"; "There's no such thing as a free lunch"; "The devil is in the details"; "If you can't beat 'em, join 'em"; and so forth. These sayings apparently arose in the past century and carry no moral sense.[12] Earlier proverbs that seem entirely practical include: "Do not cross the bridge till you come to it" and "Facts are stubborn things."[13]

"All's fair in love and war" goes one step further and seems to counsel or excuse mendacity and ruthlessness. So does "You can't make an omelette without breaking eggs," apparently a revised version of "the end justifies the means," which is now used primarily when accusing someone else of ruthlessness (*YBQ*, 617). The *Yale Book of Quotations* comments on the proverb "Throw dirt enough and some will stick": "The exact wording [of 1678] is: 'Tis a blessed saying of Machiavel—if durt enough be thrown, some will stick'" (610), which suggests that the saying was meant in an amoral sense foreign to the spirit of proverbs.

Let us call sayings that counsel the opposite of righteousness, justify immoral behavior as effective, or mock the traditional moral calculus "anti-sayings." The names Machiavelli and Talleyrand have become synonymous with the anti-saying, and one of Machiavelli's best-known examples voices the worldview of this counter-genre as a whole: "Many have imagined for themselves republics and principalities that no one has ever seen or known to be in reality. Because how one ought to live is so far removed from how one lives that he who lets go of what is done for that which one ought to do sooner learns ruin than his own preservation."[14] Other anti-sayings, whether documentable or merely attributed, circulate widely:

> Treason is a matter of dates.   —Talleyrand (*ODQ*, 453)

> When we are ready to hang the capitalists, they will sell us the rope.
> —Lenin (*YBQ*, 452)

> The broad mass of a nation . . . will more easily fall victim to a big lie than a small one.   —Hitler (*ODQ*, 389)

> If you bring me six lines written by the hand of the most honest of men, I will find something in them which will hang him.   —Richelieu (*YBQ*, 636)

> Paris is well worth a mass.
> —Henry IV (on converting to Catholicism to obtain the French throne)
> (*YBQ*, 354)

> The Pope! How many divisions has he got?   —Stalin (*ODPQ*, 345)

> One death is a tragedy, one million a statistic.   —Stalin (*ODPQ*, 345)

Not all professional maxims qualify as anti-sayings. Since the time of Hippocrates, various professions have collected core principles to be learned in the course of training or to perfect one's skill. Sun Tzu's *The Art of War* and

Clausewitz's posthumously published *On War* fall into this category. These repositories of military wisdom offer training to generals, although businessmen have also found them useful. By and large, such collections teach skills rather than morals, and so it might be possible to regard Machiavelli's *The Prince,* Saul Alinsky's *Rules for Radicals,* and other volumes of anti-sayings in this way as well, but there is still a decisive difference. Unlike most professional maxims, anti-sayings do not just offer practical rather than moral advice; rather, they set themselves against traditional morality as fit only for fools.

Variations: Saintly Sayings

A maxim that values only prudence but despises righteousness is no longer a "wise saying" (in the sense we have been using the term) at all. Machiavellian counsels express a worldview radically at odds with the moralistic spirit of the book of Proverbs: "The fear of the Lord is the beginning of wisdom" (9:10); "The fear of the Lord is to hate evil" (8:11).

On the other hand, some wise sayings value only righteousness while despising prudence. In fact, wisdom collections often include such "saintly sayings," as we may call them. They typically belong to holy men or ascetics seeking to rise above all worldly concerns.

In anthologies of the "desert fathers"—the fourth-century Christian hermits of Egypt and Palestine—saintly sayings instruct us in holiness: "Abba Theodore of Pherme said, 'The man who remains standing when he repents, has not kept the commandment'.... He also said, 'Do not sleep in a place where there is a woman.'"[15] "An elder saw a certain one laughing and said to him: In the presence of the Lord of heaven and earth we must answer for our whole life; and you can laugh?"[16] Saintly sayings call upon us to go beyond our usual desires and transcend ordinary human nature.

Variations: Reverse Wise Sayings

Numerous writers have offered what might be called "reverse wise sayings," which self-consciously find wisdom where traditional wise sayings find folly or nonsense where others find insight. One type of reverse wise saying—let's call it romantic—counsels the very opposite of prudence, caution, and moderation. Solon advised "nothing to excess," which, along with "know thyself," was probably the most cited saying of the Seven Sages. But Blake's "Proverbs of Hell"—a title that calls attention to their repudiation of traditional wisdom—instead advises us to take everything to excess and do nothing in moderation: "The road of excess leads to the palace of wisdom"; "Prudence is a rich, ugly old maid courted by Incapacity"; "The cistern contains, the fountain overflows." Blake's hellish proverbs also reverse the wise saying's traditional praise of patient lessons: "The tigers of wrath are wiser than the horses of instruction." And they praise what has been called folly so long as it is taken to a truly foolish extreme: "If the fool would persist in his folly, he would become wise."[17]

Some reverse sayings picture the world as neither providential nor even as indifferent to morality, but as *providential in reverse*. All is for the worst in this worst of all possible worlds. Schopenhauer's collection of sayings offers the most obvious example. The world according to Schopenhauer was constructed to maximize evil and suffering: "If the immediate and direct purpose of our life is not suffering then our existence is the most ill-adapted to its purpose in the world: for it is absurd to suppose that the endless affliction of which the world is everywhere full . . . should be purposeless and purely accidental."[18] If we doubt that the world's pain outweighs its pleasure, we need only "compare the feelings of an animal engaged in eating another with those of the animal being eaten" (Schopenhauer, 42). People suffer because "the world is Hell, and men are on the one hand the tormented souls and on the other the devils in it" (48).

Wise sayings purport to make sense of the world, and so yet another type of reverse wise sayings makes nonsense of it. This type resembles the deliberate witlessism except that it overtly calls attention to the traditional wise saying as the form it reverses. It gives us nonsense in proverbial form. In the chapter entitled "The Mock Turtle's Story," for instance, Alice encounters the Duchess's obsessive use of proverbs, applied or reworded in an absurd way. The Duchess's world apparently exists so that ridiculous morals can be drawn from it. Only once does she hesitate:

> "I ca'n't tell you what the moral of that is, but I shall remember it in a bit."
> "Perhaps it hasn't one," Alice ventured to remark.
> "Tut, tut, child!" said the Duchess. "Everything's got a moral, if you can only find it." (*AIW*, 70)

Longer Forms: The Moment Between

Wise sayings have generated and play an important role in a variety of longer works. Some works exploit the dialogic, others the narrative potential of the saying. Many do both, either by narrating a story containing dialogues or describing a dialogue about stories.

The most obvious way to exploit dialogic potential is to expand the dialogue of instruction. In English, John Heywood's *Dialogue of Proverbs* takes the form of an older man reciting tales, replete with proverbs, to a youth considering whether to marry a beautiful poor woman or an ugly rich one. However useful this technique may be at preserving sayings or inculcating proverbial wisdom, I know of no work using this approach that manages to achieve literary greatness.

The best works, whether dialogic, narrative, or some combination of the two, situate themselves in what might be called the "interim" or "the moment between." The work concerns the *temporal gap* between a good or bad action and its reward or punishment. After all, if the consequences of evil were immediate, no one would think he or she could get away with it, and wise sayings would not be needed. The longer the interim, and the more suffering caused by the delay itself, the greater the dramatic potential.

Some psalms calling for justice develop this dramatic potential through a dialogue with, or rather an address to, God. The psalmist himself first complains that the promise of justice is not fulfilled. He may then switch roles and, as if speaking for God, foresee the moment when it will be. Speaking from the middle of the story, he describes its end, when the interim is over.

As he complains, the psalmist reminds God of his promise. When the speaker is himself suffering, this reminder may achieve special power. So we see in Psalm 22, which opens with what will become Jesus's last words in Matthew and Mark: "My God, my God, why hast thou forsaken me?"[19] Prayers and poems may also derive emotional and rhetorical power by dramatizing the interim.

If long enough, the interim may provoke doubt that justice will ever come to pass. It seems that traditional wisdom proves unwise, as unbelievers and evildoers say. In a third dialogic form, the speaker argues directly with such an unbeliever—the "fool" or "scorner" that wise sayings often imagine. Proverbs 30:1–9 contains the model for such a dialogue. In verses 1–4 the skeptic Agur ben Yakeh (Agur, son of Jaketh) issues a challenge, which seems directed at all the assurances provided by the previous twenty-nine chapters of wise sayings. God is unknowable: "Who has ascended up into heaven, or descended? [W]ho hath gathered the wind in his fists? . . . [W]hat is his name . . . if thou canst tell?" (30:4). The believer in wisdom answers in verses 5–6: "Every word of God is pure. . . . Add thou not unto his words, lest he reprove thee, and thou be found a liar" (30:5–6). In verses 7–9 the believer prays that he never fall into such blasphemy, a prayer that implicitly acknowledges the power of the doubter's arguments. He begs for two blessings—to be far from vanity and to be neither rich nor poor, "lest I be full, and deny thee, and say, Who is the Lord? or lest I be poor, and take the name of my God in vain" (30:9).

Job as Interim Dialogue

The book of Job both expands and complicates this sort of dialogue. Though it tells a story, it consists largely of dialogues between Job as a doubter and his friends who speak for traditional wisdom. All these dialogues take place in the interim, in the period when Job suffers unjustly, before God rewards him. Interestingly enough, the wicked who are at last punished include those who have defended divine justice.

After the brief opening narrative portion, Job argues at length with the three "Job comforters" and Elihu. Repeating the logic of Proverbs, they argue that it only seems as if wickedness triumphs because we sometimes find ourselves in the moment between offense and retribution, a moment that must be short: "Knowest thou not this of old . . . [t]hat the triumphing of the wicked is short, and the joy of the hypocrite but for a moment?" (Job 20:4–5). Both sides agree that not just the fact but also the length of the delay matters.

Like the psalmist, Job complains not only of suffering but also of being mocked for his suffering. But he draws an unexpected conclusion from this mockery. It is to be blamed on wisdom itself. The very fact that traditional wisdom teaches that only the wicked suffer makes matters still worse for the innocent, because those who should offer consolation instead presume guilt. Job rebukes his friends for just this wisdom-induced cruelty.

Job calls upon God: "Behold, I cry out of wrong, but I am not heard; I cry aloud, but there is no judgment" (19:7). The very fact that his calls go unanswered proves that the traditional promise is untrue, that "there is no judgment." Job therefore speaks as both righteous victim and scorner. The force of his utterances depends on this combination of discrepant roles.

Job's friends explicitly appeal to traditional wisdom and its sources. They cite the experience of generations along with the testimony of "wise men" (15:18) and "wisdom" (15:8). Like the skeptic in Proverbs 30:1–9, Job denies the existence of wisdom: "But where shall wisdom be found?" (28:12). Interpreters of the book of Job have understandably differed as to which side of the dialogue triumphs. On the one hand, when God appears in wrath, Job repents in dust and ashes. He has been mistaken. On the other, God explicitly tells Eliphaz:

"My wrath is kindled against thee, and against thy two friends: for ye have not spoken of me the thing that is right, as my servant Job hath" (42:7). The skeptic concedes while his opponents are divinely refuted. Subsequent commentary, including literary and philosophical responses up to the present, has only extended the dialogue.

Perhaps the book of Job is best viewed as essentially dialogic: wisdom's inconclusive dialogue with herself.

Plutarch's Symposium on the Interim

Plutarch's remarkable symposium "On God's Slowness to Punish" illustrates a fourth way in which the moment between can create dialogue.[20] The delay of justice serves as the *topic* discussed by the participants.

As the work begins, the only one who denies providential justice, the Epicurean, leaves. The friends who continue the discussion try to resolve the problems posed not by the absence of justice but by its "slowness." Why does God allow an interim, and why is it often so long?

First Patrocleas cites Euripides' argument that retributive justice "comes with silent and steady tread and grabs criminals when they don't expect it," but finds such an argument wanting because it would not discourage criminals very effectively (Plutarch, 252). Since enjoyment is immediate but punishment is far off, and may even be reserved for one's descendants, crime might very well be said to pay. No less important, delay usually precludes victims from witnessing the punishment. What good does it do them if they are already dead? How does their lot differ from a complete lack of justice?

Olympichus adds "another outstandingly odd consequence of divine tardiness and slowness . . . which is that it destroys the belief in providence" (252). The traditional proverb may assure us that "the mills of God grind slowly, but they grind exceedingly small," but slow grinding makes it hard for people to connect the punishment with an act committed long before.[21] Much more likely, the wicked will see their suffering not as punishment but as entirely unconnected with its cause.

As the dialogue proceeds, each participant tries to square providence with delay. The dialogue concludes with the narrator telling the others a myth about a wicked man who dies but whose soul soon returns to his body after he witnesses what happens after death. He becomes a righteous man not because of any argument but because of what has happened between life and life. One interim provides the answer to the other.

The Providential Narrative Justifies the Interim

In some longer works based on wise sayings, a providential story demonstrates that justice prevails. Interim moments allow both doubt and traditional wisdom to be expressed until wisdom is vindicated. The more unexpected the causal pattern, the more interesting the story. In some cases, the plot justifies not only the promise of justice but also the lengthy delay.

The deuterocanonical book of Tobit offers a particularly interesting combination of wise sayings and narrative—or rather, narratives, because the resolution of several stories at once at last provides the reason for delayed justice in each of them.

The righteous Tobit suffers, despairs, and wishes for death. (This is the time depicted in Rembrandt's 1630 painting "Anna and the Blind Tobit.") Even so, when he is apparently dying, he counsels his son to accept proverbial wisdom, which promises the justice that Tobit himself has failed to receive. "For those who act in accordance with truth will prosper in all their activities. . . . Do not turn your face away from anyone who is poor, and the face of God will not be turned away from you."[22] The plot illustrates that wisdom demands confidence in justice even during the interim.

With the help of a strange companion who is really the angel Raphael, Tobias not only cures his father's blindness and collects the money owed him, but also drives out the devil who has seven times killed a young woman's bridegroom on her wedding night. Providence has in fact reserved her for Tobias, and in marrying her, he finds the very sort of bride Tobit has counseled him to marry. We at last see that justice delayed is justice multiplied. Tobit could not have known the suffering of the bride widowed seven times, nor could she have been aware of his fate. But the vindication of each righteous person can take place only when the story of the other allows.

No person can know all the stories of others or the hidden connections among them. They must have faith. It is important to recognize that the book of Tobit works by inverting the causal model we usually assume. Key events are related not because they derive from a single cause, but because they tend to a single solution. Or, as we might say, they share a *future cause. Providence works from the end backward*, which is why people, who can only detect past causes, cannot anticipate it. Tobit's wise sayings are justified in a way that itself contains important wisdom.

When Raphael reveals who he is, he, too, repeats wise sayings, now proven true: "Do good and evil will not overtake you. . . . Those who give alms will enjoy a full life, but those who commit sin and wrong are their own worst enemies" (Tobit 12:7–10).

Perhaps unexpectedly, the story draws yet another conclusion from its plot. Israel, too, is in its in-between time, and is being drawn by providence to its eschatological triumph. Itself providential, history also works backward.

On his deathbed, Tobit predicts that Nineveh will fall for its wickedness. He has no doubt that the justice promised by wise sayings applies not just to individuals but also to whole peoples. As the book of Tobit ends, we learn that Nineveh has in fact fallen. Therefore we can believe the book's other prediction: even though Israel is scattered, it will be reunited in Jerusalem just as the prophets foretold. We are assured that every word of the prophets will prove true. If so, history will be completed according to the logic of wise sayings: "Then the nations in the whole world will be converted to worship God in truth. . . . Those who sincerely love God will rejoice, but those who commit sin and injustice will vanish from the earth" (14:6–8).

The providential wise sayings Tobit affirms in his suffering hold true for all suffering. The book of Tobit's two sets of wise sayings, Tobit's and Raphael's, form the basis for a complex story justifying their logic.

Fables and Morals

Fables represent the simplest way to illustrate a wise saying. In fact, many proverbial sayings or expressions are either morals of fables or condensed allusions to them ("sour grapes," "cried wolf," "wolf in sheep's clothing").

Erasmus, citing the fourth-century fabulist Aphthonius, reminds us that the ancients considered a proverb to be "a fable in miniature." Erasmus has in mind stories with an explicit moral, like the ones attributed to Aesop (*AE*, 9). Walter Benjamin suggested we think of a proverb as "the ideogram of a story. A proverb one might say, is a ruin which stands on the site of an old story, and in which a moral twines around a happening like ivy around a wall. Seen in this way, the storyteller joins the ranks of the teachers and sages. He has counsel—not for a few situations, as the proverb does, but for many, like the sage."[23] As Benjamin suggests, some stories made from wise sayings not only illustrate but also expand their wisdom.

Moral tales may concern either beasts or people; they may be as short as jokes or considerably longer. Some reflect the heritage of sacred parables, while others, like the fables of La Fontaine, Krylov, and Gay derive from the Aesopian tradition. That tradition includes not only stories by Aesop (a semilegendary figure) himself but also many other stories authored, amended, or edited and collected from antiquity to the present. Laura Gibbs's recent collection, *Aesop's Fables*, for instance, contains versions from Greek, Roman, and medieval Christian sources.[24] Caxton published an Aesopic collection in England in 1484, and the tradition has never ceased to evolve. Aesop has long since become the name of a genre.

Some of Aesop's fables contain morals spoken by a character within the story (an endomythium). In others, the author provides the moral outside the story proper, sometimes before the narrative (a promythium) and sometimes after (an epimythium). As their morals stress, the fables typically show prudence and righteousness rewarded or folly and wickedness punished.

Folly constitutes the most common theme. In one famous fable, a fox trapped in a well coaxes a goat to leap in and taste the sweet water, then climbs out on the goat's horns and leaves the goat trapped as he was. The first-century Roman fabulist Phaedrus supplied the moral: "As soon as someone clever gets into trouble, he tries to find a way out at someone else's expense." Caxton allows the fox to draw a somewhat different moral: "And thenne the foxe beganne to lawhe and to scorne hym / and sayd to hym / O master goote / yf thou haddest be wel wyse with thy fayre berde / or euer thou haddest entryd in to the welle / thou sholdest first haue taken hede / how thou sholdest haue comen oute of hit ageyne" (Gibbs, xvi and 59–60). Seeing the outcome as a lesson in foresight, the fox adds laughter to suffering. In many fables, folly leads to self-destruction, and self-destruction itself earns ridicule. Fables of this sort tend to be pitiless.

Other fables praise moral virtues, including pity of one's fellows. Aphthonius's "The Ant, the Pigeon, and the Bird-Catcher" concludes: "The story shows that even dumb beasts experience fellow feeling and come to one another's aid" (38). The Christian rewriter of Aesop, Odo of Cheriton, directs us to see the story of "The Birds, the Peacock, and His Feathers" as a narrative "[a]gainst vanity and so on" (46). Some fables have come down to us in versions where one author draws a prudential conclusion and another a moral one (see 71–72), and morals may themselves differ.

So close is the fable to the wise saying that a large number of fables include a sage as character or narrator: Socrates, Diogenes, Thales, or Aesop himself, whom the ancients sometimes included among the Seven Sages. Demetrius of Phalerum, apparently the first to record Aesop's fables, also wrote *Sayings of the Seven Wise Men*.[25]

John Locke recommended Aesop's fables as appropriate for children, and in the nineteenth century Aesop became a children's writer, as he is now generally regarded.[26] By this time proverbs had long come to be considered below the notice of gentlemen: Lord Chesterfield commented that "a man of fashion never has recourse to proverbs or vulgar aphorisms."[27] The didactic quality of so much children's literature allows us to follow, down to our own day, the changes in what is considered wise and moral behavior.

Tolstoy's Moral Tales

In my opinion *How Much Land Does a Man Need?* is the greatest story that the literature of the world knows. I used to like also very much *Masters and Servants* in spite of a little propaganda in it.   —James Joyce[28]

It is not the priest who shatters our desires most effectively; it is the man who has known them, and loved them himself. When he derides them the world indeed turns to dust and ashes beneath our feet. Then fear mingles with pleasure.   —Virginia Woolf (on Tolstoy)[29]

Tolstoy, the greatest writer to turn his hand to moral tales, used this apparently unpromising form to produce some magnificent works.

How does one make something great out of something so simple? Does not greatness demand complexity and don't we rightly honor writers of complex works the most? Tolstoy addressed these questions in *What Is Art?*, where he explained that, contrary to sophisticated opinion, it is much harder to make the truly simple effective. To illustrate his point, he described attending an astronomer's lecture. After hearing it, Tolstoy suggested to the astronomer that it would do more good to explain something basic, like why day follows night, which most of the audience probably do not comprehend. The astronomer replied: "Yes, it would be a good thing, but it is very difficult. To lecture on the spectrum analysis of the Milky Way is far easier." Tolstoy comments:

> And so it is in art. To write a rhymed poem dealing with the times of Cleopatra, or paint a picture of Nero burning Rome, or compose a symphony in the manner of Brahms or Richard Strauss, or an opera like Wagner's, is far easier than to tell a simple story without any unnecessary details, yet so that it should transmit the feelings of the narrator. (*WIA*, 179)

Some of Tolstoy's moral tales, including "How Much Land Does a Man Need?," succeed in just this way. Like Joyce, we marvel at how an apparently simple story and moral can convey such emotional force. Other tales explicitly illustrate a proverb that serves as their title, such as "A Spark Neglected Burns the House" (*Ustupish' ogon'—ne postupish'*; more literally: Start a fire and you won't extinguish it).

Tolstoy's best moral tales accomplish still more. Rather than just illustrate, they question the logic of proverbs, but not as a skeptic or realist would. Instead of rejecting or qualifying proverbial wisdom in the light of real-world experience, they do the opposite and take that wisdom a step further. In effect, they endorse Blake's anti-proverb "If the fool would persist in his folly, he would become wise"—except that by "fool" Blake means the fool of Proverbs, whereas Tolstoy means the fool as imagined by sophisticated skeptics. For Tolstoy, traditional wise sayings promise not too much but too little. We educated folk do not usually think so because we fail to grasp the depths of the moral wisdom governing the world.

Consider one of Tolstoy's tales that he especially loved, "God Sees the Truth, but Waits to Tell." As this proverb-title suggests, the story deals with the moment between. And yet if we take the title as endorsing the promise of justice, it proves misleading.[30] The title turns out to be a decoy.

The narrative deals with a young merchant, Aksyonov, accused of murdering his traveling companion. In fact, a thief killed the companion and planted the knife on a sleeping Aksyonov. Convicted and flogged, Aksyonov finds it particularly painful when even his wife wonders whether he is guilty. Sent to Siberia, he loses wife, children, and property. Nevertheless, after his petitions fail, Aksyonov comes to accept his punishment as somehow in accordance with divine justice, which will eventually be accomplished. "Clearly, only God knows the truth, and one must turn to God alone and from God alone await mercy," he tells himself.[31]

Aksyonov comes to be regarded by prisoners and guards alike as good, humble, and truthful. After twenty-six years, the man who really committed the murder, Makar Semyonovich, is sent to the same prison and, from his chatter, Aksyonov deduces that this is the man who framed him. Thinking of his wasted life, Aksyonov grows enraged and craves revenge, which would also be justice. He gets the chance when he discovers Makar Semyonovich digging a tunnel to escape. The guards ask Aksyonov, as one who can be believed, who the culprit is, and so, at last, destiny grants Aksyonov the opportunity he has longed craved, not only to see justice done but to be its agent. This is the moment that the proverbial wisdom in which he believes has promised. Apparently, his faith in justice, and the story's proverbial title, are vindicated. God

sees the truth, but waits to tell. And yet, for some reason he does not understand, Aksyonov refuses to denounce Makar Semyonovich.

Like Aksyonov, readers demand justice. But God's plan proves much wiser
than traditional wisdom. Just where the narrative should end proves to be the
point where the real story begins. It turns out that the entire sequence of events
up to this moment has happened in order to give Aksyonov something far
more valuable than mere justice.

Because Aksyonov has refused to turn him in, Makar Semyonovich comes
to Aksyonov in the middle of the night and begs his forgiveness. Still enraged,
Aksyonov replies quite understandably: "It's easy for you to talk, but how have
I suffered! Where can I go now? . . . My wife is dead, my children have forgotten
me" (Tolstoy, *Short Stories*, 211). The past cannot be changed. And yet, when he
sees Makar Semyonovich consumed with unbearable guilt, Aksyonov forgives
nonetheless. And then he experiences a bliss he has never felt before. "His soul
grew calm. He ceased to yearn for home and no longer wanted to leave prison"
(211). Makar Semyonovich confesses to the murder for which Aksyonov was
sentenced, but by the time Aksyonov's pardon arrives, he has died. That is how
the story ends.

If this were a story about justice, as the title seems to promise, this ending
would be a mockery. It is almost worse that the truth should be revealed, and
justice done, precisely when Aksyonov dies and it no longer matters. As the
participants in Plutarch's symposium understand, delay itself—how long "God
waits"—makes a difference.

But the story's point is that justice is not what we should look for. To read
the story as one of justice at last accomplished, as so many have, is to endorse the
very belief Tolstoy wants us to overcome. God does reward Aksyonov, but not
with justice. He gives him something much better than justice, the joy that can
come only from forgiveness. Not just the greatness of the injury done to him,
but also the long delay, have made forgiveness all the more joyful. Aksyonov realizes that he has indeed lived a meaningful life in a way that he never expected
and in a way that, without his long imprisonment, he would never have had the
chance to live.

Readers also prove mistaken. Like the hero, they have misread the story of
Aksyonov's life, and precisely because they have expected the proverbial plot.
This sort of surprise serves as one of Tolstoy's favorite narrative devices. Both
hero and readers understand the story's meaning when they realize that the
story of the hero's life differs decisively from what they imagined.[32]

If "God Sees the Truth" were a tale of justice achieved, Aksyonov's death just when his pardon arrives would make no sense. But that apparent senselessness explains why the story ends this way. The ending points to a superior moral. If we grasp that moral, the ending upsets nothing. On the contrary, it shows how a meaningful life concludes.

In fact, the story has two providential endings, since Makar Semyonovich also achieves meaning when he confesses. Aksyonov's unjust suffering has saved two people.

For Tolstoy, providence is not justice and meaning is not compensation. The highest good is not justice but forgiveness. And the law of God is not righteousness but love.

∎ SARDONIC MAXIMS ∎

Having reserved the term "aphorism" for the family of short genres, and the term "apothegm" for the particular short genre discussed in Chapter 2, I choose a different term for the genre discussed here. Although these short works might well be, and often are, called aphorisms or apothegms, I shall, to avoid confusion, call them "sardonic maxims" (or simply maxims). However named, this genre works primarily as an anti-wise saying or, sometimes, as an anti-dictum or anti-witticism. The wise saying, the dictum, and the witticism depend on faith in the power of mind or the possibility of knowledge. The sardonic maxim discredits such faith as the product of vanity.

Scribes believe in the tradition they guard, scholars in the knowledge they transmit, and intellectuals in the ideas currently accepted by other intellectuals. In *War and Peace* Tolstoy observes that we have theories attributing historical change to great ideas and learned men because "history is written by learned men and so it is natural and agreeable for them to think the activity of their class is the basis for the movement of all humanity, just as it would be natural for merchants, agriculturalists, and soldiers to entertain such a belief (if they do not express it, it is only because merchants and soldiers do not write history)" (*W&P*, 1419–20). Tolstoy's comment captures the spirit of the sardonic maxim.

Whether claims to superior insight belong to sages, philosophers, or wits, and whether they take the form of wise sayings, dicta, or witticisms, they provoke sardonic maxims pointing to the egoism motivating authors and followers alike. When Harold Rosenberg referred to the intelligentsia as "the herd of independent minds," he was writing out of a tradition of sardonic maximists.[33] Consider the following classic examples:

> How a great mind, joined to a weak soul, sometimes seems to increase the weakness of the latter! The brilliant faculties of the one give reason and color to the cowardice of the other.   —Alexis de Tocqueville

> If he is a fool who at forty applies to Hippocrates for health, still more is he one who then applies to Seneca for wisdom.   —Baltasar Gracián

> A learned fool is more foolish than an ignorant fool.   —Molière

> There are two sorts of fool; those who doubt nothing and those who doubt everything.   —Charles-Joseph Lamoral, prince de Ligne

[A] school of thought is to be viewed as a single individual who talks to himself for a hundred years and is quite extraordinarily pleased with himself, however silly he may be.   —Goethe

There are no fools so troublesome as those who have wit.
                                                                —Benjamin Franklin

Stupidity consists in wanting to reach conclusions. We are a thread, and we want to know the whole cloth.   —Gustave Flaubert

The university brings out all abilities, including stupidity.
                                                                —Anton Chekhov[34]

Where others discover providence, rationality, or the possibility of intelligent control, the authors of sardonic maxims detect hubris and self-deception. Behind the ostensibly great mind is a weak soul, and where grand philosophy stakes its claim we would be wise to look for mundane psychology. People believe what it is "natural and agreeable" for them to believe. They persuade themselves that it is prudent to do what self-indulgence desires and honest to say what rage prompts. Typically, they prove most foolish where they pride themselves on their wisdom, and most cruel as they act in the name of a humane cause. Skeptical of theoretically derived schemes and professed good intentions, sardonic maxims tend to be (in this respect) conservative.

Wise sayings (and dicta) know, sardonic maxims ask why we think we know. The former presume, and the latter doubt, both the possibility and the value of wisdom or knowledge.

Sardonic maxims concern vanity in both senses of the word: futility and excessive self-regard. Their sense of the former makes them suspicious of effort and their sense of the latter of judgment.

Sardonic Maxims (Type 1): Ecclesiastes

Commentators agree that the book of Ecclesiastes (Qohelet) responds directly to the book of Proverbs and other traditional wisdom literature.[35] In several places it seems to quote a traditional proverb or wise saying and then answer it. In the Alter version, for instance, the passage beginning at 2:14 begins: "The wise man has eyes in his head, and the fool goes in darkness" (KJV: "The wise man's eyes are in his head; but the fool walketh in darkness"), which we recognize as the sort of wise saying to be found in Proverbs. It is one of those wise sayings praising wise sayings, the voice of the sage exalting sages. Alter observes that we are to read this line not as the author's assertion but as his quotation. It is the position that Qohelet means to challenge.

In Alter's view, "the statement is cast in the form of a proverb, akin to what one finds in the Book of Proverbs. . . . What follows in the second half of this verse and in the next two verses certainly looks like a challenge to this bit of proverbial wisdom" (Qohelet, 20). That challenge reads: "Yet, I, too, knew that a single fate befalls them all. And I said in my heart, 'Like the fate of the fool, it will befall me, too, and so why have I become so wise?' And I said in my heart that this, too, is mere breath [KJV: "this also is vanity"]. For there is no remembrance of the wise, as with the fool, forever. Since in the days to come, all will be forgotten. Yes, the wise man dies like the fool!" (Qohelet 2:14–16).[36]

To place too much faith in wisdom is folly. The truly wise know the limits of wisdom. As traditional wisdom literature counsels, and as Wisdom in the book of Proverbs demands, Qohelet has spent his life gathering wisdom (he has sometimes been identified with Solomon): "And I gave my heart to seek and search out by wisdom concerning all things that are done under heaven . . . saying, Lo, I am come to great estate, and have gotten more wisdom than all they that have been before in Jerusalem: yea, my heart had great experience of wisdom and knowledge" (Ecclesiastes 1:13–16). But he has acquired this wisdom with an open mind. Unlike those committed to finding evidence supporting wise sayings, he has tested them against experience and reason. And he has found wisdom unable to keep the promises made for it.

At times, wisdom even increases misery. "For in much wisdom is much worry, and he who adds wisdom adds pain" (Qohelet 1:18). Alter notes: "Here this radical Wisdom text challenges the basic premise of wisdom literature—that devotion to wisdom is the one true road to the good, fulfilled life" (Qohelet, 20).

In other passages, Qohelet questions the very possibility of knowledge or wisdom. "For there are many words that increase mere breath; what is the advantage for man? For who knows what is good for man in life, in his days of mere breath, for he spends them like a shadow?" (Qohelet 6:11–12). Here Alter again detects a dialogue with traditional wisdom literature: "Qohelet is a Wisdom writer who constantly questions the value of wisdom. He knows that a human life is likely to be bleak, that it is inherently unpredictable, may end badly, and will surely be blotted out by death. His 'wisdom' is to register this perception, but, apart from his occasional exhortations to enjoy [the moment], he does not presume to know what is good for man, unlike the purveyors of mainline Wisdom" (Qohelet, 42–43). Commentators have also pointed out that in Qohelet's vision "revelation is ruled out because there is no possibility of communication from beyond the impenetrable veil" (*ABPE*, 198). "Everywhere else—except in the words of another agnostic inquirer in Proverbs 30:1–4—the Bible affirms, not only that God is knowable, but that he has in fact made himself, his will, and his salvation known to man" (*ABPE*, 206).

Qohelet insists on the unpredictability of life in lines that are among its most famous, such as 9:11: "I returned, and saw under the sun, that the race is not to the swift, not the battle to the strong, neither yet bread to the wise, nor yet riches to men of understanding, nor yet favour to men of skill; but time and chance happeneth to them all."[37] If the world is so uncertain, then prudence may or may not be rewarded. La Rochefoucauld seems to echo these anti-proverbial lines: "We praise prudence without stint, but it cannot insure our smallest undertaking" (*LaR*, 45).

The same may be said of righteousness. Qohelet repeats that it often fails to earn the promised reward. "And I went back and saw all the oppression that is done under the sun: the tears of the oppressed who have none to console them, and from the hand of their violent oppressors there is none to console them" (Qohelet 4:1; see also 3:16 and 7:15). Unlike Schopenhauer, Qohelet does not insist on inverse providence—that we live in the worst of all possible worlds. Rather, he contends that no relation obtains between goodness and reward. To be sure, he agrees with Schopenhauer that we must not expect this reward in an afterlife: "for there is no doing nor reckoning nor wisdom in Sheol where you are going" (9:10).[38]

Like the participants in Plutarch's symposium on God's slowness to punish, Qohelet recognizes that, even when evil is eventually punished, delay itself constitutes an evil that teaches evil: "The sentence for an evil act is not carried out swiftly. Therefore the hearts of the sons of men brim over within them to do evil" (8:11).

Of course, Qohelet's best-known lines concern the utter futility of all human effort, and it is on this note that he begins. In the King James Version, "Vanity of vanity, saith the Preacher, all is vanity. What profiteth a man of all his labour which he taketh under the sun?" (Ecclesiastes 1:2–3). Where the King James gives "vanity of vanities," Alter gives more literally: "merest breath," an image that suggests ephemerality and insubstantiality as well as futility. And where the King James repeatedly has the speaker call all effort "vexation of spirit," Alter corrects to the striking image, "herding the wind." Wise sayings, whether biblical, Confucian, or any other, presume that effort matters because its results matter, but if results do not matter then neither can effort or the wisdom guiding it. Nothing is remembered, so how could anything make a lasting difference? Qohelet concludes: "And I hated life . . . for all is mere breath and herding the wind" (Qohelet 2:17). The dead are better off than the living, and those never born most fortunate of all (4:2–3).

Commentators have agreed that the pious conclusion of the work (12:9–14) belongs to another writer. It affirms tenets of traditional wisdom. "The last word, all being heard: fear God and keep his commandments, for that is all humankind" (9:13; KJV: "for this is the whole duty of man"). It also affirms that God recompenses good and evil and, not incidentally, the value of wisdom and proverbs (Ecclesiastes 9:14; Alter gives "maxims"). Commentators conclude that the real book ends as it begins, with the reference to "vanity of vanities" (or "merest breath") in 12:8.

But it is also possible to see the conclusion as an intrinsic part of a dialogic work. As Qohelet quotes and answers traditional wise men, so they answer him. And since Qohelet knows we can be sure of nothing, such a conclusion by another makes sense.

Sardonic Maxims (Type 2)

Will not a tiny speck very close to our vision blot out the glory of this world, and leave only a margin by which we see the blot? I know no speck so troublesome as self.   —George Eliot (*MM*, 402–3)

The second type of sardonic maxim focuses on vanity in the other sense of the word: self-love, or what La Rochefoucauld calls *amour-propre*. For this type of maxim, self-love governs all we do. "Whatever discoveries one has made in the realm of self-esteem, many uncharted regions still remain there" (*LaR*, 33). Out of vanity itself, we want to conceal this fact from ourselves, and so vanity necessarily begets self-deception, the other great theme of this short genre. These two facts of human nature, self-love and self-deception, work in tandem, and where one is found, the other lurks.

Nothing so impedes understanding as faith in our own intelligence. "Self-love is the greatest of all flatterers" (*LaR*, 33). Self-deception governs life, and the most learned and sophisticated succumb to it all the more because they believe they have outwitted it. "Self-love is cleverer than the cleverest man in the world" (33).

By their very nature, both vanity and self-deception hide. Just as other people are false while we are tactful, so no one believes he is vain. Others have an inflated opinion of themselves, but we ourselves appreciate, if not underestimate, our true merits. No best seller in pop psychology encourages us to value ourselves more soberly.

By the same token, self-deception can work only if it is taken to be honesty. We play a confidence game with ourselves. The sardonic maxim therefore focuses on disguises, how a failing or lack represents itself as a virtue or possession. It seeks to unmask those disguises.

Unmasking is anything but easy, because self-love is infinitely resourceful and stays one step ahead of all attempts to expose it. We expose one mask and then are deceived by the one beneath it. Among La Rochefoucauld's maxims we find one short essay, itself composed of many maxims, concerning the incredible ingenuity of self-love in hiding from itself:

> Nothing is so impetuous as its schemes, so guileful its maneuvers . . . its altered looks surpass the chameleon's. . . . There is no plumbing the depths or piercing the darkness of its abysses; darting in and out of them it escapes the sharpest eye and is often invisible even to itself. . . . But the heavy veil that hides it from itself never prevents its seeing clearly what lies outside; in this it resembles our eyesight, which can see everything but our own eyes. (140–41)

"Seeing our own eyes" suggests a sort of distortion principle in which the act of seeing, including what one arranges to notice or miss, partly determines what one discovers. Self-knowledge looks and overlooks. To see one's own eyes one might look in a mirror, and to overcome the distortion principle of self-knowledge one might seek out one's image in the eyes of others. But others are subject to the distortions of amour-propre as well, and will see everyone else in terms of their own needs.

Looking for ourselves in others, we see the mote in their eyes and not the beam in our own.

Others

That the other suffers must be learned; and it can never be learned completely.

—Nietzsche (*HATH*, 71)

It is very hard for someone to discern what another discerns in him. Not only does amour-propre distort the evidence, but people's inherent self-centeredness also resists occupying another person's position. To do so means seeing the world from the perspective of that person's "I" and seeing oneself as merely an object in the other's field of vision. One must sense the other's amour-propre and regard oneself as a means or perhaps an obstacle to its gratification. No one easily experiences himself as an object, and the pain of doing so makes one avert one's eyes.

Many well-known sardonic maxims concern the difficulty of adopting the other's perspective:

All of us have sufficient fortitude to endure the misfortune of others. [Nous avons tous assez de force pour supporter les maux d'autrui.]
—La Rochefoucauld (*ODQ*, 469)

There is nothing less sincere than the way we solicit and offer advice. When we solicit it, we seem to defer to our friend's opinion, while actually seeking approval of our own, and surety for our conduct; we seem to offer it with warm, disinterested zeal, to pay the confidence we have been honored with, though it is usually given with self-interest and self-glory uppermost in mind.
—La Rochefoucauld (*LaR*, 54)

With nothing are we so generous as with advice.
—La Rochefoucauld (*LaR*, 53)

In every age and country, the wiser, or at least the stronger, of the two sexes, has usurped the powers of the state, and confined the other to the cares and pleasures of domestic life.   —Gibbon (*DAF*, 116)

The most worthless of mankind are not afraid to condemn in others the same disorders which they allow in themselves; and can readily discover some nice difference of age, character, or station to justify the partial distinction.
—Gibbon (*DAF*, 115)

We are all of us born in moral stupidity, taking the world as an udder to feed our supreme selves.   —George Eliot (*MM*, 205)

La Rochefoucauld's famous comment on enduring another's misfortune states a truth none of us can deny. It depends for its force on its inversion of two proverbs we all know, "Bear misfortune with fortitude" and some version of the Golden Rule (from "Do unto others" to "Love thy neighbor as thyself"). We cannot do what we counsel others to do, and the moment we are in their situation the difference between "I" and "you" becomes apparent as a fundamental fact.

As a kind of anti-wise sayings, sardonic maxims often contain the traces of proverbs we can reconstruct. Proverbs promise that virtue triumphs over vice, and so it does, in a way: "Hypocrisy is a tribute which vice pays to virtue" (*YBQ*,

443). Victorious virtue receives tribute, but the victory only substitutes one evil for another.

In her insightful sardonic maxims, George Eliot often recasts proverbs explicitly. Commenting on how guilt, as a kind of negative vanity, conjures up what we most fear to see, she observes: "Solomon's Proverbs, I think, have omitted to say that as the sore palate findeth grit, so an uneasy conscience heareth innuendos" (*MM*, 289–90).

La Rochefoucauld's maxims on advice giving reveal that both parties to the transaction act insincerely but that neither is fully aware of it. If the solicitor of advice knew he was not going to defer to an opinion he would rather avoid, then he could not have the "surety" provided by one he would like. By the same token, the advice giver would not feel superior (or as in the next example, "generous") if he were aware of glorifying himself. Successful selfishness depends on self-deception. To gratify self, he needs to feel unselfish.

Each of Gibbon's sardonic maxims describes a three-stage process presented as a single fact. Males justify usurping the power of the state by appealing to their higher wisdom. But the immediate qualification, "or . . . the stronger, of the two" suggests a concession made in light of contrary evidence or a switch to the other sex's point of view. We hear the implicit objection: power *always* justifies itself as righteous. Isn't it suspicious that the speaker has chosen to invoke a supposedly impartial law—the wisest sex always dominates—as if the formulation were not partial and the rationalization palpable from the outset? Finally, the further qualification "at least" ("or at least the stronger") half takes back the concession, as if the rule of strength might after all be identical to the rule of wisdom. Taken together, these three stages dramatize in one assertion the process of self-interest warding off conscience and honesty.

Complex maxims like this are Gibbon's trademark. The second example works more simply because it describes, rather than enacts, the process of self-justification. However much we may resemble those we condemn, and however well our principles turn out to be applicable to our own bad conduct, some "nice difference" can always be discovered. "Nice" and "discover" are favorite words of Gibbon's because they suggest the process of exculpation. "Nice" points to how fine the distinction between our conduct and theirs must sometimes be, and "discover" suggests that there was no doubt of the result because, like a discovered object, it was already a given.

In other cases, Gibbon adds to the irony by a strategic use of the passive voice. When exorcisms were performed "the vanquished daemon was heard to confess" (*DAF*, 367); "fanaticism was permitted to assume the language of inspiration, and the effects of accident or contrivance were ascribed to supernatural causes" (369); for the ascetics, "the loss of sensual pleasure was supplied and compensated by spiritual pride" (375). The passive voice suggests that it would be misleading to name an agent, as if he were the cause, because the facts of human nature, which are the real cause, ensure that the action would be done by *someone*. It suggests as well one way in which self-deception and the avoidance of responsibility work: people perform actions as if done by an impersonal force independent of their will.

From the perspective of the sardonic maxim, we are all "born in moral stupidity, taking the world as an udder to feed our supreme selves." Eliot continues: "Dorothea had early begun to emerge from that stupidity, but yet it had been easier to her to imagine how she would devote herself to Mr. Casaubon, and become wise and strong in his strength and wisdom, than to conceive with that distinctness which is no longer reflection but feeling—an idea wrought back to the directness of sense, like the solidity of objects—that he had an equivalent centre of self, whence the lights and shadows must always fall with a certain difference" (*MM*, 205). No one has to be talked into seeing events from her own point of view. But we do have to be trained to imagine another's point of view and to recognize, more than theoretically, that others have "an equivalent center of self." There are degrees of recognition, and very rarely, if ever, do we truly feel the other's "selfness" with "directness of sense, like the solidity of objects." But that is precisely what the realist novel, and *Middlemarch* in particular, is designed to do.

When we *identify* with a character, we practice sensing the world from a perspective different from our own. The more that character differs from the reader, the more that reader learns to transcend her supreme self. Realist novels also allow us to practice switching perspectives from character to character, without ever quite losing our own. In doing so, we watch characters who empathize, or more often fail to empathize, with others, and see how their vanity leads them into misperceptions and unsuspected cruelties.

Precisely because he is so unappealing, Casaubon serves as Eliot's touchstone for perception that falls far short of recognizing the other. If Mr. Casaubon struck Ladislaw, Sir James, Celia, Mr. Brooke, and Mrs. Cadwallader as repellent, each for his or her own reason, then, Eliot observes, "even Milton, looking at his portrait in a spoon, must submit to have the facial angle of a bumpkin" (*MM*, 83). If readers grant the justice of this observation, they are immediately asked to apply it to themselves: "Suppose we turn from outside estimates of a man, to wonder, with keener interest, what is the report of his own consciousness about his doings. . . . Doubtless his lot is important in his own eyes; and the chief reason that we think he asks too large a place in our consideration must be our want of room for him, since we refer him to the Divine regard with perfect confidence; nay, it is even held sublime for our neighbor to expect the utmost there, however little he may have got from us" (83). Here and elsewhere with her sardonic maxims, Eliot insists that we include ourselves in the judgment we pass on others. She refers us to the emotions we feel and the observations we make in the process of reading as evidence of our tacit drawing of nice distinctions in our own favor.

Psychological Paradox

Sardonic maxims often express the complexity of our internal stratagems through paradoxes, apparent self-contradictions, or riddles.

> Everyone complains of his memory and no one complains of his judgment.
>
> —La Rochefoucauld (*LaR*, 49)

> He suddenly recalled how he had once in the past been asked, "Why do you hate so and so so much?" And he had answered them, with his shameless impudence, "I'll tell you. He had done me no harm. But I played him a dirty trick, and ever since I have hated him."   —Dostoevsky (*BK*, 99)

Why exactly would we allow our memory to be impugned more readily than our judgment? Because our judgment is closer to our sense of self. We *are* the one who judges. Memory is more easily regarded as a tool and, in any case, is, if accurate, the same for all and therefore feels less personal. For much the same reasons, "our vanity can better bear having our opinions disparaged than our tastes" (*LaR*, 35). Taste marks the self more than opinion, and opinions are more likely to be shared.

But why does the maxim say not only that we would rather have our memory criticized than our judgment, but also that we actively complain about our memory, as if a bad memory were not a lesser evil but a positive good? Why not just be silent about both? Because bad memory is a good: it can excuse cruelty, indolence, or neglect. A lapse in memory, if others accept it, minimizes the offense.

Everyone who knows Dostoevsky will recognize Fyodor Pavlovich Karamazov's comment as characteristic of Dostoevskian psychology. But as the snap of paradox suggests, its logic defies common sense. We readily understand hating someone who has injured us, but not one we have injured. After all, we have heard precepts like "Revenge not injuries" and "Forgive your enemies," but no one teaches children "Revenge not benefits" and "Forgive your benefactors." Nevertheless, people often do hate those who confer benefits, and precisely for doing so. In Dostoevsky's novels, as in life, we witness inversions of expected psychology.

These inversions take place because of La Rochefoucauld's amour-propre or, as Russians might say, the "I" behind actions. La Rochefoucauld shrewdly observes: "Men not only tend to forget benefits and injuries; they even hate those who have helped them, and stop hating those who have harmed them. The need to requite good and revenge evil becomes a slavery painful to endure" (*LaR*, 35). But for Dostoevsky, even this acute analysis leaves out something essential to human nature. Dostoevsky is perhaps the only writer who makes La Rochefoucauld look too simple.

What Dostoevsky adds to La Rochefoucauld, and what makes his maxims even more profound, is his appreciation that our sense of self depends on our *moral* self-evaluation. Life consists not only of a constant guarding of the ego but also of protecting oneself from guilt. Men call attention to their bald spots, not their cruelties.

Dostoevsky's famous "scandalous scenes," in which heroes and heroines disgrace themselves in public, illustrate that people will often injure even their amour-propre to escape moral self-reproach.

Even closer to our "I" than judgment is our sense of innocence. Perhaps more than any other author, Dostoevsky has conveyed the pain of guilt, the punishment by conscience that is worse than judicial sentence. He describes people who commit crimes so as to be punished and thereby escape from guilt. In *Crime and Punishment*, a housepainter confesses to Raskolnikov's murders for just this reason, and one way to understand this novel's title might be "crime *for* punishment." Guilt does not only arise from bad behavior, it also causes it.

Guilt and shame: these are the driving emotions for Dostoevsky, much more than vanity as we usually think of it. What is more, we feel humiliated by guilt and guilty for being humiliated. Fyodor Pavlovich's paradox demonstrates his understanding of these complexities.

Fyodor Pavlovich means: a person can hate someone he has injured because his victim has become the occasion for his guilt. As our psyches register matters, the victim has hurt the persecutor because he has made the persecutor feel guilty. To be sure, the victim has done so unwittingly, but that only makes his "offense" worse, precisely because he cannot justly be blamed for what he did not intend. The proof is that, if the injurer should subsequently discover that the victim was not as innocent as all that, or somehow intended to make his injurer experience remorse, the injurer's feelings of guilt will diminish. And that is odd because, after all, the new information changes nothing about what the injurer did or intended to do.

If a victim really is completely innocent, his innocence can provoke guilt so intolerable that it leads to hatred, which in turn provokes further injuries out of a peculiar species of revenge—revenge for offenses not committed and for sufferings wrongly endured. Had Dostoevsky written *Othello*, the hero would have discovered he was accusing Desdemona falsely and murdered her for that.

Once the offense is repeated, the consciousness of its injustice leads to another offense in an ever accelerating cycle. If this cycle takes place in public, as it often does in Dostoevsky, it drives a sequence unfolding with dizzying speed, with each horror apparently the last, until we sense a moment of almost infinite density—a moment evoking, in the reader as well as the characters, the emotion Dostoevsky calls "mystic terror." Self-referential paradoxes often entail infinities, and it was Dostoevsky's genius to discover in the paradoxes of moral self-evaluation the basis for an especially intense plot.

Fyodor Pavlovich differs from the person described by most sardonic maxims because he knows just what he is doing. Rather than conceal his perverse motives from himself and others, he announces them "with shameless impudence." The evil that others do out of self-deception becomes for him a conscious principle of action. In this respect, he is no hypocrite, and his vice pays no tribute. Perhaps that tribute is not a bad thing after all.

The Irony of Origins: Feelings

With regard to *origin*, *everything* deserves ironic reflection.

—Nietzsche (*HATH*, 155)[39]

Neither our feelings nor our convictions arise as we think they do. If we understood their true origins, feelings would alter and convictions wobble.

Sardonic maxims offer an etiology of human feelings.

Love is an agreement on the part of two people to over-estimate each other.

—E. M. Cioran[40]

Men often choose to love whom they fear, so as to be protected from them.

—Joubert (28)

Truly, a person loves to see his best friend humiliated before his eyes; on humiliation the better part of friendship is based; this is an old truth known to all
intelligent people.

—Mr. Astley, in Dostoevsky's The Gambler (PSSVTT, 5:313)

Pity is often a way of feeling our own misfortunes in those of other people: it is
a clever foretaste of the unhappiness we may some day encounter.

—La Rochefoucauld (LaR, 83)

Envy is more implacable than hatred.   —La Rochefoucauld (LaR, 95)

Nothing is more fleeting than the memory of benefits received.

—Guicciardini[41]

In most men gratitude is only a secret longing for greater benefits. [La recon-
naissance de la plupart des hommes n'est qu'une secrète envie de recevoir de
plus grand bienfaits.]

—La Rochefoucauld (LaR, 90; ODQ, 469)

[Gratitude] is a lively sense of future favors.   —Robert Walpole (ODQ, 820)

There are minds so impatient of inferiority, that their gratitude is a species of
revenge.   —Samuel Johnson (ODQ, 425)

For Cioran, love derives from needing the flattery of another demanding
the same service in return; for Joubert, it arises from fear of fear. Dostoevskian
friendship can be based on an unacknowledged mutual envy. Pity for La Rochefoucauld is less an expression of care than a form of insurance.

Gratitude figures especially prominently in sardonic maxims because we
deceive ourselves both in giving and receiving it; and because we crave it even
though we know from our own experience it is usually counterfeit. Walpole
echoes but amends La Rochefoucauld not only because he was in context referring to receivers of public offices but also because "a lively sense" is a direct
feeling whereas a secret hope is partly concealed. It is hard to say which is more
damning. In pointing out how a sense of inferiority can turn gratitude into a
species of revenge, Dr. Johnson sounds a Dostoevskian note.

It is not immediately obvious why envy should be more implacable than
hatred until we consider that we often boast of our anger, which is easily represented as a desire for justice, but are ashamed of envy because its very existence
admits inferiority.[42] Moreover, since envy expresses not a desire for what the
other has but a wish to prevent the other from having it, it necessarily testifies

to spite and mean-spiritedness. The envious person therefore envies the other's freedom from the need to envy, and so this emotion, like guilt, feeds on itself. That is why hatred can fade more readily than envy.

Irony of Origins: Beliefs

So convenient a thing it is to be a *reasonable creature*, since it enables one to find or make a reason for everything one has a mind to do.   —Benjamin Franklin[43]

As we have seen, sardonic maximists despise those who pride themselves on their intellect. "The subtlest folly," writes La Rochefoucauld, "is fabricated of the subtlest wisdom" (*LaR*, 147). Orwell observed: "One has to belong to the intelligentsia to believe things like that; no ordinary man could be such a fool" (*YBQ*, 569).

The folly of intellectuals derives from their belief in beliefs, and their still stronger belief in those who believe in beliefs—that is, in themselves. Sardonic maxims refer beliefs to psychology: theories purporting to be based on evidence in fact rationalize fears, desires, and, above all, vanity. The more closely beliefs pertain to our sense of identity, the less they depend on reason and the less they can be changed by argument. No one was ever talked out of a belief he was not first talked into. For intellectuals, identity is composed primarily of beliefs. And so, for the maximist, they are, despite their assertions to the contrary, the last people to be influenced by facts or reason.

Where believers give reasons, sardonic maxims discover etiologies, much as they do with feelings. The believer believes because it suits his interest or vanity to believe. That great etiologist of professed morals, Nietzsche, expressed particular appreciation for La Rochefoucauld and the genre in which he wrote. "Knowledge of the truth," observed Nietzsche, might gain a great deal "from a stimulating hypothesis like the one La Rochefoucauld places at the beginning of the first edition of his *Sentences et maximes morales*: 'Ce que le monde nomme vertu n'est d'ordinaire qu'un fantôme formé par nos passions, à qui on donne un nom honnête pour faire impunément ce qu'on veut' [That which men call virtue is usually no more than a phantom formed by our passions, to which one gives an honest name in order to do with impunity whatever one wishes]."[44] La Rochefoucauld can certainly sound like Nietzsche: "Love of justice, in most men, is only a fear of encountering injustice" (*LaR*, 47). The point is not that we assert what it is to our advantage to assert, or that social groups argue the justice of what advances their interests, but that people actually *believe* such assertions—or, rather, believe they believe them.

It might seem that the sardonic maximists would favor those philosophical systems that claim to unmask beliefs by finding the self-interest that has generated the arguments for them. But they don't. To take the two most obvious examples, Marxism and Freudianism speak in and express the worldview of dicta, not sardonic maxims. They claim to have at last uncovered the timeless truth. For the sardonic maxim, such confidence in one's own discoveries represents just another form of intellectual vanity, born of the very process described in others. That, I take it, is the point of Karl Kraus's most cited line: "Psychoanalysis is itself the disease it purports to cure."[45] The disease it purports to cure, but itself induces, is self-deception. Sardonic maxims delight in unmasking those who claim to unmask others.

The Nature of Beliefs

If we deceive ourselves that we believe something, but believe sincerely that we believe it, then what does it mean to believe? Do beliefs come in a spectrum of sincerity? The best authors of sardonic maxims tell us they do. Between the spectrum's extremes, we find a paradoxical state of belief that is also disbelief.

In his *Natural History of Religion* (not to be confused with his *Dialogues Concerning Natural Religion*) David Hume presents belief as a complex of contradictions and paradoxes.[46] The philosopher can identify those paradoxes and perhaps trace their origins, but the peculiar nature of each combination of opposites must ever elude his grasp. "Among idolaters," he observes, "the words may be false, and belie the secret opinion: But among more exalted religionists, the opinion itself contracts a kind of falsehood" (Hume, 178). Those more exalted religionists—implicitly including Hume's own sophisticated contemporaries—are not mere hypocrites. They do not affirm what they know to be false, but contrive to believe sincerely what they sincerely doubt. In such cases, "men dare not avow, even to their own hearts the doubts which they entertain" and so "disguise to themselves" their infidelity by all the more extreme professions.

> But nature is too hard for all their endeavours, and suffers not the obscure, glimmering light, afforded in those shadowy regions, to equal the strong impressions, made by common sense and by experience. The usual course of men's conduct belies their words, and shows, that their assent in these matters is some unaccountable operation of the mind between disbelief and conviction, but approaching much nearer to the former than the latter. (172)

The "shadowy regions" between: that is the where the sardonic maxim situates itself.

Gibbon cites Hume's argument with approval and argues in a similar vein about the sincerity of Constantine's conversion.[47] "The protestant and philosophic readers of our age," he observes, will not hesitate to describe Constantine's choice of religion as entirely a matter of political calculation, but this harsh conclusion is not justified by "our knowledge of human nature." In a way characteristic of his history, Gibbon offers a maxim along with its illustration: "Personal interest is often the standard of our belief, as well as of our practice; and the same motives of temporal advantage which might influence the public conduct and professions of Constantine might insensibly dispose his mind to embrace a religion so propitious to his fame and fortunes" (*DAF*, 573). Piety that might have been largely specious could "insensibly" develop into real devotion. In between lie the shadowy regions.

That is also where the narrator of *Middlemarch* repeatedly finds herself. The usual categories of sincerity or hypocrisy seem far too crude to apply to the people she examines.

> This was not what Mr. Bulstrode said to any man for the sake of deceiving him; it was what he said to himself—it was as genuinely his mode of explaining events as any theory of yours may be, if you happen to disagree with him. For the egoism which enters our theories does not affect their sincerity; rather, the more our egoism is satisfied, the more robust is our belief. (*MM*, 499–500)

> There may be coarse hypocrites, who consciously affect their beliefs and emotions for the sake of gulling the world, but Bulstrode was not one of them. He was simply a man whose desires had been stronger than his theoretic beliefs. And who had gradually explained the gratification of his desires into satisfactory agreement with those beliefs. If this be hypocrisy, it is a process which shows itself occasionally in us all, to whatever confession we belong. . . . This implicit reasoning is essentially no more peculiar to evangelical belief than the use of wide phrases for narrow motives is peculiar to Englishmen. There is no general doctrine which is not capable of eating out our morality if unchecked by the deep-seated habit of direct fellow feeling with individual men. (*MM*, 590–91)

These passages illustrate how novelists use sardonic maxims. Readers are first allowed to trace a character's thoughts (which occur before the passages I have cited). Then the author comments on how they are to understand them ("this was not what Mr. Bulstrode said to himself"). In case readers are inclined to attribute self-deception only to people with different beliefs, the narrator assures them all of us do the same.

At last, she formulates a maxim reflecting the general pattern: We tell ourselves our actions follow from our beliefs, but in fact we adjust our beliefs to fit our actions. We do so without conscious hypocrisy, without consciously lying to others or to ourselves; and yet we do not quite believe in what we purport to believe. Every theory can be corrupted this way, even the ones we find most moral.

Whatever skepticism we apply to others' beliefs should be redoubled in the case of our own. The cruelest actions were probably performed by people who believed, as much as we do, that they were acting in the name of justice, which is why we must trust, more than any theory, basic kindness. We must refer our beliefs and our sense of justice to decency growing from a "deep-seated habit of direct fellow feeling with individual men."

The narrator of Tolstoy's *Boyhood* inverts the usual advice to act from principle. "In my opinion the incongruity between a man's situation and his moral activity is the surest sign of his sincerity" (*PSS*, 136; translation mine). One might imagine that such incongruity would be the sign of hypocrisy rather than sincerity, but Tolstoy's point is that the only way to make one's actions and beliefs coincide is to adjust the beliefs to the actions. A sincere person will not adjust his beliefs so conveniently.

In *Middlemarch*, Lydgate worries whether he has adjusted his beliefs in this very way. When Dorothea refuses to accept he could be bribed to do a wickedness, Lydgate replies with a groan in his voice: "I don't know. . . . [T]here is a pale shade of bribery which is sometimes called prosperity" (*MM*, 730). Lydgate's self-doubt may prompt us to ask whether guilt for such "pale shades" is warranted, because it tacitly presupposes that we could act with perfect sincerity. But is it possible to act with no shade of bribery or hypocrisy at all?

At some point, accurate perception can be erroneous, and it can be unjust to judge too justly.

Zeal

Hume formulates maxims in the form of rhetorical questions: "Is it strange, when mistakes are so common, to find every one positive and dogmatical? And that the zeal often rises in proportion to the error?" (Hume, 171). The more spectacular the absurdity one wants to profess sincerely, and the more difficult the self-deception required to do so, the greater the zeal of the adherent becomes. For the sardonic maximist, zeal—of religious fanatics, of political parties, of adherents of a theory or proponents of an ideology—constitutes the greatest, and most dangerous, folly.

To justify a belief that runs contrary to evidence and common sense, the zealot contrives first to ignore counterevidence. As the delusion proceeds, he goes further: he allows, admits, and at last flaunts the greatest irrationality and the most telling contrary facts as signs of piety. Gibbon describes this process repeatedly. When cold and sullen skeptics, like those Egyptians prejudiced in favor of their traditional sacred animals, at last became believers, Gibbon explains, they allayed doubt and demonstrated contempt for their former suspiciousness by professing the most extreme assertions and performing the rashest actions. "As soon, indeed, as Christianity ascended the throne, the zeal of the barbarians obeyed the prevailing impulsion: the cities of Egypt were filled with bishops and the deserts of Thebais swarmed with hermits" (*DAF*, 393).

The paradox of "swarming hermits" reflects the same law of human nature that creates welcome persecution. Tertullian wrote a treatise, "filled with the wildest fanaticism and the most incoherent declamation," in which he argued that any flight from persecution was a form of apostasy, while others "according to the lively expression of Sulpicius Severus, desired martyrdom with more eagerness than his contemporaries solicited a bishopric" (436). Ignatius beseeched Roman Christians not to rescue him from execution by wild beasts, whom he resolved to provoke.

In the course of such descriptions, Gibbon advances another sardonic principle of human belief. The monks of succeeding ages who described the great number and exquisite kinds of tortures suffered by the early Christians largely spun fictions out of the air, and yet they believed what they were saying for a reason natural to us all. "The total disregard for truth and probability in the representation of these primitive martyrdoms was occasioned by a very natural mistake. The ecclesiastical writers of the fourth or fifth centuries ascribed to the magistrates of Rome the same degree of implacable and unrelenting zeal which filled their own breasts against the heretics or idolaters of their own times" (*DAF*, 421). La Rochefoucauld discerns that "those who cannot commit great crimes do not easily believe it possible of others" (*LaR*, 151), and Gibbon tells us that those who easily believe in the great crimes of others are usually capable of them themselves. In either case, the standard of plausibility is the thoughts we ourselves indulge. For Dostoevsky, that is why former victims make the worst tyrants.

From similar examples, Hume deduces a different sardonic law of human nature. Whenever a controversy among religious or ideological factions occurs, the outcome can usually be foretold: "Whichever opinion . . . is most contrary to plain sense is sure to prevail; even where the general interest of the system requires not that decision. Though the reproach of heresy may, for some time, be bandied about among the disputants, it always rests at last on the side of reason" (Hume, 166). "Even where the general interest of the system" would dictate a different result: Hume explicitly sets his law *against* one based on rational self-interest. Is it any surprise that the Bolsheviks defeated the other socialists? As another well-known sardonic maxim instructs, "The Revolution is like Saturn—it devours its own children."[48]

Where ideology is concerned, bet on the outcome most "contrary to plain sense." If economists took Hume's principle into account, they would be more cautious in extending their "rational choice" model outside of economics proper.

For organizations no less than for individuals, numerous vanities—but especially zeal—easily trump reason. "To oppose the torrent of scholastic reason by such feeble maxims as these, that *it is impossible for the same thing to be and not to be*, that *the whole is greater than a part*, that *two and three make five*, is pretending to stop the ocean with a bulrush. Will you set up profane reason against sacred mystery?" (Hume, 166).

And so reason itself tells us that faith in reason is as deluded as any other superstition. *The Natural History of Religion* may be considered a series of variations, usually expressed in sardonic maxims, on this lugubrious outcome of enlightenment reason.

The Maximist

Maximiste, pessimiste.   —Joseph Roux (*OBA*, 1)

Who, then, is the maximist? Or rather, what image of the maximist do the conventions of the genre create?[49]

The maximist speaks from experience, which counts more than reasoning or theory, and has evidently had plenty. We sense him as old, though not very old. He has lived through what surprises younger people and has reflected upon it. Having moved among the urbane and sophisticated, he knows his conclusions have been tested by demanding judges. In this sense, the maximist is aristocratic, as well as world-weary. He speaks out of what one commentator has called "cool disdain." The maximist expects his readers to be as old and sophisticated as himself, and to recognize from experience, rather than proof or argument, the truth of what he says. If they don't, no argument will substitute.

Maxims create the impression they were produced as La Rochefoucauld's apparently were. It seems that the guests in Madame Sable's salon played a game in which worldly comments were made about human behavior, emotions, and deceptions. Each promising comment was passed around, so others could refine it into something pithier. When the company had gone as far as it could, La Rochefoucauld would take the result home and work it over and over again in his study, perhaps for years. He was guided by the instinct famously described by Joubert: "If there be a man tormented by the cursed ambition to put a whole book into a page, a whole page into a phrase, and that phrase into a word, I am that man" (Joubert, 206). Economy of expression reflects precision of observation.

Unlike witticisms, which convey the sense that they were spoken on the spot, maxims are essentially a *written* form and demand we recognize the process of constant reflection and revision. Witticisms would be ruined by any reminder that they follow the conventions of a genre with a set of learnable techniques, for the more we recall the techniques the less spontaneous the witticism seems. But maximists display constant awareness of their genre. We cannot miss La Rochefoucauld's consciousness of the tradition in which he was writing.

Witticisms aspire to achieve the perfection of maxims without assiduous reworking. They want us to marvel that they were spoken spontaneously yet perfectly. Of course, they are often perfected later by others, which is why so many—like the best of Mark Twain's—have come down to us in both more and less polished forms. Maxims, by contrast, disdain the pretense of spontaneity as they disdain all pretense. They demand to be taken as written, not just to show the value of reflection but also to avoid the wit's boastfulness.

Maximists favor self-reference and reversal: "They are most often wrong who cannot bear to be"; "What alone should astonish is that we can still be astonished"; "We often forgive those who bore us; we cannot forgive those whom we bore." With such locutions maximists demonstrate that they refuse to exempt themselves from the critical gaze they fix on others. By convention, they despise all attempts to occupy an "Archimedean" position outside the world of human flaws they describe.[50]

Sentimentalities Undone

Sardonic maxims typically reflect misanthropy. Their authors sense the evil in human nature, and nothing so provokes their derision as the idea that people are fundamentally good. All sentimentality irritates them, and they readily discover sentimentality. As Qohelet is provoked by Proverbs, maximists find intolerable the intellectual commonplaces of their day, which is why they tend to be despised as reactionaries.

We have a remarkable book, not intended to be one, by Holbrook Jackson and G. K. Chesterton. When Jackson published a collection entitled *Platitudes in the Making*, he sent a copy to Chesterton, who wrote his comments in the margin. The copy was discovered in 1955 and a facsimile was published in 1997 under the title *Platitudes Undone*.

Jackson explained his title in the first "platitude": "All ideas aspire to the condition of platitude." As the subsequent entries make clear, he saw history as inevitable progress, so that the eccentricities of one age become the platitudes of another. The title therefore promises to speak for the future. Such presumption is bound to irritate a maximist.

Chesterton regarded Holbrook's sayings as platitudes in the pejorative sense, that is, as the empty truisms of an intelligentsia prone to socialism, Nietzscheanism, and other distressingly familiar advanced views. Chesterton scribbled answers. And so the book gives us a dialogue of wise sayings in the contemporary mode with sardonic maxims in response. "Every custom was once an eccentricity; every idea was once an absurdity," writes Jackson; and Chesterton answers: "No, no, no. Some ideas were always absurdities. This is one of them" (*PU*, 50).

> Jackson: The great revolution of the future will be Nature's revolt against man.
> Chesterton: I hope Man will not hesitate to shoot. (*PU*, 66)

> Jackson: Goodness and happiness are synonymous terms in a healthy animal.
> Chesterton: True: and man is never a healthy animal. (*PU*, 35)

> Jackson: Morality is the child of self-consciousness.
> Chesterton: No wonder self-consciousness is a little vain. A fine child. (*PU*, 35)

> Jackson: Reason is the dotage of instinct.
> Chesterton: Said the sheep haughtily, as they followed each other to the slaughter house. (*PU*, 75)

The Spectator

Precisely because the maximist knows society all too well, and readily detects human evil, maxims often read as if, however they may have begun, they were finished in seclusion. The maximist has (as we say today) seen it all, and has withdrawn to reflect. Qohelet has been able to try everything because he has been king of Jerusalem, and later maximists have evidently experienced enough to conclude that the sole novelty possible is a new kind of tedium. The only thing that astonishes the maximist is that he can still be astonished.

It takes self-control, as deft as the maximist's control over language, to remain alone as a mere observer. "In France," writes La Bruyère, "it takes much firmness of spirit and a great breadth of understanding to do without offices and positions, and be willing to stay alone and do nothing."[51] Chamfort, who became famous as a dandy, revolutionary, and self-mutilator, reflects that the ability to say "no" and "the ability to live to oneself are the only two ways of preserving one's liberty and one's character" (Epstein, "Chamfort," 174).

As Samuel Johnson repeats, if one cannot attain a modicum of happiness in one's own heart, no external stimulus will secure it. Teach oneself obedient passions and a will resigned: "With these celestial wisdom calms the mind, / And makes the happiness she does not find."[52] Unlike the wise saying, the sardonic maxim cautions us not to expect justice but to accept injustice with philosophic calm. Gibbon repeatedly identifies wisdom with the stance of what he calls "the philosopher," the person of temperance, moderation, courage, thoughtful skepticism, and "calm suspicion" (DAF, 571).

The Long Maxim

The deep pessimism of both types of sardonic maxim has blossomed into a profusion of longer forms, which have, in turn, supplied yet more well-known maxims. Gibbon offers his history as stories to instruct, and draws the lessons of a weary wisdom from each example of folly, fantasy, and fanaticism. One might view The Decline and Fall of the Roman Empire as the world's longest sardonic maxim.

The sensibility that inspired Ecclesiastes has generated numerous works affirming the futility of human action and the absurdity of existence. For the existentialists, of course, the lessons of Ecclesiastes were self-evident. Like the myth of Sisyphus, they expressed the absolute futility of being. The existentialists also loved Tolstoy's Confession, perhaps the greatest modern version of Ecclesiastes.

As Qohelet surveys the world from his place of knowledge and power, Tolstoy speaks from a position of authority and fame, as the acknowledged sage of his day. There came a time, he writes, when I saw that all my works meant nothing, because

> death . . . destroys all things including my work and its remembrance; but soon I saw that this too was a fraud. . . . And I sought for an explanation of these problems in all the branches of knowledge acquired by men. . . . I sought in all the sciences, but far from finding what I wanted, I became convinced that all who like myself had sought in knowledge for the meaning of life had found nothing. And not only had they found nothing, but they had plainly acknowledged that the very thing which made me despair—namely the senselessness of life—is the one indubitable thing man can know. (*TC*, 21–23)

Tolstoy finds meaning only when he ceases to look for it among the "wise" and ceases to believe it results from effort.

Juvenal's tenth satire considers "the vanity of human wishes," a theme that became a commonplace of the formal verse satire. Originally a Latin creation, the verse satire served as a vehicle for poetic maxims about the futility of achievement. Samuel Johnson's greatest poem, "The Vanity of Human Wishes: The Tenth Satire of Juvenal Illustrated," portrays all desires, individual or collective, as producing more misery than happiness. "By darling schemes oppress'd" are fools and nations doomed by fond request; for wavering power politicians rise, while envy and revenge dispute the prize; the scholar's fame the literate ills assail, "toil, envy, want, the patron, and the jail" (*SJ*, 51). Foolishly we pray for long life, but forget that age brings the shame of feebleness, desires frustrated by incapacity, and the distress of loved ones wishing for release.

Old age inspires verse satires not only because it shows the vanity of our most cherished hopes but also because it constitutes a natural unmasking of the weaknesses we most fear. La Rochefoucauld offers celebrated maxims on the theme: "Old fools are worse than young ones"; "Old age is woman's hell"; "Few people know how to be old" (*LaR*, 115, 139, 111). We imagine the true self to be our young and vigorous self, but old age, or even the prospect of it, shows that the essence of flesh is weakness and subjection to time.

Still more horrible to self-love is dementia, because it takes away the self itself. Swift's "Verses on the Death of Doctor Swift," as well as Juvenal's and Johnson's satires, dwell on the theme of old age, and we remember that when Gulliver expatiates on the happiness of an indefinitely extended life, he is confronted with the unspeakable horror of the Struldbrugs, who cannot die but forever decay. "They were the most mortifying sight I ever beheld. . . . The reader will easily believe, that from what I had heard and seen, my keen appetite for perpetuity of life was much abated."[53]

Progress

You cannot fight against the future. Time is on our side.

—William Gladstone (*MDQ*, 451)

We've made great medical progress in the last generation. What used to be merely an itch is now an allergy.   —Anonymous (*MDQ*, 450)

As earlier maximists ridiculed the notion of Providence, more recent ones have questioned its modern substitute, progress. For the maximist, no law guarantees that later is better. The future is not a force; it does not exist until we make it. The myth of progress—that history has an inherent direction toward the better—has obsessed Western thought at least since the seventeenth century. The sardonic maximists have bravely, perhaps perversely, refused to go along. For them, "progress" is a myth that excuses lack of thought. Instead of weighing evidence, the believer in progress favors whatever seems "later" and more "up-to-date."

If anything, maximists incline to some version of Malthusianism, and Malthus himself employs the form. Optimists inspired by "the great and unlooked for discoveries that have taken place of late years . . . and particularly that tremendous phenomenon in the political horizon, the French revolution[,]" had come to believe in "the perfectibility of society," Malthus explains; but such a belief makes as much sense as claiming people are being transformed into ostriches. His *Essay on the Principle of Population* reads like a grand restatement of Ecclesiastes. "It has been said the great question is now at issue whether man shall henceforth start forwards with accelerated velocity towards illimitable, and hitherto unconceived improvement; or be condemned to a perpetual oscillation between happiness and misery, and after every effort remain still at an immeasurable distance from the wished for goal."[54]

In this debate between optimism and futility, futility wins. Society cannot escape the principle of population: "Population, when unchecked, increases in a geometrical ratio [while s]ubsistence increases only in an arithmetical ratio." So long as people need to eat and so long as the sexes attract each other with the same force, "perpetual oscillation" must result (Malthus, 13). What has been is what shall be; one generation passeth away and another generation cometh; the sun also rises.

No fashionable idea provoked Tolstoy's contempt as much as the law of progress, which he called a mere superstition. "To subordinate history to the idea of progress," he wrote, "is just as easy as to the idea of regress, or to any other historical fantasy that you like. I will say more: I see no necessity whatsoever to seek out general laws of history, not to mention the impossibility of doing so" (*PSS* 8:333). All you have to do to find a law of progress is to ignore counterevidence or rule it out as (in the Hegelian phrase) "nonhistorical." In short, "progress is the general law for all mankind, they say, with the sole exception of Asia, Africa, America, Australia, with the exception of one billion people. . . . To say that progress is the law of humanity is just as unfounded as to say that all people are blond with the exception of those with black hair" (8:332–33).

Progress has proven attractive because it flatters the vanity of the believer. After all, if later is better, then we surpass all the geniuses of history. I pronounce every word I say at the latest moment of history. What is more, progress always conforms to the preferences of the progressives. According to several of Tolstoy's maxims, Europeans believe in progress for the same reason that aristocrats believe in status and capitalists justify wealth. In *War and Peace*, he explains that European historians presume that humanity is being led to a goal known to the historian, namely "the welfare and civilization of all humanity, by which is generally meant those people that occupy the small northwest corner of a large continent" (*W&P*, 1413).[55] By the same token, intellectuals believe that history is guided by ideas (1420). Historians presume they can judge people of the past "according to whether they promoted *progress* or *reaction*," that is, according to whether they favored processes leading to the historians themselves.

In the *Confession*, Tolstoy describes how at a particular time in youth he accepted the law of progress and development toward greater complexity: "It was just the time when I was myself becoming more complex and was developing . . . and feeling this growth in myself it was natural for me to think that such was the universal law in which I should find the solution of the question of my life" (*TC*, 25). But then I began to age, Tolstoy explains: "I felt that I was not developing, but fading, my muscles were weakening, my teeth falling out, and I saw that the law not only did not explain anything to me, but that there never had been or could be such a law" (25).

We might also suppose that intellectuals believe society progresses because what intellectuals produce—knowledge—progresses. But progress in knowledge may easily lead to regress in human welfare. When Swift's Houyhnhnms contemplate the possibilities of Yahoos with reason, they understand that such creatures would use it to produce more and more monstrous weapons: "[T]he corruption of the faculty might be worse than brutality itself" (Swift, 473). In his polemic against intellectuals and the law of progress, Dostoevsky's Underground Man echoes this thought: "Civilization only produces a greater variety of sensations in man—and nothing more." "The subtlest slaughterers have almost always been the more civilized gentlemen, to whom the various Attilas and Stenka Razins could never hold a candle" (NFU, 21). "Progress," observed Kraus, "makes purses out of human skins" (PDE, 323).

Maxims in the Form of Laws

When examining dicta, we saw that "moral Newtonians" have contended that they would soon discover, or had already discovered, social laws of the same explanatory power as Newton's laws of motion. Inasmuch as sardonic maxims also make general statements of a lawlike character, numerous maximists have phrased their insights as parodic "laws." We have already considered Hume's law that in theological or ideological disputes, the position most opposed to reason will eventually win out. Consider the following:

> But the human character, however it may be exalted or depressed by a temporary enthusiasm, will return, by degrees, to its proper and natural level, and will resume those passions that seem the most adapted to the present condition.
>
> —Gibbon (DAF, 376)

> [Parkinson's Law:] Work expands to fill the time available for its completion.
>
> —C. Northcote Parkinson[56]

> [The Law of Triviality:] ... [in committee meetings] the time spent on any item of the agenda will be in inverse proportion to the sum involved.
>
> —C. Northcote Parkinson (24, 30–32)

> [The Peter Principle:] In a hierarchy every employee tends to rise to his level of incompetence.   —Laurence J. Peter and Raymond Hull[57]

> [The Darwinian Extension of the Peter Principle:] Sooner or later, man must reach his level of life-incompetence.
>
> —Laurence J. Peter and Raymond Hull (136)

Misery increases to meet the means available for its alleviation.

—Theodore Dalrymple[58]

[The Law of Tension:] The first muscle stiffened [in his opponent by the Games-
man] is the first point gained.   —Stephen Potter[59]

Public definitions of a situation (prophecies or predictions) become an integral
part of the situation and thus affect subsequent developments. . . . The self-
fulfilling prophecy is, in the beginning, a *false* definition of the situation evoking
a behavior which makes the originally false assumption come true. The specious validity of the self-fulfilling prophecy perpetuates a regime of error. For
the prophet will cite the actual course of events as proof that he was right from
the beginning.   —Robert K. Merton[60]

As the maxims of La Rochefoucauld show the real feelings behind a display of
virtue, "laws" such as these show the real dynamics behind apparent rationality,
purposefulness, or social order. These maximists do for sociology what La Rochefoucauld does for psychology. The rational performance of necessary functions
no more explains society than rational choice theory explains individuals.

Parkinson begins his book: "To the very young, to schoolteachers, as also
to those who compile textbooks about constitutional history, politics, and current affairs, the world is a more or less rational place. . . . To those, on the other
hand, with any experience of affairs, these assumptions are ludicrous. Solemn
conclaves of the mind are mere figments of the teacher's mind" (Parkinson,
vii). Instead of the schoolteacher image of civil servants, Parkinson offers to
"provide . . . a glimpse of reality" (viii). This glimpse reveals disguise and the
facts disguised.

Parkinson's Law invites us to consider the circumstances behind any bureaucrat's claim that more staffing is needed. To the bureaucrat, an overwhelming
amount of work justifies the claim, but in fact the addition of more staff does
nothing to alleviate matters because it creates more work for the new staff to
perform. No matter how much staff is provided, sooner or later still more will
be required to do the same job. Indeed, staff increase will take place even if the
job supposedly performed has disappeared. The staff of the colonial office will
grow when there are no more colonies, and federal agencies draining swamps
will increase in size even when other agencies have been established to preserve
the same swamps as valuable wetlands. And yet each bureaucrat's insistence that
he or she needs more staff is entirely sincere. Dalrymple's law, evidently based
on Parkinson's, applies similar thinking to the claims of social reformers.

Parkinson's Law of Triviality, which he presents as a contribution to "comitology" (the scientific study of committees), purports to elucidate the difference between supposed and actual allotment of time. Gibbon has given us an early example of an equilibrium principle, in our time a favorite model for economic understanding. Also indebted to Parkinson's Law, the famous Peter Principle does for "hierarchiology" what Parkinson did for comitology. It explains not the functioning but the malfunctioning of the social world ("why things always go wrong"). The Darwinian Extension of the Peter Principle seems especially relevant in an age attracted to sociobiology. Stephen Potter's books on "gamesmanship" state laws in the form of strategic principles for winning at games, including social games, by shaking another's self-possession.

Few users of the term "self-fulfilling prophecy" know that it was coined by Robert K. Merton, who was both a great sociologist and an occasional satirist. His concept explains yet another way in which people misperceive the world and how some mistakes ensure their perpetual acceptance. The idea that folly creates its own justification (or that prognosticators make their own predictions come true) belongs to the tradition of sardonic maxims and satiric literature. Gulliver praises the "skill at prognostics" shown by British doctors who, when they anticipate death, prove remarkably accurate even when indications seem to go the other way.[61] As we saw with Dostoevskian guilt, sardonic maximists understand positive feedback loops for negative qualities.

Keenly aware of his debt to the great sardonic writers, Merton modeled one study on Sterne's *Tristram Shandy* and, in the course of its argument, cites one of Tristram's laws:

> I am thoroughly mindful of what Tristram reports about the singular behavior of hypotheses, that, "it is the nature of a hypothesis, when once a man has conceived it, that it assimilates every thing to itself as proper nourishment; and from the first moment of your begetting it, it generally grows the stronger by every thing you see, hear, read or understand." . . . Since the truth of Tristram's hypothesis is exemplified by its own enunciation, any further report of the versatile uses of hypothesis would be altogether superfluous.[62]

Such hypotheses cannot be disconfirmed because they "assimilate" all apparent counterevidence. Karl Kraus, who readily detected such assimilative reasoning, devoted several of his most famous maxims to its use by psychiatry and psychoanalysis. The concept of "resistance," for instance, easily transforms all disproof into proof: "The psychiatrist unfailingly recognizes the madman by his excited behavior on being incarcerated"; "If I tell the analysts to kiss my ass, they tell me I have an anal fixation."[63]

Tristram's law of the gobbling hypothesis echoes a long tradition of sardonic maxims explaining the unshakeable attachment of intellectuals (or as the ancients called them, "philosophers") to absurdities. The self-confirming hypothesis represents another variation on the logic of the self-fulfilling prophecy and guilt-inducing guilt. Merton took that logic seriously in his studies of the sociology of ideas and theories.

It was Merton who drew the famous distinction between "manifest" (presumed) and "latent" (unconscious) functions.[64] Social institutions that fail to perform their official function may nevertheless flourish because they perform other, unacknowledged functions. Even if those other functions prove harmful to society at large, they may be beneficial to the institution's staff and supporters. Merton's theory of "latent" functions not only challenged traditional functionalism but also reworded in sociological terms the essential unmasking logic of sardonic maxims. Merton may be viewed as the La Rochefoucauld of the twentieth century.

Maxims as Definitions

Some satirists have composed definitions giving not the manifest meaning (as found in other dictionaries) but the latent meaning, the way the word is actually used. They define the word by the disguised purpose of it: self-interest masquerading as virtue, vanity distorting perception, or desires leading to self-deception.

In Ambrose Bierce's *Devil's Dictionary* we find: "*Impunity*, n., Wealth"; "*Hers*, pron., His": and "*Egotist*, n., A person of low taste, more interested in himself than in me."[65] Chamfort gives us: "*Ambition*: serious imbecility"; "*Love*: agreeable folly"; "*Celebrity*: the advantage of being known by those who do not know you."[66] Dr. Johnson's dictionary defines "Whig" as "the name of a faction" and "pension" as "an allowance made to anyone without an equivalent. In England it is generally understood to mean pay given to a state hireling for treason to his country."[67] Johnson famously called patriotism "the last refuge of a scoundrel" (Boswell, 222); Bierce in response insists it is the first (Bierce, 155). George Eliot explains that "what we call our despair is often only the painful eagerness of hope" (*MM*, 478).

Flaubert's *Dictionary of Received Ideas* works somewhat differently. It explains to readers the proper thing to say or think about a given word or concept.

What is proper is not necessarily ignorant but always conforms to the clichés of the educated: "*Académie Française*: Denigrate it, but become a member if you can." "*Accident*: Always 'deplorable' or 'unfortunate'; as though anyone might find some cause to rejoice in misfortune"; "*Age, the present age*: Denounce vigorously. Lament its unpoetic tone. Call it 'an age of transition, of decadence.'" He draws the book's epigraph from Chamfort: "I wager that every public notion, every received orthodoxy is a piece of foolish nonsense, since such great numbers have found it to their taste."[68] I choose these definitions, of course, because the clichés they transmit survive.

Misanthropology

Literary works have drawn on the sardonic maxim to create a kind of inverse celebration of human nature. In answer to lovers of humanity, to believers in human perfectibility, to philosophers presuming the rationality of human behavior, satiric works have offered maxims of misanthropy.

Ancient menippean satire, which exalted the laughing philosophic misanthropes Democritus and Menippus, also created the misanthropic hero. Like the eponymous central figure of Lucian's *Timon*, this hero hates all gods and men. The satire illustrates the reasons. When Hermes, whom Zeus sends to Timon, asks the goddess Wealth why, if she is so ugly, she has so many lovers, Wealth replies that she always comes in disguise and accompanied by blinding vices like Delusion, Stupidity, and Arrogance, all of which aid Self-Deceit.[69] Guided by those vices, humanity behaves viciously.

In the hands of the Earl of Rochester, the verse satire goes beyond exposure of vanity to complete rejection of human nature. Rochester's late seventeenth-century "Satyr against Mankind" prefers beasts to people. "Pressed by necessity, they kill for food; / Man undoes man to do himself no good. / . . . Inhumanly his fellow's life betrays; / With voluntary pains works his distress, / Not through necessity but wantonness" (*EPP*, 38). Could it be, as Dostoevsky was to suggest, that cruelty does not just occur as a by-product of self-interest, but also directly, as an irreducible principle of human behavior?

Perhaps the most familiar way to construct a narrative around misanthropic maxims is to tell the story of a lover of humanity who confronts its real nature. That is the story of Lucian's Timon, while Gulliver, who repeatedly assures us that "there were few greater lovers of mankind, at that time, than myself," provokes from the wise and good a rather different judgment (Swift, 452). The King of Brobdingnag concludes from Gulliver's own account of human beings that they are "the most pernicious race of little odious vermin that nature ever suffered to crawl upon the surface of the earth" (342). The Yahoos Gulliver encounters in book 4 constitute a sort of maxim come to life: they are human beings as they really are. The Yahoos embody the reverse of the "noble savage," a phrase coined by Dryden for a concept that goes back at least to Tacitus. In that sunny kind of thinking, people stripped of civilization would be stripped of vice, but for Swift, and the maximists generally, they would be stripped of all restraints on vice.

Swift offers us what might be called a misanthropology. For some reason the Houyhnhnms cannot grasp, Yahoos fight for little shining stones and battle each other "without any visible cause" (486), but Gulliver understands all too well that he is seeing human nature in its primal form. Sometimes Yahoos subject the deposed favorite of their leader to a ceremony in which "young and old, male and female, come in a body and discharge their excrements upon him from head to foot. But how far this might be applicable to our courts and favourites, and ministers of state, my master said I could best determine" (486).

Voltaire's *Candide* and Johnson's *Rasselas* also contain maxims to reeducate optimists. So do many Russian stories about "going to the people."[70] When Gulliver at last realizes what people are, he goes mad and, in his insane pride, condemns his fellow humans for pride. The only thing wrong with his judgment is that he exempts himself.

It is important to recognize that Swift does not rely here on the distressingly familiar trope of the man who sees because he is mad. Quite the contrary, here the hero is mad because he sees.

Dostoevsky: The Maximist as Hero

You know, dear boy, there was an old sinner . . . who declared that, if there were no God, he would have to be invented. . . . And what's strange, what would be marvelous, is not that God should really exist; the marvel is that such an idea, the idea of the necessity of God, could enter the head of such a savage, vicious beast as man.   —Ivan Karamazov (*BK*, 278)

To examine the maxim's worldview, one might narrate the story of a maximist. That is what Dostoevsky does in his greatest work, *The Brothers Karamazov*. Ivan Karamazov crafts memorable maxims, while the narrative subjects his philosophy to an unwelcome but respectful critique. As a result, the book exploits this short genre's potential without succumbing to its vision.

In the novel's symposium of genres in interaction, the maxim poses the strongest challenge. So strong has that challenge proven that critics have argued ever since whether the novel's Christian sayings adequately meet it.

Often the author or narrator of realist novels voices sardonic maxims, but sometimes a character speaks them. If realism is not to be compromised, the character must have more than ordinary insight. One accepts maxims in the style of La Rochefoucauld from Lydgate or Farebrother, as one would not from Rosamond Vincy. In *Karamazov*, several characters use the form, which supplies the book's most cited lines.

Father Zossima surprises the characters gathered in his cell with maxims reflecting psychological sophistication that, one might think, would not easily be acquired in a monastery. He responds to Fyodor Pavlovich's aggressive self-humiliation with pithy comments about shame and self-deception. "It is sometimes very pleasant to take offense," he observes. Going one better (or worse), Fyodor Pavlovich adds that at some moments "it is not so much pleasant as distinguished [literally, beautiful] to be insulted" (*BK*, 48).

Such maxims instruct Alyosha, the novel's Christian hero, in human nature. Even the passionate brother, Dmitri, speaks in maxims. In his ecstatic despair, Dmitri concludes from his combination of idealism and self-degradation that "there is beauty in Sodom" and that ugliness itself may be as alluring as beauty. "A man with lofty mind and heart begins with the ideal of the Madonna and ends with the ideal of Sodom," he explains. "What's still more awful is that a man with the ideal of Sodom in his soul does not renounce the ideal of the Madonna, and his heart may be on fire with that ideal, genuinely on fire" (127). These paradoxes, typical of the maxim, evoke Dmitri's horror.

La Rochefoucauld to the contrary, virtue and vice can exist together without hypocrisy. The maximist's idea that the former simply masks the latter may be too simple. The contradictions of the human heart are not so easily resolved. There "all shores meet and all contradictions stand side by side" (127). At times virtue masks vice, but at times the reverse. People are often ashamed of their *good* impulses.

Could it be that maximists exaggerate the evil of the world so that they can feel the superiority that comes from unmasking it? For intellectuals, perhaps the devil's most potent temptation is not wealth or power but the gratifying confidence in one's own clear-sighted and worldly sophistication. The paltry devil who haunts Ivan mocks him precisely for the delusions of superiority shaping his sardonic vision. "You are wounded, in the first place, in your aesthetic feelings," the devil taunts him, "and, secondly, in your pride. How could such a vulgar [*poshlyi*] devil visit such a great man as you?" (786).

The Maxims of "Rebellion" and
"The Grand Inquisitor"

Ivan self-consciously adopts the stance of the sardonic maximist. Like the devil who haunts him, he has read the literature of misanthropy. Knowing the tradition, he has labored over his own maxims. He tries them out in salons, in his published articles, and, most important, in his unpublished works. In the novel's core sequence, Ivan recites to Alyosha two of these works, the diatribe in "Rebellion" and his "poem" "The Grand Inquisitor." Hoping to shock Alyosha out of his piety, Ivan places him in the position of the naïve believers in traditional wisdom, who justify God or love humanity.

One of literature's greatest misanthropes, Ivan has mastered all Dostoevskian psychology. "Rebellion" offers a series of terrifying stories leading to sardonic maxims about human nature, which in turn lead to even more terrifying stories in an accelerating spiral of misanthropy.

Some maxims concern the difficulty of caring for others. Such care reflects not genuine love of others but the pride that comes from self-sacrifice, "from the self-laceration of falsity, for the sake of charity imposed by duty" (281). After all, Ivan explains, "another can never know how much I suffer, because he is another and not I." "A man is rarely ready to admit another's suffering (as though it were a distinction)" (281–82).

"Love thy neighbor" is a command impossible to obey. In Ivan's view, one can love only the idea of others, not specific other people with all their shortcomings. "For any one to love a man, he must be hidden, for as soon as he shows his face, love is gone" (281). One feels pity for "the poor," abstractly considered or far away, not the repulsive sufferer before one's eyes. "Beggars, especially genteel beggars, ought never to show themselves, but to ask for charity in the newspapers. One can love one's neighbors in the abstract, or even at a distance, but at close quarters it's almost impossible" (282). Fundraisers know this truth well.

Like other maximists, Ivan argues that people are worse than animals: "People talk of bestial cruelty, but that's a great insult to the beasts; a beast can never be so cruel as a man, so artistically cruel" (283). Cruelty is its own reward. No change in education or social conditions will ever eliminate our taste for it. The helplessness of children does not just provide child abusers with an opportunity but is itself what makes abuse appealing. "It's just their helplessness that tempts the tormentor, just the angelic confidence of the child who has no refuge and no appeal. . . . In every man, of course, a demon lies hidden" (287). We are evil all the way down, and when the devil appears to Ivan, he inverts the sentimental saying "I am human, and nothing human is alien to me": "I am Satan," he declares, "and nothing human is alien to me."[71]

In "Rebellion," Ivan subjects Alyosha to misanthropic stories and maxims; in "The Grand Inquisitor" Ivan's fictional character, the Inquisitor, does the same to Jesus. Ivan's Jesus mistakenly believes in the goodness of humanity and the Inquisitor confronts Him with misanthropic counterevidence. His argument is well known: Christianity depends on free choice but "the fundamental secret of human nature" is that people want not freedom but only the belief that they are free while having everything decided for them (301). They wish to claim the dignity of the term "freedom" without suffering the doubt and guilt that freedom necessarily entails. "Nothing is more seductive for man than his freedom of conscience, but nothing is a greater cause of suffering" (302). "Man is tormented by no greater anxiety than to find some one quickly to whom he can hand over that gift of freedom with which the ill-fated creature is born" (302). "There are three powers, three powers alone, able to conquer and to hold captive for ever the conscience of these impotent rebels for their happiness . . . miracle, mystery, and authority" (303). These three powers work by concealing the truth, because the only possible human happiness requires social, as well as individual, self-deception.

On the Other Side

And by chance there came down a certain priest that way; and when he saw him, he passed by on the other side. And likewise a Levite, when he was at the place looked on him, and passed by on the other side.   —Luke 10:31–32

The novel's plot turns on Ivan's stance as maximist. The consequences of that stance lead him, and us, to question the genre's vision. Maxims typically subject beliefs to an irony of origins, but Dostoevsky's novel subjects the maxim to an irony of outcomes.

Having seen and understood "too much," Ivan has withdrawn into lonely meditation on human folly and cruelty. As we have seen, the maximist typically adopts the role of spectator, and Ivan publishes his satiric reflections, sometimes disguised as serious arguments about topics of the day, under the pseudonym "Observer." He thinks of himself as *one who looks on* but does not participate.

For much the same reason, Ivan has perfected a rhetoric of spectatorship. He speaks from outside human affairs and refuses to commit himself to any position within them. His rhetoric abounds in paradoxes, which in their self-contradictions allow him to hide and offer him a loophole. When others ask what he believes, he answers half (but only half) jokingly, and if pressed, jokingly denies that he is joking. Retrospectively, he dismisses his earlier assertions as mere provocations. When Alyosha asks whether Ivan's profession of atheism was serious, he replies:

> "I said that yesterday at dinner on purpose to tease you and I saw your eyes glow. But now I've no objection to discussing with you, and I say so seriously. I want to be friends with you, Alyosha, for I have no friends and want to try it. Well, only fancy, perhaps I too accept God," laughed Ivan, "that's a surprise for you, isn't it?"
> "Yes, of course, if you are not joking now."
> "Joking? I was told at the elder's yesterday I was joking." (278)

Even among other people, Ivan always stands at one remove, a spectator not only of others but also of himself. It is as if participation requires the belief in life he has long since overcome. Dmitri remarks that "Ivan is a tomb"—as dark and remote as death—but Alyosha offers Ivan a better comparison: "I say of you, Ivan is a riddle. You are a riddle to me even now" (273). Ivan responds to this declaration with still darker enigmas.

Paradoxically, Ivan's refusal to act creates the novel's central actions. What he doesn't do matters. Without allowing himself to realize it, Ivan encourages his father's murder by absenting himself. In his heart he consents to remain a mere spectator of what he could prevent. As the proverb has it, he gives that consent silently. While he is doing nothing and only *watching* his father, he signs on to the plot, which, as it happens, is also the novel's plot. "That 'action' [of just watching] all his life afterwards he called 'infamous,' and at the bottom of his heart he thought of it as the basest action of his life" (327). The quotation marks around "action" indicate that doing nothing can be doing something and that responsibility can indeed be incurred by only observing.

Ivan is at last driven mad by his guilt for the consequences of his mere wishes. This guilt represents Dostoevsky's demonstration that the Sermon on the Mount, far from naïvely idealistic, is psychologically true. Wishes do have moral value, and we hold ourselves responsible for them.

Later in the novel, a drunken peasant accidentally falls on Ivan, who in his withdrawal from others reacts with disgust to being touched and abandons the peasant to freeze to death. But shortly after, when his guilt for nonactions at last becomes clear to him, Ivan returns to rescue the peasant. The incident repeats the parable in Luke of the people who pass by a man fallen among thieves and left half dead (Luke 10:25–37).

The answer to the maximist's stance is the good Samaritan. Coming upon the injured man ignored by others, "a certain Samaritan . . . when he saw him, he had compassion on him. And went to him, and bound up his wounds, pouring in oil and wine, and set him on his own beast, and brought him to an inn, and took care of him" (10:33–34).

The Samaritan response acknowledges all the sardonic maxim asserts, but encourages us to rise above it and value compassion.

5

TWO KINDS OF TRIAL

▮ THE SUMMONS ▮

Then let us rise, my friends, and strive to fill
This little interval, this pause of life,
(While yet our liberty and fates are doubtful,)
With resolution, friendship, Roman bravery,
And all the virtues we can crowd into it.

—Cato, in Addison's *Cato: A Tragedy*

When an enemy threatens a group's survival, a leader may summon the people to defend itself. In the ensuing conflict, episodes of defeat or fading hope may demand an inspiring call to continue the struggle, preserve the people, and defend its highest values.

The group may become aware of those values, or they may first achieve conscious expression, in the course of preserving them from extinction. During and after the crisis, persuasive expression becomes the highest form of literature. If the point of philosophy is to guide life, then the crisis tests commitment to philosophy's teachings. True nobility can discover no better way to fill this "little interval" of life.

Probably every culture experiences such moments. Recollections of it, however accurate, easily achieve the status of myth. Reflecting on their past, people recall the leader's appeal to their sense of who they are, and those recollections themselves become an intrinsic part of who they have become. In the name of their identity they met a challenge, and now their identity includes the meeting of it. They are the people who responded to that summons. Identity and crisis, literature and philosophy, fuse.

Schoolchildren of all lands memorize such inspiring appeals. When the ancient classics were considered an essential part of education, heroic pronouncements from antiquity extended identity into the remote past. People aspired to continue Roman bravery. In their battles with each other, the nations of Europe and America appealed to the same great speakers much as they invoked the same God. For each, past crises provided models for a new summons.

Adults, too, often experience a thrill as they remember the moving words spoken at moments that defined who they are. Americans of my parents' generation remember President Roosevelt's "day of infamy" speech and, before that, his first inaugural, which addressed the unprecedented economic crisis as a mortal threat. Roosevelt's genius lay in his ability to summon the people to view the crisis as if it were a foreign invasion.

The recollection of such moments may irritate the next generation, which becomes a mere inheritor of its predecessor's achievements. In any case, the skepticism and irony that often accompany advanced education may make the language of the summons, and its appeal to patriotism, seem hopelessly naïve. No matter what their political beliefs may be, sophisticated people find it hard to speak of America's enemies, however repressive, as an "axis of evil." To them, national founders and military heroes almost belong to another world, only one step from the figures of the Old Testament, and reverence for their words testifies to a touching childishness. What American today ever hears of John Paul Jones, and who would repeat his once universally known declaration, supposedly made when his ship was already sinking, "I have not yet begun to fight"?

But it is hard to do without heroes. Just as those who denounce traditional morality as oppressive wince when others ignore practices ensuring social justice, and defenders of personal choice legislate against habits injurious to health and the environment, so skeptics of old heroes create new icons of virtue. There are no unbelievers at Whole Foods. Instead of Washington's and Jefferson's words, they may remember those of Andrei Sakharov or Martin Luther King, Jr.

Their Finest Words

We can all think of heroic pronouncements. I do not cite the Gettysburg Address, because I imagine that Americans know its opening by heart and can at least recognize the rest of it. When a classical education held sway, Pericles' funeral oration offered a model:

> In short, I say that as a city we are the school of Hellas; while I doubt if the world can produce a man, who where he has only himself to depend on, is equal to so many emergencies, and graced by so happy a versatility as the Athenians. . . . Rather, the admiration of the present and succeeding ages will be ours, since we have not left our power without witness, but have shown it by mighty proofs; and far from needing a Homer for our eulogist, or others of his craft whose verses might charm for the moment only for the impression which they gave to melt at the touch of fact, we have forced every sea and land to be the highway of our daring, and everywhere, whether for evil or for good, have left imperishable monuments behind us. Such is the Athens for which these men, in the assertion of their resolve not to lose her, nobly fought and died; and may every one of their survivors be ready to suffer in her cause.   —Pericles, Funeral Oration[1]

> So died these men as became Athenians. You, their survivors, must determine to have as unaltering a resolution in the field. . . . [Y]ou must yourself realize the power of Athens, and feed your eyes upon her from day to day, till love of her fills your hearts; and then when all her greatness shall break upon you, you must reflect that it was by courage, sense of duty, and a keen feeling of honor in action that men were enabled to win all this. . . . For this offering of their lives, made in common by them all, they each of them individually received that common renown which never grows old, and for a tomb, not so much that in which their bones have been deposited, but that noblest of shrines wherein their glory is laid up to be eternally remembered upon every occasion on which deed or story shall be commemorated. For heroes have the whole earth for their tomb.
> —Pericles, Funeral Oration (Thucydides, 115)

The sense of a struggle between absolute good and absolute evil inspired Bernard of Chartres and his summons to "holy rage":

> You cannot but know that we live in a period of chastisement and ruin; the enemy of mankind has caused the breath of corruption to fly over all regions; we behold nothing but unpunished wickedness. . . . Remembering that their triumph will be

a subject of grief to all ages and an eternal opprobrium upon the generation that has endured it, Yes, the living God has charged me to announce to you that He will punish them who shall not have defended Him against His enemies. Fly then to arms; let a holy rage animate you in the fight. . . . [A]bandon then the things that perish, to gather unfading palms, and conquer a Kingdom that has no end.

　　　　　　　　—Bernard of Chartres, call for the second Crusade, 1146 (*WGS*, 63–64)

The struggle with Napoleon, then with the Germans in the Great War, helped define what it is to be British:

Before this time tomorrow I shall have gained a peerage or Westminster Abbey.

　　　　　　　　　—Horatio, Lord Nelson, before the Battle of the Nile, 1798 (*ODQ*, 558)

England expects that every man will do his duty.

　　　　　　　　　　　—Horatio, Lord Nelson, at Trafalgar, 1805 (*ODQ*, 558)

We are fighting against barbarism. . . . [I]t will be a terrible war; but in the end we shall march through terror to triumph. We shall need all our qualities— every quality that Britain and its people possess—prudence in counsel, daring in action, tenacity in purpose, courage in defeat, moderation in victory; in all things faith.

　　　　　　　　—David Lloyd George, "Appeal to the Nation," 1914 (*WGS*, 203–4)

Franklin Delano Roosevelt transformed the Great Depression into a test of the American people's character:

The only thing we have to fear is fear itself.

　　　　　　　—Franklin Delano Roosevelt, inaugural address, 1933 (*YBQ*, 653)

In our time, Churchill above all others thrilled with his call to fight the Nazis and the odds:

I have nothing to offer but blood, toil, tears and sweat.

　　　　　　　—Winston Churchill, 1940, after becoming prime minister (*HIQ*, 845)

We shall not flag or fail. We shall go on to the end. We shall fight in France, we shall fight on the seas and oceans, we shall fight with growing confidence and growing strength in the air, we shall defend our island, whatever the cost may be. We shall fight on the beaches, we shall fight on the landing grounds, we shall fight in the fields and in the street, we shall fight in the hills; we shall never surrender.

　　　　　　　　　　　　　—Churchill, 1940, after Dunkirk (*HIQ*, 845)

If we fail, then the whole world . . . will sink into the abyss of a new dark age
made more sinister, and perhaps more protracted, by the lights of a perverted
science. . . . Let us therefore brace ourselves to our duty, and so bear ourselves
that, if the British Commonwealth and Empire last for a thousand years, men
will still say, "This was their finest hour."   —Churchill, 1940 (*HIQ*, 846)

Never in the field of human conflict was so much owed by so many to so few.
                                                     —Churchill, 1940 (*HIQ*, 846)

With the Second World War still recent, and the Cold War underway, John F.
Kennedy invoked the tradition of the summons:

Let every nation know, whether it wishes us well or ill, that we shall pay any
price, bear any burden, meet any hardship, support any friend, oppose any foe
to assure the survival and success of liberty. . . . In the long history of the world,
only a few generations have been granted the role of defending freedom in its
hour of maximum danger. I do not shrink from this possibility—I welcome it.
                                        —John F. Kennedy, inaugural address, 1961

I chose these examples precisely because they are so familiar, at least in Great
Britain and the United States. I imagine that a similar collection could be made
elsewhere. The fact that they have been so often quoted has itself become part
of them. We hear them as lines that have resonated for many. We know them
because they have made us—whether for evil or for good, as Pericles says—
who we are.

Sometimes pronouncements like these are short enough that everyone can
learn them by heart. At other times, the summons extends to several sentences,
with one or two well-known phrases serving as a sort of précis or epitome of
the whole, which people recognize even if they cannot repeat it word for word.
"We will fight them on the beaches"; "Four score and seven years ago"; "A day
that will live in infamy": these lines inspire with the context they recall.

Pericles exemplifies one important element of the summons. He reminds the
people of their essential qualities, or, at least, attributes those qualities to the people as if reminding them. Pericles boasts of the Athenians for their democratic institutions, their freedom, their meritocracy, their interest in culture. He insists on
Athenian "exceptionalism," as we have come to call it: "[O]ur constitution does
not copy the laws of neighboring states; we are rather a pattern to others than
imitators ourselves" (Thucydides, 112). Athenians cultivate "refinement without
extravagance, knowledge without effeminacy," and value wealth not for show but

for its use. Athenians alone, "fearless of consequences, confer their benefits not from calculation of expediency, but in the confidence of liberality" (113–14). It is for these reasons that Athens is a "school," that is, a model, for Hellas.

In his speech to the young men of Italy, Mazzini called for Italian patriotism out of love—"but let your love be the love taught you by Dante . . . the love of souls that aspire together" (*WGS*, 100). The mention of Dante—I imagine no equivalent American speech has ever mentioned Walt Whitman or Emily Dickinson—indicates that poetry, no less than love, belongs to Italianness. Lloyd George appealed to "every quality that Britain and its people possess." The very brevity of Nelson's comment points to English pride in understatement and unboastful dedication. It implicitly contrasts itself with Napoleon's grandiose appeals to the French. Lincoln's Gettysburg Address frames the war in terms not of a people's character but of its beliefs. For Americans are people not of a common origin but of a common idea: the proposition that all men are created equal, along with its consequence, government of the people, by the people, and for the people.

In his speech of 1941, once much more famous than it now is, Roosevelt's secretary of the interior Harold Ickes summoned Americans to resist totalitarianism in the name of essential American qualities. "What constitutes an American? Not color nor race nor religion. . . . An American is one who will sacrifice property, ease and security in order that he and his children may retain the rights of free men" (*WGS*, 568).

Who We Are Not and Who They Are

The summons often defines identity negatively, in terms of the enemy qualities that must be resisted. For Bernard of Chartres, the enemy is nothing less than the breath of corruption and unpunished wickedness. Lloyd George summons England to resist German "barbarism" and cynicism. Churchill summons us to fight against a "new dark age" made all the worse by "perverted science." "What is our policy?" Churchill asked right after promising "blood, toil, tears, and sweat." "To wage war against a monstrous tyranny, never surpassed in the dark, lamentable catalogue of human crime" (*ODQ*, 221). Ickes warns that the struggle today "is not merely another old-fashioned war. It is a counter revolution against our ideas and ideals, against our sense of justice, and our human values" (*WGS*, 569). What is at stake is the very possibility of an American future—"a future, not of concentration camps, not physical torture and mental straightjackets . . . a future when free men will live free lives" (*WGS*, 568).

Of course, rhetoric excoriating the monstrous evil of an enemy morally far worse than we are has been used so frequently that, even when true, it may ring false. It was common for those who heard such descriptions of the kaiser's Germans to doubt Churchill's charges against the Nazis. Over a million Soviet citizens defected to the Germans because they believed that since Stalin was the ultimate evil, Hitler could not be as bad as all that. Sometimes the devil is worse than he is painted. When the portraitist is another devil, the picture, no matter how truthful, seems like caricature.

When too freely used, the rhetoric of evil, like currency minted to profusion, loses its value.

The Time of Crisis

These are the times that try men's souls. The summer soldier and the sunshine patriot will, in this crisis, shrink from the service of his country; but he that stands it *now*, deserves the love and thanks of man and woman.

—Thomas Paine, *The American Crisis*, December 19, 1776 (*YBQ*, 576)

The summons understands its time as crisis. Everything depends on *this* moment in history. We live or die, and if we fail, the extreme of evil triumphs, perhaps forever. The tropes of eschatology shadow the rhetoric of crisis, but with one important qualification. There is no guarantee of victory.

"No one can guarantee success in war, only deserve it," Churchill wrote in 1940. Even Bernard of Chartres, who knows God's will, does not foresee an inevitable outcome. The summons rejects the language of inevitability, because if the result were already given, the moment would not be critical.

We may lose, and if we do, chaos is come again: such a perspective creates the maximum of urgency. Everything depends on *this* moment, "this little interval, this pause of life, (While yet our liberty and fates are doubtful)." When our child is dying, we do not count the cost or care about the odds, we commit all our energies to doing anything possible. We tax ourselves to "the last full measure," and know that, even if our efforts should fail, they were worth it. They are what we *must* do.

Caution, as counseled by proverbs, is entirely beside the point. However senseless, we shall resist even when it is hopeless; we shall fight them on the beaches, in the cities, on the hills; we shall never give in. Kennedy's inaugural represents the Cold War this way, as one of the few moments "in the long history of the world" in which the people have the task of "defending freedom in its hour of maximum danger."

As the summons understands it, the crisis stands out as a radically different moment, a time unlike other times. But it is not an isolated moment. On the contrary, it has meaning precisely because we are supremely aware of the heritage of the past, which may now be destroyed, and a future that may never come to be. Today we know that if the Greeks had lost at Thermopylae and Marathon, the culture that made the West would have perished. Jews affirm that if Moses had not split the Red Sea, they would still be slaves in Egypt. And just as the future of the past, which we can see, was at stake then, so an equally important future we cannot see is at stake now.

The hinge between past and future, a hinge that can turn either way: that is how the summons understands its moment. Garibaldi summons his soldiers "to finish worthily the marvelous design of the elect of twenty generations" (*WGS*, 102). If the British Empire exists for a thousand years, the people to come will recognize the importance of this moment and call it their finest hour. If we lose, government of, by, and for the people will perish from the earth.

Test and Temptation

The summons belongs to the literature of the *test*. Just as stories of martyrs narrate the test of the saint's devotion, and Greek romances test the hero's and heroine's fidelity, so crisis time tests a people as a whole. It's as if the devil had led the whole tribe into the wilderness to tempt them.

The most important thing about a test is that it cannot be avoided. To avoid it is already to fail it. Time will not wait. We must act in the nick of time, not a moment later, and the nick of time is now.

The temptation to which we must not yield is the natural desire for peace. The summons must ward off the desire to temporize, to delay a decision, or to accept a compromise. In his appeal to the House of Commons for resistance to Napoleon, William Pitt the Younger insisted that to negotiate now would be "to palsy at once the arms of Russia, or of Austria, or of any other country that might look to you for support." Even if we could reach a separate peace, Napoleon's next attempt would find us without allies and "would leave us only the option of submitting without a struggle to certain loss and disgrace" (*WGS*, 169–70). In his first speech to the Athenians, Pericles also equates negotiation with slavery (Thucydides, 80–85). Churchill stressed that it was precisely Chamberlain's attempt to negotiate "peace with honor," "peace in our time," that had made the crisis all the more critical. As Pitt stresses, the danger lies not in negotiation as such but in negotiation at the moment of test and crisis. At some moments we must stop talking and decide to act. If not we, who? And if not now, when?

We know that at the time that tries men's souls, we must be prepared to sacrifice everything. That is what the test requires. "What we obtain too cheaply, we esteem too lightly," Thomas Paine explains. "Heaven knows how to set a proper price upon its goods; and it would be strange indeed, if so celestial an article as *freedom* should not be highly rated" (*YBQ*, 576). We hear of no sunshine patriots at Iwo Jima.

The speaker of the summons is not himself the one tested. Rather, he speaks for the people. He voices not his own opinion but the resolve of all. A force larger than himself—God, history, freedom, the people—has made him its prophet. Pericles stresses that the Athenians chose him for the customary funeral oration. God has chosen Bernard to call upon Christians. The speaker of the summons ceases to be a mere individual and becomes a tribune.

Honor

The speaker summons the people to exhibit the qualities that will enable them to pass the test. Those qualities include not only their national characteristics, but also, and always, the courage to resist despair. Despair, fear, terror: these emotions represent yet another temptation, the carrion comfort on which we must refuse to feed. No matter the odds, we must not lose hope. According to Herodotus, a few hundred Spartans resisted a hundred myriad Persians, and we must be prepared to do the same.

One summons after another proclaims: the more desperate the situation, the more harmful is despair. The more fearful the forces arrayed against us, the less can we give in to fear. The only thing we have to fear is fear itself. "Don't despair, not even over the fact that you don't despair."[2] Churchill swears we will not flag or fail, and will fight the invaders in every street, hill, and field.

The test demands faith, courage, and daring. The crisis tests faith—"in all things faith"—because what makes it an existential moment in the first place is that defeat looks more than possible. However dire matters appear, we must believe that "unfading palms" await. Courage overcomes discouragement, and so enables a people to endure. The leader has nothing to offer but "blood, sweat, and tears," as Churchill and everyone else came to amend this famous phrase. Courage in turn inspires daring. The world is "the highway of our daring," Pericles tells the Athenians, and Danton implores the French assembly: "To conquer we have need to dare, to dare again, ever to dare!" (*WGS*, 77).

All these values depend on the one that sustains them: honor. Above all, the summons appeals to our sense of what is honorable and dishonorable. Honor requires above all that, regardless of circumstance, one does one's duty, and so these two concepts are inseparably linked. Pericles appeals to "courage, sense of duty, and a keen feeling of honor." England expects every man, not to be a brilliant and effective soldier, but to do his duty. People a thousand years from now will remember this as our finest hour if we "brace ourselves to our duty." Doing what one is supposed to do simply because that is what one does: that lesson is what Wellington meant when he (allegedly) said that "the battle of Waterloo was won on the playing fields of Eton."[3]

Honor, the resolve to do one's duty in the face of danger, constitutes a supremely aristocratic value. The summons calls upon even ordinary people to aspire to the values of aristocrats. It is as if Nelson is saying that each Englishman is an aristocrat by virtue of being English. Democracies appeal to a meritocracy of honor, which everyone may join if worthy. In every society, nothing earns dishonor so much as cowardice.

What Is That Honor?

But why be honorable? Many have regarded honor as an empty concept, a sham value used to get people to sacrifice their lives. "War, he sung, is toil and trouble; / Honor but an empty bubble."[4] Let others have the bubble, and me preserve my life. Honor is the opiate of the aristocrats.

Educated people often wince at the rhetoric of honor. When they hear the summons, they reflexively doubt that the moment is as critical as all that. No intellectual ever lost the respect of his peers by underestimating the need for war. Even when it is needed, honor is not the point. The summons may be used to rally the unwashed, but for intellectuals it is an embarrassment.

As wise sayings hear scorners, the summons knows this discrediting voice. That voice sounds like Falstaff:

> Can honour set to a leg? No. Or an arm? Or take away the grief of a wound? No. Honour hath no skill in surgery then? No. What is honour? A word. What's in that word "honour"? What is that honour? Air. A trim reckoning! Who hath it? He that died a-Wednesday. Doth he feel it? Doth he hear it? No. 'Tis insensible, then? Yea, to the dead. But will it not live with the living? No. Why? Detraction will not suffer it. Therefore I'll none of it. Honour is a mere scutcheon—and so ends my catechism.[5]

Why suffer without needing to? Why die if death can be avoided? The summons claims that for life to be meaningful we must esteem some value as worth suffering and dying for. The summons believes in heroism.

Falstaff, of course, does not believe in heroism at all. The dead could not possibly benefit from honor. They do not sense it. Save your blood, sweat, and tears. By contrast, the summons presumes that meaning comes from life as a whole, and the whole of any story can be assessed only with its ending. As Solon tells Croesus, one can regard no life as fortunate—that is, well lived—until it is over. What is more, in this view a person can be harmed after his death because his reputation is part of him. That is why heroes who value honor die for glory. Let me die but my glory live on. Only a cynic regards monuments solely in terms of their function for the living. Epics see life entirely in terms of glory (*kleos*). The summons calls us to a life and death of epic significance.

The Battlefield

Where better than a battlefield to celebrate sacrifice and proclaim the glory it has earned? The tomb or monument of the honored dead: this locale particularly favors the summons. There Pericles extols the sacrifice and inspires the Athenians to do what these men, and all heroic ancestors, have done. They have achieved that "renown which never grows old," not just in this place and at this monument, but at "that noblest of shrines wherein their glory is laid up to be eternally remembered upon every occasion on which deed or story shall be commemorated. For heroes have the whole earth for their tomb" (Thucydides, 115).

It is for us, the living, to demonstrate that these dead have not died in vain. Lincoln at Gettysburg doubtless had Pericles' funeral oration in mind. Pericles begins with what would become a commonplace of the genre: words cannot adequately commemorate the dead. Words are needed, but they are too easy and must always fall short. The heroes have given their lives, but in speaking of them we risk nothing. "The worth that displayed itself in deeds," declares Pericles, should be honored by deeds.

Lincoln affirms the propriety of commemorating the dead but also the larger sense in which we, speaker and audience, "cannot dedicate—we cannot consecrate—we cannot hallow—this ground." Because honor is more than a word, words can never be equal to it.

Modesty

Pointing to the dead and their deeds, Lincoln's speech directs attention away from itself. We are asked to think not of his words but of the events that have prompted them.

A summons must strive for modesty, and the speaker must above all avoid self-aggrandizement. To the extent that it calls attention to itself, and to the extent that we sense the orator's display of his rhetorical powers, the summons fails. This genre idealizes a peculiar modesty. Its rhetorical power seems to arise solely from the glory of the heroes it celebrates and from its sacred purposes: honoring the dead, inspiring courage, and summoning resolve.

The fame of Lincoln's address derives in part from its apparent, or real, unself-consciousness. It seems as if Lincoln did not know he had composed a masterpiece, and that moment of ignorance makes the speech a still greater masterpiece. Whether the received story is true or folklore does not matter, because, no matter how truthful, its significance is mythic.

The main event that day was an oration by Edward Everett, and Lincoln, as president, was to provide just a few concluding dedicatory remarks. He was to speak briefly, and did. The address's brevity achieved the peculiar modesty to which the genre aspires. The many legends that grew up around the speech, including its composition at the last moment on the back of an envelope, contribute to the same effect. The very fact that such myths arose indicates the genre's aspiration. There are no such legends surrounding successful witticisms, proverbs, or maxims. The summons, like courage itself, disdains the fame it wins.

Kennedy's Long History of the World

I do not know whether my reaction is unique, but John F. Kennedy's inaugural address strikes me as failing in just the way the Gettysburg Address succeeds. The president strains to represent the moment as more critical than it was in order to deliver a speech like Churchill's. "In the long history of the world," he proclaimed, "only a few generations have been granted the role of defending freedom in its hour of maximum danger." Why exactly was January 1961 such an "hour," and why precisely is this generation one of few in world history? What made *this* moment in the Cold War, which had been going on for years and, so far as could be told, would continue for many years more, different from all the others? For that matter, did this generation face a danger as grave as that faced by the generations who fought World War I, lived through the

Great Depression, resisted Hitler, or died in Korea? Kennedy might have done better to speak of a *century* testing freedom, but that would have diminished the urgency he claimed for 1961.

"I do not shrink from this possibility—I welcome it." Kennedy's reference to himself strikes a false note. If this moment is so critical in the history of freedom, it does not matter whether he, John F. Kennedy, welcomes it or not. The fact that he thinks that matters makes the declaration of crisis seem contrived.

Once these doubts arise, the speech borders on the pretentious. The torch that is passed, the trumpet that summons, the light that glows: these clichés call attention to themselves as rhetoric. The self-conscious reversals ("Let us never negotiate out of fear, but let us never fear to negotiate"; "Ask not what your country can do for you, ask what you can do for your country") read as if the young president was showing off how well he could make a speech.

In retrospect, one wants to ask: Did Kennedy's taste for crises help create them? How much did it affect his decisions in the Bay of Pigs invasion and the Cuban missile crisis? Could his rhetorical promise—to pay any price and bear any burden to "support any friend, oppose any foe to assure the survival and success of liberty"—have shaped his thinking about Vietnam? In a crisis, one needs a summons, but a needless summons can create a crisis.

Honor Preens and Glory Kills

In *War and Peace*, which satirizes heroic pronouncements, Alexander and Napoleon preen themselves on their own rhetoric. In the received account of Alexander's response to Napoleon that Tolstoy had at his disposal (Mikhailovsky-Danilevsky), the tsar, learning at a ball of Napoleon's invasion, utters heroic words that Russians all remember:

> Then the Emperor sent for Shishkov, the Secretary of State, and said to him: "It is necessary to write an order to the army immediately, and also to send to Count Saltykov in Petersburg, telling him of the enemy's invasion. Say that I will not make peace as long as a single enemy remains on our soil."[6]

Tolstoy mocks these grand words as he mocks conventional heroism in all its forms. He does so by making Alexander so proud of his own words that he repeats and calls attention to them.

To be sure, when Balashev informs Alexander that Napoleon's army has invaded, Alexander spontaneously replies: "To enter Russia without declaring war! I will not make peace so long as a single armed foe remains in my country"

(*W&P*, 739). But having said these bold words, Alexander becomes mightily impressed by them, and contrives to show off his great rhetoric on every possible occasion. The passage derived from Milhailovsky-Danilevsky reads: "On returning home from the ball at two o'clock in the morning, he sent for his secretary Shishkov and told him to write an order to the troops, and a rescript to Field Marshall Saltykov, in which he *insisted on inserting the words* that he would never make peace so long as a single armed Frenchman remained on Russian soil" (739; italics added). It is almost as if the rescript were a pretext for the bombast. The next day, Alexander summons Balashev and entrusts him with a letter to deliver to Napoleon. "As he dismissed Balashev, he repeated to him his declaration that he would never make peace so long as a single armed foe remained on Russian soil, and told him that *he was to repeat those words* to Napoleon without fail" (740; italics added). By this time heroic pronouncement has become self-indulgent farce.

The Dissident's Summons

The genre's rule of modesty does not apply to one type of summons. Rather than direct attention away from itself to the deeds of others, this type of summons calls attention to itself.

For the dissident's summons, as we may call it, words are as important as deeds because they *are* deeds, often the only possible deeds. Their speakers do not describe the courage of others, they exhibit courage by their speech or writing. In the face of danger, the dissident dares voice what others are afraid to say. He enunciates heresy and risks the consequences. In doing so, he places himself, usually deliberately, in the tradition of the Hebrew prophets and of ancient predecessors extending back to Socrates.

If the dissident summons succeeds, the heretic may become a heresiarch, the leader or symbol of a new movement. He must exhibit courage to qualify for leadership. Martin Luther's famous refusal at the Diet of Worms to retract his beliefs ("Here I stand. I can do no other") draws on a tradition of refusing to deny one's faith under pressure. It became, and not just for Protestants, an iconic utterance, symbolizing all courageous dissent. Thomas More, his Catholic counterpart, demonstrated heroic faith not just by his example but also by his words. Roper's biography reports that he said of the Tower, "Is not this house as nigh heaven as my own?" and even at the block bid the executioner not to be afraid: "[M]y neck is very short; take heed therefore thou strike not awry, for saving of thine honesty" (*ODQ*, 548). It is entirely possible to identify with both Luther and More if one thinks not of the beliefs they professed but of the brave dissent they exhibited. As the summons is a genre of its own, so dissent can itself be an ideology.

So much do we demand the fulfillment of this pattern that when a hero does recant to save his life, legends to the contrary arise. Shown the instruments of torture, Galileo acceded to the Inquisition's demand that he renounce his adherence to the Copernican belief in the Earth's motion. But legend tells us that Galileo then whispered, "Eppur si muove" (And yet it moves), thereby fulfilling the genre's demands. A moment's reflection ought to tell us that there could be no evidence for such an event. If no one heard it, it would not have a witness, and if others did hear it, he would have been an idiot to have said it. Such legends show us the genre's expectations and the strength of their appeal.

Soviet and East European dissidents risked their lives to speak out against their regimes, and many were executed, tortured, or imprisoned in insane asylums. Our admiration for them seems more than warranted. Nevertheless, it also reflects the magnetic power of the dissenter's image. For obvious reasons, the image figured prominently in Russian culture even before the Soviets. Soviet dissidents used the genre's conventions and located themselves in its traditions. Often enough they answered, and repeated, earlier dissidents' calls to speak out. Words responding to words and conjuring words: the dissident's summons reflects its core belief, the power of the word.

To use Václav Havel's phrase, the dissident's summons demonstrates "the power of the powerless."[7] Accepting a peace prize in Germany, Havel observed of lines like his own: "I really do inhabit a system in which words are capable of shaking the entire structure of government, where words can prove mightier than ten military divisions" (*ODQ*, 374).

Words matter. I speak, therefore we are. Solzhenitsyn dedicated his Nobel lecture to this conception of the word. He stressed the responsibility of those who have mastered words—writers—not to give way to fashionable cynicism. Rather, they must respect their gift by acting with faith, courage, and honor, by risking their lives in the name of basic human values.

> The simple act of an ordinary courageous man is not to take part, not to support lies! Let *that* come into the world and even reign over it, but not through me. Writers and artists can do more: they can vanquish lies. . . . Lies can stand up against much in the world, but not against art. . . . In Russian, proverbs about truth are favorites. They persistently express the considerable, bitter, grim experience of the people, often astonishingly:
>
> One word of truth outweighs the world.[8]

The Summons and Long Forms: History and Drama

Remember, O my friends, the laws, the rights,

The generous plan of power delivered down,

From age to age, by your renowned forefathers,

(So dearly bought, the price of so much blood,)

Oh let it never perish in your hands!

But piously transmit it to your children.

Do thou, great liberty, inspire our souls,

And make our lives in thy possession happy,

Or our deaths glorious in thy just defense,   —Cato, in Addison's *Cato*[9]

Among longer works, histories and biographies offer the readiest way to develop this genre's worldview. The summons thrives in stories combining valorous "deeds and sayings." The narrative portion of these stories provides the crisis to which the hero responds, and the words record the lesson for us to remember. Reading them, honor and glory inspire us. Herodotus begins the first Western history: "This is a publication of the researches of Herodotus of Halicarnassus, in order that the actions of men may not be effaced by time, nor the great and wondrous deeds displayed both by Greeks and barbarians deprived of renown" (*H*, 1). Plutarch hopes his *Lives* offer us "the clearest discoveries of virtue and vice in men" (*PL*, 801).

In much the same spirit, national histories often preserve the people's finest actions and greatest sayings. They piously transmit them to children. At critical moments such as these, the histories instruct, someone rose to the occasion and inspired us to show our true qualities. Those qualities always include the heroic virtues of courage and honor.

Valerius Maximus's first-century classic, *Memorable Deeds and Sayings*, offers the reader an easy compendium of great stories and sayings from many sources. "Other authors have dealt with these stories at great length, but this makes it impossible to learn about them in a short period of time, so I have decided to make a selection of them from the most famous writers."[10] The book enjoyed immense popularity in antiquity and, it seems, was one of the most widely copied prose works of the Middle Ages and Renaissance. It served as a short course in Roman virtues and, as one critic has observed, became "a sort of reference book for would-be gentlemen . . . who needed a quick exemplary history to provide a sort of 'instant ancestry'" (Valerius, xxi n.52). As we have seen, Roman history became a sort of instant ancestry for many European peoples. Cato was French, English, and American, as well as Roman.

The "deeds and sayings" in Valerius include many examples of courage, endurance, and honor in a crisis. Its modern translator gives us a sense of its appeal when he observes: "Fortunately, we do not need Valerius to teach us how to live. We have gradually developed our own traditions . . . of role models. We have Gandhi and Mandela as well as Brutus the Liberator and Cato of Utica" (xiii). Evidently, we still need the sort of inspiration Valerius and Plutarch provide, even if we do not expect historians or scholarly biographers to provide it. We rely on journalism and various other sources for uplifting entertainment. The deeds and sayings of our modern heroes circulate in versions that we regard as just possibly true or more or less true. In either case, we pledge ourselves to follow their example and realize their dream.

The Literature of Drama

The will to do, the soul to dare.   —Walter Scott (*BFQ15*, 430)

Anecdotes concerning critical moments also shape historical plays, novels, and narrative poems—broadly speaking, the literature of dramatic speech and action. As fictions, these forms offer ample opportunity to imagine situations to which a summons responds, but as quasi-factual they have nevertheless contributed to national legend. It is as if Richard the Lion-hearted, Rob Roy, Henry V, and General Kutuzov actually behaved and spoke as Scott, Shakespeare, and Tolstoy imagined them.

As Henry V, the former Prince Hal rejects Falstaff's depreciation of honor. Before Agincourt, Henry expands on the tropes of the summons. For him, nothing less resembles a mere word or feels more palpable than honor.

Herodotus relates that before Thermopylae, Dieneces, a Spartan soldier, heard that "when the Persians let fly their arrows, they would obscure the sun by the multitude of the shafts, so great were their number." "Not at all alarmed at this, . . . holding in contempt the numbers of the Medes," Dieneces replied: All the better, for in that case the Spartans would "fight in the shade" (*H*, 488). But even Dieneces does not wish the odds against the Spartans to be still longer, as Henry does. The famous line about "we few, we happy few, we band of brothers" occurs just after Henry proclaims, "the fewer men, the greater the honor," and bids that anyone without the stomach for the fight should be permitted, nay encouraged, to leave. So precious is honor that he is jealous of sharing it. He craves it, covets it, almost sinfully. "But if it be a sin to covet honour, / I am the most offending soul alive." Henry looks forward to appreciating Saint Crispin's day as the day of Henry's glory. "Then shall our names, / Familiar in the mouth as household words" be celebrated. "And Crispin Crispian shall ne'er go by / From this day to the ending of the world / But we shall in it be remembered."[11]

Of course, these words occur in a play written long after the event. Henry's speech is addressed to an audience that, unlike Henry, knows the outcome and the truth of his prediction. The drama makes the speech a self-fulfilling prophecy. Our attendance at this speech confirms that Henry earned the glory he anticipated. Shakespeare's double perspective, which allows us to hear the words simultaneously at the moment of crisis and in the time of remembrance, provides the answer to Falstaff's mockery. It also contrasts with Qohelet's despair that "there is no remembrance of former things" (Ecclesiastes 1:11).

The Devil's Summons

As writers have recognized, the power of the summons makes it subject to abuse. After all, evil leaders also summon their people to what they see as right. "Italy! Italy!! Entirely and universally Fascist! The Italy of the black shirt revolution, rise to your feet, let the cry of your determination rise to the skies," Mussolini addressed his people on the eve of the Ethiopian invasion. "It is the cry of Italy which goes beyond the mountains and the seas out into the great world. It is the cry of justice and of victory" (*WGS*, 489). We cannot hear Mussolini's words without a shiver. Did Churchill's summons sound to the Fascists as Mussolini's sounds to us? How did Southerners respond to the Gettysburg Address?

We must beware of what most moves us. The devil hath power to make a thrilling speech. So Milton reminds us when Satan and the demons speak in books 1 and 2 of *Paradise Lost*. They use the summons to forge the demons' identity and rouse them to further resistance. The evil multitudes respond to Satan's defiant call:

> He spake: and to confirm his words, out-flew
> Millions of flaming swords drawn from the thighs
> Of mighty Cherubim; the sudden blaze
> Far round illumin'd hell: highly they rag'd
> Against the Highest, and fierce with grasped Arms
> Clash'd on thir sounding shields the din of war,
> Hurling defiance toward the Vault of Heav'n.[12]

The devils resolve to resist the tyranny of heaven, never give in to the deceit that tempted their attempt against it, and forge from the depths of defeat a new resolve. Precisely because things seem so hopeless, they can earn still more glory. "From this descent / Celestial Virtues rising will appear / More glorious and more dread than from no fall" (Milton, *Paradise Lost*, bk. 2, ll. 14–16).

Milton makes the comparison with heroic literature explicit. When the devils, "downcast and damp," despair, the sight of their chief "not in despair" allows them to find "themselves not lost / In loss itself." Then Satan, "his wonted pride / Soon recollecting, with high words, that bore / Semblance of worth, not substance, gently rais'd / Thir fainting courage, and dispell'd thir fears." Soon the devils respond to "the warlike sound / Of Trumpets and Clarions." They move "in perfect Phalanx" to the Dorian mood of music

> such as raised
> To highth of noblest temper Heroes old
> Arming to Battle, and instead of rage
> Deliberate valor breath'd, firm and unmov'd
> With dread of death to flight or foul retreat,
> Nor wanting power to mitigate and swage
> With solemn torches, troubl'd thoughts, and chase
> Anguish and doubt and fear and sorrow and pain
> From mortal or immortal minds. (bk. 1, ll. 523–59)

If immortals cannot resist such a call, people must be all the more wary of its "power to mitigate and swage anguish and doubt."

The Summons of Regret

Sometimes the failure to heed the summons, duty neglected from cowardice, provides the theme for a speech. Such a summons of regret, as we might call it, reproaches the people: We feared to answer the call, and that is why we face destruction.

The most powerful lines of *Beowulf* speak this way. Wiglaf summons the Gaets to contemplate the consequences of their cowardice and loss of honor. "Then a stern rebuke was bound to come / from the young warrior to the ones who had been coward. / Wiglaf, son of Weobstan, spoke / Disdainfully and in disappointment."[13] "Anyone ready to admit the truth" would tell you of all Beowulf did for us, he declares, "but when the worst happened / too few rallied around the prince":

> So it is goodbye now to all you know and love
> On your home ground, the open-handedness,
> The giving of war-swords. Every one of you

With freeholds of land, our whole nation,
Will be dispossessed, once princes from beyond
Get tidings of how you turned and fled
And disgraced yourselves. A warrior will sooner
Die than live a life of shame. (ll. 2884–91)

The Summons Replies to Other Short Genres

The summons expresses a sense of life radically at odds with that of other short genres. For the summons, honor and high ideals define all life's meaning. By contrast, wit mocks ideals. One type of maxim suspects them of self-love, while the other treats them as exercises in futility.

The summons knows these objections. It does not so much answer as disdain them; but to disdain something is also to be aware of it. The sounds of mockery and the voice of skepticism leave their mark, which we detect in the very effort to ignore them.

To the disparagement of honor as self-love, the summons tacitly replies: so much the better for self-love, if it leads to cherishing one's honor. It answers the wit's cynicism by pointing to courageous deeds, compared with which witticisms seem trivial. Charged with futility, the summons leaves no doubt that the results of such thinking are paralysis and destruction. No one wants Qohelet at Gettysburg. The difference between a world conquered by the enemy and the present one, however numerous its flaws, provides all the justification that resistance requires. For the summons, there is no doubt that struggle matters; perhaps it is what matters most. Struggle is what life is all about.

In *War and Peace*, Bilibin the wit mocks Prince Andrei's desire to rejoin the army at its darkest hour. Either you will not reach the army in time or you will share in its defeat, he advises, but Prince Andrei replies as heroism demands, with cool disdain.

> "I cannot discuss it," said prince Andrei coldly, but he thought: "I am going in order to save the army."
> "*Mon cher*, you are a hero," said Bilibin. (*W&P*, 208)

Bilibin's reply is of course ironic, as is everything he says. But Andrei is nothing if not courageous. And, interestingly enough, he also responds to Napoleon's summons to French soldiers. Andrei mentally repeats Napoleon's words, "and they aroused in him amazement at the genius of his hero, a feeling of wounded pride, and a hope of glory. 'And should there be nothing left but to die?' he thought. 'Well, if need be, I shall do it no worse than another'" (209). Andrei thinks of dying itself as another contest for honor.

Before Austerlitz, Andrei contemplates honor and glory, which he recognizes can be terrible goals. Unlike most heroes, he does not shrink from the dark side of heroism:

> I shall never tell anyone, but, my God, what do I do if I care for nothing but glory and men's love? Death, wounds, the loss of my family—nothing holds any terror for me. And dear and precious as many persons are to me—father, sister, wife, those who are most dear, I would sacrifice them all, dreadful and unnatural as it may seem, for a moment of glory, of triumph over men, for the love of men I do not know and shall never know. . . . Yes, that's how it is, I love and value nothing but triumph over all of them, value only this mysterious power and glory that is hovering over me in the mist. (324–25)

Glory can be sensed, directly and palpably. Andrei knows that he is not just answering a call to defend his homeland and thereby earn glory. No, glory has become a goal in itself. Tolstoy regards this transformation of a noble urge as terrible.

So does Andrei seven years later, the night before Borodino. He blames chivalry, honor, and the cult of military glory—all valued by heroic pronouncements—for all the slaughter and destruction. Guided by these values, soldiers

> "meet, as we shall meet tomorrow, to murder one another; they kill and maim tens of thousands of men, and then hold thanksgiving services for having slaughtered so many (they even exaggerate the number). . . . How God can look down and hear them!" cried Prince Andrei in a shrill, piercing voice. (933)

Paradoxically, Andrei's horror at the glorification of killing leads him to want the army to take no prisoners, just kill.

How does horror at bloodshed lead to abandoning all humane rules of war? As Andrei sees the matter, those rules belong to the cult of honor and chivalry, which cause most wars. "Eliminate the humbug," he demands. "If there were none of this chivalry in war, we should go to war only when it was worth going to certain death, as now" (932).

Prosaic Heroism

At Austerlitz, Andrei behaves as heroically as he has hoped. Then, unexpectedly, he is thrown on his back and contemplates the clouds drifting peacefully across the battlefield sky. The sky has always been there, but he has not seen it. The sight of it teaches him that "all is vanity, all is delusion except those infinite heavens. There is nothing but that." This line alludes to the words of Ecclesiastes, but Andrei detects the possibility of another meaning not yet discovered. That meaning, Tolstoy makes clear, resides where Andrei is least likely to look for it, in the common practices of daily life.

In *War and Peace*, the inspiring words of Napoleon and Alexander sound empty, but not because the author means to reject heroism. Rather, he redefines it. For Tolstoy, heroism is to be found where adherents of conventional accounts least expect it, in ordinary acts of ordinary men and, especially, women.

Truly heroic acts respond to no summons but the heart's whispers, and they earn no glory.

▮ THE THOUGHT ▮

That observation is my own;—and was struck out by me this very rainy day,
March 26, 1759, and betwixt the hours of nine and ten in the morning.

—Tristram Shandy[14]

Expansive Brevity

We can best understand the genre I call the "thought" as an opposite of the summons. While it is common for an author of one short genre to compose others, it is rare for anyone to master both the summons and the thought. They belong to different worlds, both formally and conceptually. Indeed, in one key respect, the thought stands apart from all other short genres.

Short genres are by definition brief, but thoughts seem to test the limits of brevity. Aphorisms, we feel, should be memorizable, but some thoughts barely qualify. For this reason, quotation anthologies usually include relatively few of them, even though the form has appealed to several great writers. They more readily find a home in anthologies of "great thoughts," or other collections that include more than can be accommodated by ordinary memory. Thoughts may be included apologetically, even guiltily, testifying to the presence of the norm they may violate. Thoughts find their identity on the boundaries of brevity.

Or we might say that thoughts embody a paradox: they belong to the family of short genres while more closely resembling an unfinished longer one. The masters of the form have made the most of this paradox.

Aristotle explained that prose can be either "free-running" or "compact." Free-running style, like most of Herodotus, "has no natural stopping-places, and comes to a stop only because there is no more to say on the subject. This style is unsatisfying just because it goes on indefinitely" and people like to see a stopping point ahead of them, much as runners pace themselves toward a known goal. By contrast, compact style is easier to follow, more readily remembered, and more likely to satisfy its audience because it "has in itself a beginning and an end being at the same time not too big to be taken in at a glance. Language of this kind . . . is satisfying because it is the reverse of indefinite." With the compact but not the free-flowing style, the audience "always feels that it is grasping something and has reached some definite conclusion."[15]

The thought straddles this boundary. It works as a short genre in a free-running style. It is hard to say just where the thought as a genre ends and the essay begins. Many resemble the germ, or else the residue, of an essay.

Brevity is the soul of wit, but belongs to the thought only half accidentally. No one contemplates writing expansive apothegms, wordy proverbs, or digressive maxims, but thoughts appeal precisely because they seem to have no natural stopping point. They break off rather than end.

How can such digressive brevity prove appealing? Just because thoughts seem unfinished, they capture the very process of thinking.

Thinking in the Present

The rhetoric of thoughts tends to diffuseness. Poised on a threshold, thoughts seem ready to head off in more than one direction but to be hesitating which one to choose. They remain uncommitted, and we catch them in the act of choosing. One could not speak a summons this way.

The thought records, or purports to record, thinking itself. Like the witticism, it has not been prepared in advance, but unlike the witticism, it does not emerge fully formed. The thought seems to flounder, to question itself, and to struggle for clarity of insight and expression. We catch the authors as an idea first occurs to them and observe their process of thinking it through.

Authors may try out several formulations, each expressing a somewhat different idea, and they may explore implications first in one direction, then in another. They know the idea may entail surprising results when applied to different topics and have not yet decided whether to believe it. This not-yet-ness belongs to the form's essence. So does openness to starting over. Authors often seem to backtrack, to reword, and to be about to try again.

For the reader, the thought excites an almost voyeuristic interest. *This* is how the author's mind worked before he or she was willing to share achievements. Thinking seems to be going on in the real present of the creative process, and the thought apparently records that process, with all its fits and starts. If the author has covered up a logical flaw by artful language or an abrupt change of topic, we detect him or her doing so. We are let in on a secret.

The thought offers much the same pleasure as rough drafts of a great novel, but in considerably fewer words. Thoughts may be as short as a small paragraph or extend considerably longer.

Jewels in Sand

Occasionally the author hits upon an expression that, if removed from the flow of thinking, could stand on its own as an apothegm or maxim. In that case, anthologizers may reproduce the happy phrase by itself and present it as if composed as a free-standing work. In so doing, they reassign it from one short genre to another and so change its meaning. The author may seem to be more committed than he or she was. The tone of "what if," present in the untransmuted thought, disappears from the extracted apothegm or maxim.

Many of Pascal's well-known apothegms and maxims have undergone such a change. We may regard them as the joint product of Pascal still working things out and an editor searching for a presentable finished product. We may choose to take such an extract both ways, valuing it as a jewel adroitly set and as one we have just discovered in the sand.

Some thoughts make it into anthologies without condensation. Large volumes of quotations, like Bartlett's or the *Oxford Book of Quotations*, can devote space to unabbreviated thoughts, especially when they are relatively short. Or they may shorten a thought without losing its essential spirit. Nevertheless, the relative length of thoughts makes it more convenient to include them in anthologies devoted to a single author, where we are prepared to encounter selections of varying length. We may also find thoughts copied into an author's commonplace book, which may later be published and then mined by other authors. Or thoughts may find a home in collections of "great thoughts." Such collections, like the famous one compiled by George Seldes, may begin as an anthology of favorite short aphorisms but then, step by step, and edition by edition, come to include longer and less finished extracts.[16]

Such a complicated history, which we can sometimes sense, seems to continue the author's own struggle for expression. The author gave birth to the thought but it developed on its own. It may even expand beyond the limits of any short genre. That possibility is always present, and constitutes an essential part of the thought as a genre testing the limits of brevity.

In fact, Pascal's *Pensées*—from which I have taken the term "thought" to designate this genre—rewards reading not in two but in three distinct ways: for brief apothegms, for longer "thoughts," and taken as a whole, as a notebook for an unwritten book we may try to guess at.

We sense Pascal aiming at a finished work, but Lichtenberg, another great master of the thought, did not imagine using his "waste-books" that way. Rather, he recorded thoughts as they occurred to him for his own private use. Here, too, readers experience the voyeuristic pleasure of being there while thinking is happening. For obvious reasons, diaries and letters lend themselves to the thought, as would any kind of expression understood to be tentative, experimental, or not yet ready for public inspection.

Thought versus Summons: Two Kinds of Trial

The author of a thought withholds full commitment to it. As Bakhtin would say, he has not yet "signed" it, and may not do so. But nothing could express more commitment than a summons.

By its very nature, the summons addresses a public, whereas the thought is, or at least pretends to be, private. The thought sprawls, while the summons strives for concision so that key phrases can resonate in memory. Standing before the House of Commons, Churchill did not fumble to express an offer of only sanguinary, horrendous conflict, along with lots of hard work without immediate reward, and while we are at it, expressions of bodily effort and fatigue, and, how shall I put it? lots of sorrow, either expressed or left in silence. No, Churchill had nothing to offer but blood, toil, tears, and sweat, and even that expression proved not economical enough. He and the public soon amended it to the much better "blood, sweat, and tears."

Churchill and the summons imagine time as a trial, a test of the people. Pascal's thoughts imagine time as a trial in a quite different sense: it is a pause for trying things out.

In the course of writing, Pascal sometimes finds himself surprised by an objection that has just occurred to him. He tries to state it cogently, and then to see if he can answer it. Addressing the nation or the House of Commons, Churchill will not be surprised. The summons calls upon its audience to cease questioning and devote all its energies to resistance.

The thought invites revision, and continually revises itself. The summons will not be shaken; we can refuse it but cannot alter it. The summons is final, the thought unfinalizable. The thought is always ready to retreat, while the summons will never surrender.

Only one conclusion can be drawn from a successful summons: the resolve to fight. But it is part of the very nature of a thought that it could be the midpoint of several arguments with different conclusions. It resembles a posting station where travelers come from many directions and depart to many destinations.

Thought and Apothegm

Both the apothegm and the thought intimate further development, but in quite different ways. The apothegm is a complete statement about the impossibility of complete understanding, but the thought is itself incomplete. The apothegm asserts the fragmentariness of human knowledge but is not, like the thought, fragmentary. When we follow an apothegm leading from mystery to mystery, we are still within the apothegm, but the thought reaches outside itself.

Nietzsche's Experiments

The very sign of *great* health, an excess that gives the free spirit the dangerous privilege of being permitted to live *experimentally* and to offer himself to adventure.
—Nietzsche (*HATH*, 7–8)

Not all thoughts reach the public contrary to the author's intent. Just as one can write a "private" diary with the intent of publishing it, so one can compose thoughts as a literary form. An author who has read Pascal and Lichtenberg might be motivated to strive consciously for the effect they achieved unwittingly. That, in fact, is what Nietzsche, the third great master of the form, did. He discovered in this experimental genre the vehicle for his appeal to "live experimentally." Often enough, his thoughts reflect on the genre's premises, above all the peculiar value of incompleteness and sheer process:

> *Unfinished thoughts.* Just as youth and childhood have value *in and of themselves* (as much as the prime of life) and are not to be considered a mere transition or bridge, so too do unfinished thoughts have their own value . . . as if the road to various other thoughts were still open. We stand on the threshold. . . . [I]t is as if a lucky trove of profundity were about to be found. The poet anticipates something of the thinker's pleasure in finding a central thought and in doing so makes us covetous, so that we snatch at it. But it flutters past over our heads, showing the loveliest butterfly wings—and yet it slips away from us. (*HATH*, 125)

> If one considers, then, that a man's every action, not only his books, in some way becomes the occasion for other actions, decisions, and thoughts; that everything which is happening is inextricably tied to everything which will happen; then one understands the real *immortality*, that of movement. (*HATH*, 125–26)

> *The incomplete as the effective.* As figures in relief sometimes strike the imagination so powerfully because they seem to be on the point of stepping out of the wall and, hindered by something, suddenly come to a stop; so the relieflike, incomplete presentation of a thought, or a whole philosophy, is sometimes more effective than its exhaustive realization. More is left to the effort of the viewer; he is incited to continue developing what comes so intensely lit and shaded into relief before him, to think it through, and to overcome himself the obstacle that hindered until then its complete emergence. (*HATH*, 120)

As childhood is more than a preparation, so the process of thinking has value in itself. An arrested thought may belong to our literary heritage.

At the end of a life, earlier moments may seem to have been leading inevitably to later events, but that impression is a fallacy of retrospection. We see the possibilities realized and not the ones that merely could have been realized, and so we mistake invisibility for nonexistence. To understand a child is to grasp his or her potentials and to imagine the different things that he or she could become.

As a child contains many potentials, so a thought leaves open "the road to various other thoughts." We stand on the threshold of difference, experience potentials in all their multiplicity, and mentally project first one development and then another. Yet the best thoughts still escape us; we snatch at them, but like beautiful butterflies, they show us only a glimpse of wing and fly away.

The incomplete effort can stimulate our imagination as powerfully as a finished product, much as a sketch or cartoon for a painting may have a beauty all its own. That beauty does not arise from considering it only as a finished work of a different kind—a drawing—but also as an idea in development. So, too, a figure in relief can be either just that, a complete artistic work, or something quite different, an arrested moment of an incomplete process, like "an insect in amber" (*HATH*, 126).

Reading a thought, we find ourselves on a road, not to a distant destination securely ahead of us, but to more crossroads, more choices, and no already determined outcome. Perhaps all that lies ahead are more roads. Nietzsche emphasized that the reader of a thought desires to continue the author's work and see where the thought might go. The reader wants "to think it through, and to overcome himself the obstacle that hindered until then its complete emergence." But whatever extension the reader makes will be just one of many that could have been made; and he is invited to return and try again.

Lichtenberg: On the Boundary

Lichtenberg's name for the notebooks containing his thoughts, "waste-books," adapts a term from English, as one of these thoughts explains:

> Merchants have a waste-book (*Sudelbuch, Klitterbuch*, I think it is in German) in which they enter from day to day everything they have bought and sold, all mixed up together in disorder; from this it is transferred to the journal, in which everything is arranged more systematically; and finally it arrives in the ledger, in double entry after the Italian manner of book-keeping. . . . This deserves to be

imitated by the scholar. First a book in which I inscribe everything just as I see it or as my thoughts prompt me, then this can be transferred to another where the materials are more ordered and segregated, and the ledger can then contain a connected construction and the elucidation of the subject that flows from it expressed in an orderly fashion.[17]

Lichtenberg's waste-books record first impressions. Ideas appear as they occur to him, "all mixed up together in disorder." Most are destined to be discarded, but a few will be reworked and presented in a more "connected construction." Reading Lichtenberg, we catch his thinking on the fly.

Critics have credited Lichtenberg with introducing the aphorism into German literature, but unlike his French predecessors, he intended to compose no such thing. He wrote the waste-books for his own use, and they became a collection of "aphorisms" only posthumously. Most of the best-known ones appear in the midst of a lot of "waste."

Some ideas occur several times, as he works them out in different ways, and the more famous ones have less felicitous counterparts.[18] The reader sees the preparatory steps and the in-between states of what became a great saying.

"I have jotted down a host of little thoughts and sketches," Lichtenberg writes, "but they are awaiting not so much a final revision as a few more glimpses of the sun that will help them blossom" (Lichtenberg, 28). The jottings are not close to being finished and require not another look but enough glimpses to make them blossom into something unexpected. An in-between state commands interest not only because it can develop more than one way but also because in-betweenness commands an interest all its own.

As we might have guessed from his description of waste-books, many of Lichtenberg's thoughts concern the fascination of in-between states. He draws our attention to the interesting time "between dreaming and waking, and at the drawing near of the divinity Bacchus" when "the recollection of long-departed sensual delights often leaps in our souls with quite heavy ardor" (29). Transitionality, indefiniteness, and contradiction, with their suggestion of the unknown, intrigue him: "Man is perhaps half spirit and half matter, as the polyp is half plant and half animal. The strangest creatures lie on the boundary" (48).

Like each person, humanity must be understood as "in between." Lichtenberg expresses irritation at someone who regards people as already defined: "He is another of those who believe man is already finished and complete, so that the Last Day might as well dawn right away" (172). Wisdom for Lichtenberg consists in imagining ever more possibilities and never remaining smugly content that we have seen everything worth seeing. "Even the mistakes we so frequently make are useful in that in the end they accustom us to believing that everything may be different from what we imagine it to be" (168).

How Many Natures

Pascal constantly tries out ideas, sees where they lead, draws a tentative conclusion, reflects on it, and then amends it or tries another. He speculates on society or human nature and then, questioning himself, offers a skeptical reply, which leads to further qualification and, often enough, to skeptical reflections about skepticism itself. He may then proceed to declare custom the only arbiter, until the variety of customs provokes new skepticism:

> Three degrees of latitude upset the whole of jurisprudence and one meridian determines what is true. Basic laws change when they have been in force only a few years, law has its periods, the entry of Saturn into the house of the Lion marks the origin of a given crime. It is a flimsy sort of justice whose limits are marked by a river; true on this side of the Pyrenees, false on the other. (P, 46)

This passage leads to another about attempts to ground the variety of custom in some more fundamental principle, "but the joke is that man's whims have shown such great variety that there is not one" (46). Custom can neither be rejected nor grounded. "Anyone who tries to bring it back to its first principle destroys it. Nothing is so defective as those laws which correct defects" (46). "The art of subversion, of revolution" is to present customs as mere injustices, but "there is no surer way to lose everything; nothing will be just if weighed in these scales" (47). Since people nevertheless respond to such subversive arguments, Augustine may have been correct that they should sometimes be deceived for their own good. And perhaps what "came about originally without reason has become reasonable" (47).

I summarize this passage at length to give a sense of the way in which many passages proceed. Arguments lead to more arguments in a potentially interminable process. We watch an internal debate unfolding, with ancient thinkers sometimes participating through quotations. Cited separately, the line about three degrees of latitude has become one of Pascal's most famous apothegms, but in context it reads as one moment of restless thinking.

As with Lichtenberg, some of Pascal's apothegms occur in different versions, sometimes because he is trying to get his thought right and sometimes because the idea seems to arise unexpectedly in a new context suggesting a different meaning.

The famous "thinking reed" quotation went through several versions:

Thinking reed. It is not in space that I must seek my human dignity, but in the ordering of my thought. It will do me no good to own land. Through space the universe grasps me and swallows me like a speck; through thought I grasp it. (*P*, 59)

Man's greatness comes from knowing he is wretched: a tree does not know it is wretched.

Thus it is wretched to know one is wretched, but there is greatness in knowing one is wretched. (*P*, 59)

Man is but a reed, the weakest thing in nature, but he is a thinking reed. The entire universe need not arm itself to crush him; a vapour, a drop of water is enough to kill him. But even if the universe were to crush him, man would still be nobler than his slayer, because he knows that he is dying and the advantage the universe has over him. The universe knows nothing of this.

Thus all our dignity consists in thought. It is on thought that we must depend for our recovery, not on space and time, which we could never fill. Let us then strive to think well: that is the basis of morality. (*P*, 95)

[At the end of a two-page passage:] All bodies, the firmament, the stars, the earth and its kingdoms are not worth the least of minds, for it knows them all and itself too, while bodies know nothing.

All bodies together and all minds together and all their products are not worth the least impulse of charity. This is of an infinitely superior order.

Out of all bodies together we could not succeed in creating one little thought. It is impossible, and of a different order. Out of all bodies and minds we could not extract one impulse of true charity. It is impossible, and of a different, supernatural order. (*P*, 125)

The idea of "the thinking reed," of conscious man contrasted with the unconscious universe, recurred to Pascal, and he approaches it from different angles. The order of these jottings is uncertain, but their differences are apparent. In the first I have cited, space seems suitable for exploring the difference: the universe contains infinite space, but it does no good for us to own land. We can in thought grasp the infinity of space that unconsciously grasps us.

In the second extract Pascal introduces the idea of greatness: we know we are wretched, which makes us truly wretched, but also gives us greatness.

The third formulation, the most famous, stresses the implications of awareness of mortality, of knowing one dies. It defines the essence of human life as vulnerability combined with knowledge, which together confer nobility.

Pascal's consideration of the lowliness of Jesus precedes the fourth passage. He therefore arrives at his key idea by a different route. As Jesus was worth more than the world that mocked and killed him, so mind outweighs all physical existence. And by the same token, charity is worth more than all minds. "Out of all bodies and minds we could not extract one impulse of true charity. It is impossible, and of a different, supernatural order." One gift of love outweighs the world. Now the famous idea about the thinking reed represents an in-between step to a quite different conclusion.

Because thoughts are trials, we often need to read many. Only then can we detect a surprising new development of it. Unlike a volume of maxims, a collection of thoughts demands weak as well as strong ones, or where would the sense of trying out come from? For difficult success to rise impressively from failure, failure must be present. Pascal's impressive lines seem all the more powerful because we witness his struggles to formulate them. We contrast them with less impressive versions, or wonder if there could be still better ones. "How many natures lie in human natures!" Pascal observes, and his *Pensées* provokes us to add: "How many thoughts lie in human thoughts!"

What If . . . ?

"Man grows used to everything, the scoundrel!" He sank into thought. "And what if I am wrong," he cried suddenly after a moment's thought. "What if man is not really a scoundrel, man in general, I mean, the whole race of mankind—then all the rest is prejudice, simply artificial terrors, and there are no barriers, and it's all as it should be."

Raskolnikov, in Dostoevsky's *Crime and Punishment* (*C&P*, 28)

Because thoughts offer themselves not as certainties but as ideas worth considering, they may take the form of *provocations*. They state an idea in extreme or paradoxical form and ask: What if this scandalous possibility should be true?

Nietzsche often phrases his thoughts in this way. A man who becomes a free spirit, he suggests, indulges in the curiosity of imagining forbidden alternatives:

Behind his ranging activity (for his journeying restlessly and aimlessly, as in a desert) stands the question mark of an ever more dangerous curiosity. "Cannot *all* values be overturned? And is Good perhaps Evil? . . . Is everything perhaps ultimately false? And if we are deceived, are we not for that very reason also deceivers? *Must* we not be deceivers, too?" Such thoughts lead and mislead him, always further onward, always further away. (*HATH*, 7)

Readers of Nietzsche will recognize his delight in such provocations.

The "provocation" may be defined as a thought that proposes we consider some shocking position—just entertain it as a possibility—and learn to appreciate such hypothetical thinking. Are truths possibly camouflaged as falsities? Could it be that . . . ? Is something really its opposite? Even if it isn't, what could we learn by imagining it is? To understand what is, you must imagine what might be. To grasp reality you must consider possibility.

Thoughts suggest that we cultivate the imagination and learn the power of asking, what if . . . ? Provocations add that the best way to do so is to pose extreme and highly unlikely solutions. It is only by considering the improbable that we come to think in terms of the possible.

To educate, the provocation "leads and misleads," and leads by misleading. It offers itself as the starting point of many journeys.

The Wager

How appropriate, then, that the greatest master of the provocation should have also invented probability theory, the branch of mathematics concerned with might-bes! Suppose a game was stopped before it was over: what are the chances that each of the participants would win? How should the pot be divided? It was just such a question that led Pascal to his mathematical discoveries. Mathematics had always dealt with certainties, so it must have been shocking to see it adapted to mere possibilities.

No matter how things have turned out, they could have turned out differently, and no matter what they are, they could become something else. Only one future will be, but many could be. Thoughts invite us to consider something else. What if a present falsity should become a future truth, or what if a past truth had been different? If Cleopatra's nose had been shorter, the face of the world would have changed: this provocation exemplifies the genre's very spirit.

Pascal's most famous provocation—the "wager"—shocks us by applying mathematics to establish faith. If the existence of God is improbable, should we bet on it? The wager proposes, not entirely seriously, that we consider an improbability by applying probability theory.

This proposal arises, as provocations often do, unexpectedly, in the course of pursuing a different argument. Pascal has been maintaining against the "philosophers" that Christianity not only cannot be proved but also entails its own unprovability. Christianity by its very nature requires faith, and faith entails doubt. It follows that if someone proved Christianity, it would have been disproven. Christians move in a world of uncertainties. "It is by being without proof that they show they are not without sense" (*P*, 150).

Pascal next imagines someone responding that such an argument can satisfy only someone who is already a believer. Nonbelievers may question whether, in the absence of proof, they should spend their lives earning a salvation that may be entirely illusory. To answer this objection, Pascal offers his provocative wager, which, quite literally, treats faith as a gamble.

Pascal explains that a smart bet measures rewards against odds. If the chances of winning are 1 in 3, but the reward for winning is 5 to 1, the bet is a good one. By the same logic, if the odds are 100 to 1 against, but the reward is 10,000 to 1, the bet is even better because the "expected return" (what would happen if the game could be played over and over again) is even greater. Now ask: Are the odds of God's existence even? or perhaps 100 to 1, or even 1,000 to 1, against? It does not matter how long the odds against God's existence might be, because the reward for winning is infinite. An infinite number divided by a finite number must still be infinite. Therefore, no matter how unlikely the truth of Christianity might be, one should bet on it.

But someone might object: Why bet at all? Ah, but you *must*, one way or the other. The game has begun, and you are already playing. You are alive, and so "you must wager. There is no choice; you are already committed" (*P*, 150). Gambles are uncertain, but one must certainly gamble.

But how can one believe by deciding belief is a good bet? One can't, but one can bet on believing by doing what is more likely to induce belief.

Life *is* a gamble, and so one must learn to think in terms of probabilities. As we negotiate a labyrinth of uncertain paths, provocations teach us to consider less than obvious choices. They are "what ifs" about the value of asking, "What if . . . ?"

The Literature of Potential

The question "What if . . . ?" suggests one way in which the logic of the thought can generate longer works. Just as a thought can be taken in many directions, so some events can lead to many outcomes. By drawing more than one line from a starting point, the author of a thought or a story can dramatize the richness of potential.

The literature of potential, as we might call it, shows us a world with might-have-beens. It intimates that however inventive people may have been, still more inventions were overlooked. We do not know what we have missed, but we might just know we have missed something.

"I don't know what I may seem to the world," Isaac Newton mused about his life's work, "but as to myself, I seem to have been a little boy playing on the sea-shore and diverting myself in now and then finding a smoother pebble or a prettier shell than ordinary, whilst the great ocean of truth lay all undiscovered before me" (*ODQ*, 572). For the literature of potentiality, each idea we entertain, and each choice we make, is but a pebble before the ocean of alternatives. Truth includes *all* alternatives, the ones that see the light of day and the others that could but do not. These unrealized possibilities are not quite invisible because, if we look closely enough, we can detect the dim shadows they cast. Actuality is shadowed by possibility, and reality consists of both.

In this kind of literature, each moment, like each thought, contains more possible continuations than are actualized. A storyteller can contrive not only to show the course of events taken but also to suggest alternative paths that could have been taken. He provides glimpses of happenstances that did not happen. Dreams, rumors, fantasies, or explicit narration of the events that would have taken place "if only" a chance occurrence had not diverted the story: all these methods and more allow the author to trace one path and then go back and trace another. First we see the face of the world as it is and then we delineate its features had Cleopatra's nose been shorter. Pascal, Lichtenberg, and Nietzsche detect more than one implication in an idea, and so they repeatedly return to it. By the same token, Sterne and Dostoevsky unsettle our sense of inevitability.

The literature of possibility teaches that to understand an event is to grasp not only what did happen, but also what could have. We live in a world made of probabilities. If we imagine otherwise, it is only because we find it difficult to detect, or disturbing to imagine, what did not happen. What becomes of the dream of predictability if time ramifies? What if prior causes merely narrow down options, but do not limit them to one, as a determinist would insist? In that case, although each outcome has a reason, at least some lack what Leibniz called a "sufficient reason" ensuring that it, and only it, could have happened.

The same is true of individual people. I am not only what I am but also what I might have been. And I am not only what I will be but also what I might be. The lessons of morality and psychology converge: Love thy neighbor as thyself because thy neighbor is thy alternative self. There but for the grace of God go I. For just these reasons Dostoevsky identified Christianity with a theory of time. Because each of us could have been others, "everyone is responsible for everyone and for everything" (BK, 334).

We live in a world that has not two but three kinds of events: not only actualities and impossibilities, but also real possibilities: events that genuinely could have happened even if they did not. Reality includes its unactualized possibilities. But how can one make visible the shadows cast by real but unactualized events?

The Ghost of Events

Oddly enough, Christmas stories typically belong to the literature of possibility. The day celebrating the birth of the Lord becomes an occasion to reflect on one's choices and one's future. Sometimes the hero regrets his life and is shown the world as it would have been had he not existed, as in the famous Jimmy Stewart film *It's a Wonderful Life* and in Philip van Doren Stern's story "The Greatest Gift," on which the film was based. Stern's story ends with the hero discovering an object which, in the alternate reality, he had sold the woman who did not become his wife but which, when he returns to his original life, she somehow still possesses. The alternative possibility has left its mark on actuality. It apparently does so to show that it is not a hallucination but a genuine might-have-been.

In the most famous Christmas story, Dickens's *A Christmas Carol*, Scrooge changes his life after seeing his life and death as his choices have made them. He begs the spirit for a world in which an alternative reality is possible, and at first the spirit refuses.

> "Before I draw nearer to that stone to which you point," said Scrooge, "answer me one question. Are these the shadows of the things that Will be, or are they the shadows of the things that May be, only?"
>
> Still the Ghost pointed downward to the grave by which it stood.
>
> "Men's courses will foreshadow certain ends, to which, if persevered in, they must lead," said Scrooge. "But if the courses be departed from, the ends will change. Say it is thus with what you show me."
>
> The Spirit was immovable as ever.
>
> . . .
>
> "Good Spirit," he pursued, as down upon the ground he fell before it: "Your nature intercedes for me, and pities me. Assure me that I may yet change these shadows you have shown me by an altered life!"
>
> The kind hand trembled.[19]

Dostoevsky's story "A Boy at Christ's Christmas Party," doubtless influenced by Dickens, also projects a possible reality to draw a Christmas lesson.

Virtual History

The enduring achievement of historical study is a historical sense—an intuitive
understanding—of how things did not happen.   —Lewis Namier[20]

The literature of potential also includes an increasingly popular form, "virtual history." If the Nazis had won the Second World War, if Napoleon had triumphed in Russia or turned back sooner, if John F. Kennedy had not been assassinated, what would the course of history have been? Filmmakers, science fiction writers, and academic historians have posed such questions and narrated the might-have-beens. Their efforts have been collected in volumes with titles such as *Roads Not Taken: Tales of Alternative History*, *What If?: The World's Foremost Military Historians Imagine What Might Have Been*, and *What Might Have Been: Leading Historians on Twelve "What Ifs" of History*.[21] Each of these volumes contains a preface defending the value of looking at alternative possibilities and insisting that what actually happened did not have to happen.

Niall Ferguson's introduction to the collection he edited, *Virtual History: Alternatives and Counterfactuals*, offers the most substantial defense of this genre. Ferguson concludes: "The world is not divinely ordered. Nor governed by Reason, the class struggle, or any other deterministic 'law.' . . . The fact of human consciousness (which cannot be expressed in terms of equations) only adds to the impression of chaos. Under these circumstances, the search for universal laws of history is futile. The most historians can do is to make tentative statements about causation with reference to plausible counterfactuals, constructed on the basis of judgments about plausibility" (Ferguson, 89).

Many who practice or justify counterfactual history cite Borges's famous story "The Garden of Forking Paths," which imagines time not only as constantly *di*verging into ever more causal lines, but also as occasionally *con*verging, with distinct causal lines leading to the same result. Or is it the same, if a moment consists not only of itself but also of the path by which it got there? At the story's climax, the hero senses the present as such a moment of convergence. "It seemed to me," he explains, "that the humid garden that surrounded the house was infinitely saturated with invisible persons" who are really the "same" persons "busy and multiform in other dimensions of time."[22]

The Incompleteness of the Moment

The thought as a genre pulsates with present possibility. Regardless of where it eventually leads, its fascination lies in the sense that it could lead in many directions. It asks us to place ourselves in its, not our, present. Virtual history makes a similar request. Ferguson cites Johan Huizinga: "The historian must . . . continually put himself at a point in the past at which the known factors will seem to permit different outcomes. If he speaks of Salamis, then it must be as if the Persians might still win; if he speaks of the coup d'état of Brumaire, then it must remain to be seen if Bonaparte will be ignominiously repulsed" (Ferguson, 1).

Presentness without a secure future, a moment that can lead in many directions: this is also the sense cultivated by certain serially published works that, like Sterne's *The Life and Opinions of Tristram Shandy, Gentleman* or Dostoevsky's *Writer's Diary: A Monthly Publication,* give us what occurs to the author as it occurs to him. These works come as close as possible to the present of the creative process.

Thoughts and events show their rich potentials. Both Tristram's "opinions" and his "life" lead in many directions, and Tristram continually circles back over and over to the same starting point. This novel, if it can be called that, develops the potential of "thought" and open-ended story together.

Much the same idea governed Dostoevsky's serialized *Writer's Diary,* a "new genre" he invented. Each monthly issue was supposed to contain short works in diverse genres, all reflecting on a key event in the news. A particularly fascinating crime inspires Dostoevsky's thoughts, revisions of these thoughts in future issues, guesses and reconsidered guesses as to the consequences for those involved, sketches for various stories that could be written about the incident, and, occasionally, a finished work of fiction. If read in context, this work's plot unfolds against the shadows of other works and other plots that the same theme might have suggested.

In one article, Dostoevsky remarks on how difficult it is to place oneself in a past moment as if it were present. To do so, he explains, one has to forget what came next and not treat it as if it were accomplished fact. Otherwise "the event will *necessarily* be imagined in its completed aspect, i.e. with the addition of all its subsequent developments that had not yet occurred at the historical moment in which the artist is trying to depict a person or event" (*AWD1,* 79).

The short genre of the thought, and the longer literature of possibility, allow us to capture the moment while it is still "incomplete." We sense the potential for more developments than could ever actually take place. And we ask, what if some other one had?

6

PROSAIC APOTHEGMS

Glory be to God for dappled things. . . .
Whatever is fickle, freckled (who knows how?)
            —Gerard Manley Hopkins, "Pied Beauty"[1]

The world is nothing but variety and dissimilarity.
            —Montaigne (*CEM*, 244)

Mystical Apothegms

In addition to the apothegms we have already examined, we may identify a
second kind. Both types describe the world as ultimately unknowable, but for
different reasons.

The apothegms discussed in Chapter 2—let us call them "mystical apothegms"—trace the inadequacy of our mental powers to the world's fundamental mystery. The ultimate principle of things lies beyond language, beyond
logic, beyond all the distinctions we draw and, indeed, beyond distinction itself. The universe baffles human intelligence. The way that can be spoken of is
not the true way.

Mystical apothegms intrigue by posing ultimate questions forever beyond
our abilities. They strive not to find the answers but to deepen the questions. To
do so, they formulate paradoxes of learned ignorance, of consciousness imprisoned in body, of finite lives against the backdrop of eternity, of belief in the un-
believable, and many others. They neither affirm nor deny, but give enigmatic
signs. Like Zen, they gesture beyond thought.

Mystic apothegms teach us to cultivate our sense of mystery, "the gateway
to the manifold secrets." God does not reveal himself in the world.

Prosaic Apothegms

Like mystical apothegms, prosaic apothegms, as we may call them, regard the
presumption of a universe conforming to our ways of knowing as anthropo-

morphic, if not hubristic. But they trace the world's incomprehensibility to a different source.

For prosaic apothegms, what obstructs our understanding is not any mystery, ineffable power, or unresolvable paradox. The obstruction lies neither before time, nor in the world of spirits, nor in categories made present before the universe was created, but in the world right before our eyes. We fail to grasp things because they are so complex.

Not some inaccessible principle but the sheer diversity of qualities defies simplification. Causes do not reduce to a few underlying laws, everything shifts before our eyes, and we ourselves differ from moment to moment. When we examine things finely enough, they baffle us with ever finer distinctions. When the world, especially the human world, seems uniform, stable, or simple, it is usually because we are not looking at it closely enough. The prosaic apothegm asks us to look and teaches us to see.

Early in *Middlemarch*, the author asks whether there was any single cause for Mrs. Cadwallader's frenetic matchmaking. "Was there any ingenious plot, any hide-and-seek course of action which might be detected by a careful telescopic watch? Not at all." If a telescope could follow Mrs. Cadwallader's phaeton, it would detect nothing. "In fact, if that convenient vehicle had existed in the days of the Seven Sages, one of them would doubtless have remarked, that you can know little of women by following them about in their pony phaetons" (*MM*, 59).

We fail to find a hidden cause or motive not because it is buried in the unconscious or obscured by sociological conventions but because the very concept of cause on which we rely is far too crude.

> Even with a microscope directed at a water-drop we find ourselves making interpretations which turn out to be rather coarse; for whereas under a weak lens you may seem to see a creature exhibiting an active voracity into which other smaller creatures actively play as if they were so many animated tax-pennies, a stronger lens reveals to you certain tiniest hairlets which make vortices for the victims while the swallower waits passively at his receipt of custom. In this way, metaphorically speaking, a strong lens applied to Mrs. Cadwallader's matchmaking will show a play of minute causes producing what may be called thought and speech vortices to bring her the sort of food she needed. (59)

"A play of minute causes": that is what the prosaic apothegm shows us. Where we are inclined to see singularity, it shows us multiplicity and complexity, and behind that complexity, still more complexity, without end. The closer you look, the more discriminations you need to make.

To treat our usual categories as if they were anything more than conveniences is to mistake labels for individuals. "Nature creates, not *genera* and *species*, but *individua*," writes Lichtenberg, "and our shortsightedness has to seek out similarities so as to be able to retain in mind many things at the same time. These conceptions become more and more inaccurate the larger the families we invent for ourselves are" (Lichtenberg, 3). Because it is easier to manipulate a few generalities than a myriad specificities, we readily endow the generalities with the solidity of nature. "Men have made subdivisions for themselves in this eternally moving, unending, intermingled chaos of good and evil," declares the narrator of Tolstoy's story "Lucerne." "They have traced imaginary lines on the ocean, and expect the ocean to divide itself accordingly" (*LTSS*, 330). Intellectuals above all expect overarching theories to account for, and guide the remaking of, the immense diversity of life. But employing theories in this way resembles—to use one of Wittgenstein's most striking similes—trying "to repair a torn spider's web with one's fingers" (*PI*, 46e).

Fibre on Fibre

One may understand Wittgenstein's shift from the *Tractatus* to the *Philosophical Investigations* as a change in genre, from the mystical to the prosaic apothegm. In both books, he confronts the insufficiency of philosophy, but the nature of that insufficiency changes. In the *Tractatus*, philosophy confronts its limit because "the sense of the world must lie outside the world" (*TLP*, 71). We must transcend all propositions, including the ones in the *Tractatus* itself, to see the world aright (74). By contrast, the *Philosophical Investigations* locates the reasons for philosophy's failure *inside* the world. It teaches us to avoid the snare of simple explanations, as if, because we can use a single name, it must correspond to a single thing.

Most famously, Wittgenstein responds to the demand that he provide the essence of language by saying that "these phenomena have no one thing in common which makes us use the same word for all," just as all the different kinds of games share no single quality (*PI*, 31e). "Don't say, 'There *must* be something common, or they would not be called *games*,'—but *look and see* whether there is anything in common to them all" (31e). In many aspects of life, there is not.

If we "look and see" we find a multiplicity and a diversity, numerous discrepant things linked to each other by "family resemblances." We call some things numbers (or games, or language), and then, when we confront something new that shares some of the qualities of numbers, we apply the term to that, too, and so on. "And we extend our concept of number as in spinning a thread we twist fibre on fibre. And the strength of the thread does not reside in the fact that some one fibre runs through its whole length, but in the overlapping of many fibres" (32e).

The *Philosophical Investigations* itself proceeds in this way, laying fibre upon fibre, and that is one reason Wittgenstein writes in prosaic apothegms.[2] A treatise subsuming everything into a generality and a structure would defeat his purpose, which is to teach us to look and see, to detect fine differences, and follow surprising discoveries wherever they lead. That is what each short apothegmic paragraph does. It responds to what has just been uncovered. Taken together, the sequence of paragraphs intimates what many of them show: there are no wholes, boundaries are vague, discrimination is endless, and philosophy provides not answers but therapies. Philosophy as prosaic apothegm *prompts* us to see what we have missed and, as Wittgenstein says, *reminds* us of what experience already teaches.

Undefining the Words Again

For the mystical apothegm, language fails because it belongs to this world while truth lies outside the world. For the prosaic apothegm, language is not worldly enough. Our ways of speaking do not match the real complexities of experience. They fail to discriminate the fine differences we see and still finer ones we might see.

Much as Wittgenstein warns against mistaking single names for single things, he also ascribes philosophical difficulties to using words outside their proper sphere. We apply what is specific to one "language-game" universally. Then, as he likes to say, "language goes on holiday" (19e). It resembles "an engine idling" (41e): "The confusions which occupy us arise when language is like an engine idling, not when it is doing work" (51e).

Other prosaic apothists show us how we confuse different emotions by applying the same word, take an empty generality for a specific cause, or lose our way in metaphors stretched too far. These and similar failures of language provide the theme of many prosaic apothegms:

> What Bacon said of the perniciousness of systems could be said of every word. Many words which express whole classes or every step of an entire scale are em-

ployed as though they represented a single step, that is as *individua*. This means undefining the words again.   —Lichtenberg (40)

There are many wonderful mixtures which are alike called love, and [so] claim the privilege of a sublime rage which is an apology for everything (in literature and drama).   —Eliot (*MM*, 290)

Mr. Casaubon had imagined that his long studious bachelorhood had stored up for him a compound interest of enjoyment, and that large drafts on his affections would not fail to be honoured; for we all of us, grave or light, get our thoughts entangled in metaphors, and act fatally on the strength of them.
                                                                      —Eliot (*MM*, 84)

[The historians ask:] Why did it happen in this way instead of some other way? . . . "*Chance* created the situation; *genius* utilized it," says history. But what is *chance*? What is *genius*? The words *chance* and *genius* do not denote anything that exists. . . . I do not know why a certain event occurs; I think that I cannot know it; so I do not try to know it and I talk about *chance*. I see a force producing effects beyond the scope of ordinary human agencies; I do not understand why it occurs and I talk of *genius*.   —Tolstoy (*W&P*, 1354–55)

Yet in the majority of these cases general historians still employ the concept of power as a force which in itself produces events, and treats it as their cause.
                                                                  —Tolstoy (*W&P*, 1417)

A word is not a crystal, transparent and unchanged, it is the skin of a living thought and may vary greatly in color and content according to the circumstances and time in which it is used.
                                        —Oliver Wendell Holmes, Jr. (*YBQ*, 367)

Always suspicious of generalities, Lichtenberg distrusts words, because they apply one term to many phenomena and therefore smooth out potentially significant differences. Here and elsewhere, Tolstoy exposes the use of words that seem to have content when they are in fact mere placeholders. Like Molière's medical student, who imagines he has explained why poppy makes you sleep by saying it contains a "soporific principle," Tolstoy's historians invoke chance, genius, and power. Why could Napoleon do these extraordinary things? Because he was a genius. What does it mean to say he was a genius? It means he could do extraordinary things. To explain events as resulting from "power" is like saying they happened because they happened, or were caused by Causality.

For Eliot, a feeling that would not otherwise justify our behavior comes to do so because of what we call it, and so we use words expansively. Metaphors easily seem more than metaphoric. What consequences have ensued because we chose to call certain feelings and behaviors mental *illness*, by analogy with physical illness, instead of, let us say, mental *deficit!*

For Holmes, words carry with them meanings accumulated over time and therefore cannot be adequately understood in terms of a dictionary defini- tion. Prosaic apothists could not differ more from those putative reformers of language, who, like Leibniz, would purify words of merely historical accu- mulations so that we could reason with them as we do with numbers. That aspiration reflects the spirit of the dictum, which aspires to purity and perfect knowledge, but for the prosaic apothegm impurity is ineliminable.

Montaigne Tastes Nothing Pure

For the prosaic apothegm, one errs by imagining that things are pure until impu- rities are introduced. On the contrary, the fundamental state of things is impure, and purity can be achieved only with hard work and never completely. By the same token, the fundamental state of the world is mess, while order requires work. A principle analogous to entropy governs the social and psychological worlds.

Some thinkers, and the dictum as a genre, regard complexity and impurity as merely apparent: look deeper, and you will find simple laws. Other think- ers, and the prosaic apothegm, presume the opposite. The deeper one looks, the more inconsistency, uncertainty, ephemerality, and lack of clarity one dis- covers. "But pure and absolute sorrow is as impossible as pure and absolute joy," Tolstoy observes in one of the more famous apothegms in *War and Peace* (1286). Such apothegms show Tolstoy's debt to the writer who most consis- tently discovered new kinds of human inconsistency, Montaigne.

In his essay "We Taste Nothing Pure," Montaigne attributes impurity not only to things but also to our perceptions of them. Even those few things we encounter in their natural simplicity come into our experience corrupted, de- based, and tinged with their opposites:

> Profound joy has more seriousness than gaiety about it; extreme and full con- tentment, more soberness than sprightliness. *Even felicity, unless it tempers itself, overwhelms* [Seneca]. Happiness racks us. (*CEM*, 510)

> "The gods sell us all the good things they give us." That is to say, they give us noth- ing pure and perfect, none that we do not buy at the price of some evil. (*CEM*, 510)

It is likewise true that for the uses of life and for the service of public business there may be excess in the purity and perspicacity of our minds. That penetrating clarity has too much subtlety and curiosity about it. These must be weighed and blunted to make them more obedient to example and practice, and thickened and obscured to relate them to this shadowy and earthly life. (*CEM*, 511)

When I confess myself religiously to myself I find that the best goodness I have has some tincture of vice. And I fear that Plato in his most verdant virtue . . . if he had listened to it closely—and he did listen to it closely—would have sensed in it some false note of human admixture, but an obscure note, perceptible only to himself. *Man, in all things and throughout, is but patchwork and motley.* (*CEM*, 511; italics added)

Tincture, admixture, subtlety; temper, obscure, blunt: these words, along with many synonyms, recur in Montaigne's essays and in prosaic apothegms generally. So do comparatives chosen in place of absolutes: things are more or less of a certain quality. Prosaic apothegms favor locutions like Aristotle's repeated qualification—"on the whole and for the most part"—or Tolstoy's frequent statement that an event happened just "for some reason."

The Patchwork of Will

Like people, human intentions are all patchwork and motley. If an ethical act must be performed, as Kant insists, simply because it is the right thing to do, then there are no ethical acts. For prosaic apothists, that conclusion demonstrates the falsity of the demand for purity of motive in the first place. All motives are mixed. We must be willing to call some actions good even if they are not wholly good, because real human goodness consists in making the moral best of psychological mixture.

In his essay "Of the Inconsistency of Our Actions," Montaigne offers example after example of our perplexing inconsistency and unpredictability. Our complexity exceeds any theory or description of us:

Those who make a practice of comparing human actions are never so perplexed as when they try to see them as a whole and in the same light; for they commonly contradict each other so strangely that it seems impossible that they have come from the same shop. (*CEM*, 239)

Even good authors are wrong to insist on fashioning a consistent and solid fabric out of us. (*CEM*, 239)

Nothing is harder for me than to believe in men's consistency, nothing easier than to believe in their inconsistency. He who would judge them in detail and distinctly, bit by bit, would more often hit upon the truth. (*CEM*, 239–40)

Those supple variations and contradictions that are seen in us have made some imagine that we have two souls, and others that two powers accompany and drive us, each in its own way. . . . [F]or such sudden diversity cannot well be reconciled with a simple subject. (*CEM*, 240)

We are all patchwork, and so shapeless and diverse in composition that each bit, each moment, plays its own game. And there is as much difference between us and ourselves as between us and others. (*CEM*, 244)

With his remarkable ability to discover the complexity of human motivations and intentions—or, as he liked to say, will—Montaigne deserves to be classed with literature's greatest psychologists, La Rochefoucauld, Tolstoy, and Dostoevsky. None sees intentions or personalities as wholes. Man "is a compound personality, and therefore it is somehow difficult to blame him as an individual," observes Dostoevsky's Underground Man (*NFU*, 20).

Montaigne attributed our inconsistencies not only to the pressure of contingent circumstances, which shape our will despite our will, but also to the composite nature of will itself. For both reasons, our intentions remain divided. Although we can will, we cannot will what our will will be. Only sometimes, and by dint of long-developed habits, can we choose what we shall choose.

We think of what we want only at the moment we want it, and we change like that animal which takes the color of the place you set it on. What we have just now planned, we presently change, and presently again we retrace our steps: nothing but oscillation and inconsistency:

> Like puppets we are moved by outside strings.
> HORACE

We do not go, we are carried away. . . .

We float between different states of mind; we wish nothing freely, nothing absolutely, nothing constantly. (*CEM*, 240)

Not only does the wind of accident move me at will, but, besides, I am moved and disturbed as a result of my own unstable posture. . . . I give my soul now one face, now another, according to which direction I turn it. If I speak of myself in different ways, that is because I look at myself in different ways. . . . [T]he strangeness of our condition makes it happen that we are often driven to do good by vice itself. (*CEM*, 242)

Shaping the Motley

The shape of Montaigne's essays reflects his inconsistency, as he weaves from topic to topic. Sometimes the topic strays to how he strays. "I take the first subject that chance offers. . . . And I never plan to develop them completely. For I do not see the whole of anything . . . I give it a stab. . . . Scattering a word here, there another, samples separated from their context, dispersed, without a plan and without a promise, I am not bound to make something of them or to adhere to them myself without varying when I please and giving myself up to doubt and uncertainty" (*CEM*, 219).

Like Wittgenstein, Montaigne writes by laying fibre to fibre. And from edition to edition, he added to each essay in much the same way, with digressions inserted as they suggested themselves. Doing so fits the spirit of the prosaic apothegm.

Montaigne exemplifies one way in which a long form can develop from the prosaic apothegm. Its spirit generates a certain type of essay—in Montaigne's sense of a trying out—and those essays in turn contain many prosaic apothegms. They wander from one to another.

Lengthen these essays still more, and you get another burgeoning masterpiece, Burton's *Anatomy of Melancholy*. Combine its digressive argument with an equally digressive plot, and you arrive at works like *Tristram Shandy* and *Don Juan*. The home of the thought easily doubles as the home of the prosaic apothegm, and the two compatible genres often occur together.

Friction

Now assume a square cow . . .   —Social science paper[3]

Theorists who aspire to a hard scientific account often proceed by abstraction. As Galileo arrived at his laws of falling bodies by thinking away the effects of friction and air resistance, so would-be social scientists try to arrive at a pure or ideal case. There they expect to discover the laws behind the noise of daily life.

Prosaic apothists respond that sometimes the supposed noise belongs to the phenomenon under examination. To think away the noise may be to think away the phenomenon itself. "Friction" (a metaphor often used) may be intrinsic:

> Everything in war is very simple, but the simplest thing is difficult. The difficulties accumulate and end by producing a kind of friction that is inconceivable unless one has experienced war. . . . Friction is the only concept that more or less corresponds to the factors that distinguish real war from war on paper.
>
> —Carl von Clausewitz[4]

Guicciardini sees politics much as Clausewitz views war:

> It would certainly be desirable to do or carry out things perfectly; that is, to have
> them free of the slightest defect or disorder. But that is very difficult. And so it is
> a mistake to spend too much time polishing things up, for very often, opportu-
> nities will flee while you are losing time trying to make something precisely the
> way you want it. Indeed, even when you think you have succeeded, you notice
> later that you were wrong. For the nature of things in this world is such that
> nearly everything contains some imperfection in all its parts.
>
> —Guicciardini (73)

For Oliver Wendell Holmes, Jr., law can least of all be understood as a consistent whole. It displays the sort of contingencies that testify to historical process:

> The law embodies the story of a nation's development through many centuries,
> and it cannot be dealt with as if it contained only the axioms and corollaries of
> a book of mathematics.   —Oliver Wendell Holmes, Jr. (*YBQ*, 365)

> The truth is, that the law is always approaching, and never reaching, consis-
> tency. It is forever adopting new principles from life at one end, and it always
> retains old ones from history at the other, which have not yet been absorbed
> or sloughed off. It will become entirely consistent only when it ceases to grow.
>
> —Oliver Wendell Holmes, Jr. (*YBQ*, 365)

In discussing language, Wittgenstein also invokes the metaphor of necessary
friction:

> When we believe that we must find that order, must find the ideal, in our actual
> language, we become dissatisfied.... The more narrowly we examine actual lan-
> guage, the sharper becomes the conflict between it and our requirement [of the
> ideal]. (For the crystalline purity of logic was, of course, not a *result of investiga-
> tion*: it was a requirement.) ... We have got on to slippery ice where there is no
> friction and so in a certain sense the conditions are ideal, but also, just because
> of that, we are unable to walk. We want to walk: so we need *friction*. Back to the
> rough ground!   —Wittgenstein (*PI*, 46e)

Some thinkers have attempted to find a science of war, of law, of politics, of psychology, of social life, or of history as a whole. By constructing an ideal model,
they posit an equivalent of Newton's laws, formulas that can substitute for the
messiness and variability of educated judgment. Holmes cautions us that to
think this way is to mistake what law is all about. Guicciardini tells us much the
same about politics, and Clausewitz about battle.

In *War and Peace*, Prince Andrei at first accepts the scientific view of battle held by General Pfühl. Experience disabuses him of his belief in Pfühl's military dicta and teaches him prosaic apothegms. At one council of war, Andrei reflects on the generals' faith in science and pure theory:

> What science can there be in a matter in which, as in every practical matter, nothing can be determined and everything depends on innumerable conditions, the significance of which becomes significant a particular moment, and no one can tell when that moment will come? (*W&P*, 775)

Before the Battle of Borodino, he develops this insight:

> "You talk about our position: the left flank weak, the right flank extended," he went on. "That's all nonsense, doesn't mean a thing. But what are we facing tomorrow? A hundred million diverse chances, which will be decided on the instant by whether we run or they run, whether this man or that man is killed." (*W&P*, 930)

If any human activity is disorderly, it is war. Battle magnifies the essential messiness of life. "As in *every* practical matter": there can be no science of anything human. "At a particular moment," "on the instant": one reason there can be no such science is that presentness matters. Moments do not derive automatically from prior moments. They contain the capacity for surprise.

In a world of friction, contingency reigns.

Alertness

When one sees the world through the glass of prosaic apothegms, decision making changes its character. Numerous prosaic apothegms concern the futility of advance planning, either for life as a whole or in a situation of radical uncertainty—that is, one in which not even probabilities can be calculated. The more radically uncertain the situation, the less the value of advance planning and the greater the value of alertness: psychological presentness and the flexibility to respond to unforeseeable contingencies.

> Time is that wherein there is opportunity, and opportunity is that wherein there is no great time.   —Hippocrates (*ODQ*, 389)

> Some men write discourses on the future, basing themselves on current events. And if they are informed men, their writings will seem very plausible to the reader. Nevertheless, they are completely misleading. For since one conclusion

depends upon the other, if one is wrong, all that are deduced from it will be mistaken. But every tiny, particular circumstance that changes is apt to alter a conclusion. The affairs of this world, therefore, cannot be judged from afar but must be judged and resolved day by day.   —Guicciardini (70)

What good does it do a man to lay in a supply of paints if he does not know what he is to paint? No one makes a definite plan of his life; we think about it only piecemeal.   —Montaigne (*CEM*, 239)

The causes of good and evil, answered Imlac, are so various and uncertain, so often entangled with each other, so diversified by various relations, and so much subject to accidents which cannot be foreseen, that he who would fix his condition upon incontestable reasons of preference, must live and die inquiring and deliberating.   —Samuel Johnson, *Rasselas* (*SJ*, 542)

Many things difficult to design prove easy to performance.
                              —Samuel Johnson, *Rasselas* (*SJ*, 537)

"Gentlemen, the disposition for tomorrow—or rather for today, for it is past midnight—cannot be altered now," he said. . . . "And before a battle, there is nothing more important . . ." he paused, "than a good night's sleep."
                    —Kutuzov, in Tolstoy, *War and Peace* (*W&P*, 323)

One cannot plan one's whole life, which is why young people are taught not to close off too many options too soon. What is more, in some situations advance planning fails because the multiplicity, entanglement, and obscurity of causes create hopeless unpredictability. Even when some calculation is possible, time and opportunity will not wait. In all such cases, alertness and the readiness to act on previously considered experience matter most.

Herodotus

Long genres may develop the wisdom of prosaic apothegms by narrating a story with a prosaic moral. We have already considered Herodotus's account of Mardonius's feast, which concludes with a mystical apothegm. Herodotus also offers us splendid stories ending with prosaic apothegms. Sometimes, the same narrative includes both.

In Herodotus's complex history of Smerdis and Darius, Otanes and others ascertain that an imposter occupies the Persian throne. Smerdis the Magus, with the help of his brother magus and palace steward Patizithes, has impersonated the true Smerdis, the brother of King Cambyses. Because few people know that the real Smerdis is dead—although far away from the capital Cambyses has had his agent Praxaspes murder his brother—the magus Smerdis can take advantage of his extraordinary physical resemblance to the royal Smerdis.

Just as Otanes and other conspirators have pledged to remove the imposter, Darius arrives, and they ask him to join them. He agrees, but only on condition that they act at once, for delay would invite betrayal. Otanes regards Darius as rash: the conspirators number too few and, in any case, have developed no plan. How are they to kill the magi, how convince the people that the ruler is an imposter, how even gain access to the palace? Action demands knowledge, and they remain ignorant.

Darius replies with a prosaic apothegm: "There are many things that cannot be made clear by words, but may by action; and there are other things that seem practicable in description, but no signal effect proceeds from them" (H, 202).

For reasons no one could have foreseen, Darius proves correct. Unknown to the conspirators, Praxaspes has chosen just this moment to reveal to the people that he killed the real Smerdis and that an imposter rules; and the palace guards for some reason do not prevent the conspirators from entering. Where plans would prove of no use, sheer accident helps.

In the Mardonius story, knowledge does no good to its possessor because it cannot be acted upon. In the Smerdis story, by contrast, knowledge is not to be looked for because it cannot be had in time. Instead of knowledge, timeliness matters. So do alertness and the ability to make the most of fleeting chances. Sometimes action creates its own opportunities. The conspirators seize the moment, exploit each surprising turn as it takes place, and, against all expectation, succeed.

Herodotus: The Story's Other Moral

Upon reflection, the Smerdis story includes yet another surprise. In addition to Darius's prosaic apothegm, it suggests a mystical one as well. The story contains a double moral.

Why does the magus bear the same name as the man he impersonates? After all, he manages to impersonate Cambyses' brother because he looks so much like him, not because he has the same name. Had the magus been named anything else, he could have assumed the name Smerdis as easily as he assumes the rest of the royal identity. Contingency seems to exceed the need for it.

This coincidence, however, does prove important in one respect. When away campaigning, Cambyses has had his brother killed because of a dream:

a messenger arrives to tell him that Smerdis now rules. Cambyses interprets this dream to mean that his brother plans to seize the throne from him, but the dream proves true with a different Smerdis on the throne. In much the same way, Cambyses accepts as true a prophecy that he will die in Ecbatana. "He therefore believed he would die an old man in Ecbatana of Media, where all his treasures were," but the oracle proves correct when Cambyses dies in the insignificant Ecbatana of Syria (*H*, 198). Again, the sheer chance of a repeated name governs events.

The Smerdis story works differently from other stories of oracular prediction. In the *Oedipus* and in the tale of Mardonius, fate dictates a result that will happen regardless of what one does. Whether one consults the oracle or not, the result is given. Even if one knows the outcome in advance, the most one can do is modify the route to it.

But in the Smerdis story, prediction itself seems to cause the outcome. Smerdis dies only because Cambyses believed his dream. The prophecy is, quite literally, self-fulfilling. No dream, no murder of Smerdis.

Stranger still, fate guarantees the outcome only in a trivial sense. No matter what happens, "Smerdis" will rule. But that is not because a single state of affairs must obtain but because both rulers happen to have the same name. Fate does not dictate, it puns. If in other stories contingency serves the whim of fate, here fate serves the whim of sheer contingency.

We wonder: is the world so ordered that apparent contingency really reflects a plan? Or is fate itself sometimes subject to sheer chance? We cannot possibly know. We must recognize the inadequacy of mind on which both kinds of apothegm rest.

Herodotus: The Two Morals of Solon and Croesus

Herodotus's most famous tale, which concerns the encounter of the sage Solon with the wealthy king Croesus, contains the best-known version of the mystical apothegm concluding the *Oedipus*: Count no man happy until he is dead. In both play and history, the apothegm points to purposes and powers beyond human understanding. Therefore wisdom demands what Croesus so markedly lacks, humility.

Like Oedipus, Croesus imagines that, with his power and intelligence, he can control events, but this very confidence marks him for destruction. The gods prove eager to demonstrate the fallibility of human reason. So Solon warns: "Croesus, do you inquire of me concerning human affairs—of me, who knows that the divinity is always jealous, and delights in confusion?" (*H*, 13). After Croesus dismisses Solon as foolish, "the indignation of the gods fell heavily upon Croesus, probably because he thought himself the most happy of men" (15). We now read about the death of Croesus's son, a story proving what Oedipus also learns: divine purposes exceed the ken of even the most fortunate and most intelligent. We act in obscurity and dwell in mystery.

As Herodotus tells the tale of Solon and Croesus, it also illustrates, as a second moral, a prosaic apothegm. Not just divine mystery but also the sheer variety of the world prevents our knowing it. Nothing reduces to simplicity, and predictions overlook surprising factors. Even if there were no gods, the uncertain nature of events in this world would mock confident reason.

Solon explains to Croesus:

> Now I put the term of man's life at seventy years; these seventy years, then give twenty-five thousand two hundred days, without including the intercalary month; and if we add that month to every other year in order that the seasons arriving at the proper time may agree, the intercalary months will be thirty-five more in the seventy years, and the days of these months will be one thousand and fifty. Yet in all this number of twenty-six thousand two hundred and fifty days, that compose these seventy years, one day produces nothing exactly the same as another. (13–14)

How then is prediction possible? Guicciardini makes a similar point: "To judge by example is very misleading. Unless they are similar in every respect, examples are useless, since every tiny difference in the case may be a cause of great variations in the effects. And to discern these tiny differences takes a good and perspicacious eye" (Guicciardini, 71).

Today we think of this insight as the basis of chaos theory with its idea of "sensitive dependence on initial conditions." In his classic 1963 paper on meteorology, Konrad Lorenz commented: "One meteorologist remarked that if the theory were correct, one flap of a seagull's wings would be enough to alter the course of the weather forever." By 1972, he changed the seagull to a butterfly in a paper titled "Predictability: Does the Flap of a Butterfly's Wings in Brazil Set Off a Tornado in Texas?"[5] The butterfly effect—like Guicciardini's "tiny differences" that may cause "great variations" or Solon's days that never exactly repeat—depends on no mystery from beyond, only the dizzying complexity we encounter daily.

No two moments are ever the same, and no two places exactly resemble each other. For Solon, as for Herodotus, geography as well as history instructs in diversity. Just before concluding that no man should be considered happy until we have seen his end, Solon again appeals not to mystery but to motley-ness: he that has one piece of good fortune lacks another.

> Now it is impossible for any one man to comprehend all these advantages: as no one country suffices to produce every thing for itself, but affords some and wants others, and that which affords the most is the best; so no human being is in all respects self-sufficient, but possesses one advantage, and is in need of another; he therefore who has constantly enjoyed the most of these, and then ends his life tranquilly, this man in my judgment, O King, deserves the name of happy. We ought therefore to consider the end of everything, in what way it will terminate; for the Deity having shown a glimpse of happiness to many, has afterward utterly overthrown him. (*H*, 14)

No person and no land is self-sufficient: nature places its bounties on the right hand and on the left. The very existence of trade shows our incompleteness. Every country is a patchwork of advantages and disadvantages; the motleyness of time and space answer to each other. The reference to the Deity seems en-tirely perfunctory and serves as a mere trope for the inconstant and amazingly various nature of things.

Montaigne's essay devoted to Solon's apothegm, "That Our Happiness Not Be Judged Until after Our Death," interprets it in the prosaic, rather than mystical, spirit. He judges Herodotus's moral to be the one Montaigne himself so often conveys: "the uncertainty and variability of human affairs, which the slightest shift changes from one state to another entirely different" (*CEM*, 54).

This story also suggests another moral common in prosaic apothegms. What matters most, what makes a life good or bad, is not the grand but the ordinary things. Croesus, the world's richest man, represents the opposite view. His pride reflects not only personal vanity but also a misunderstanding of human experience.

Confident of his splendid lot, Croesus demands Solon state who is the hap-piest of men, and becomes enraged when the sage names ordinary people. "My Athenian friend," he objects, "is my happiness, then, so slighted by you as noth-ing worth, that you do not think me of so much value as private men?" (*H*, 13). Solon replies that what is most important are the ordinary things that even a moderate person may possess, and that happiness is most readily found in the familiar. He urges upon Croesus a change in perspective. In so doing, he looks forward to many prosaic apothegms offering similar advice: direct your eyes to daily happenings, unremarkable people, immediate circumstances, and quotidian moments.

Rasselas

Good and ill are universally intermingled and confounded; happiness and misery, wisdom and folly, virtue and vice. Nothing is pure and entirely of a piece. . . . The draughts of life, according to the poet's fiction, are always mixed from the vessels on each hand of Jupiter.

—David Hume, *The Natural History of Religion* (183)

Writers may expand on prosaic apothegms by telling a story about the search for perfect wisdom, blinding happiness, or the timeless key to all mysteries. The hero or heroine discovers that such a search must end in failure. He or she arrives instead at what is possible, modest wisdom and middling happiness—the "gold in sand," as Tolstoy calls it (*AK*, 277). The story illustrates the qualified truths of prosaic apothegms.

In Samuel Johnson's *Rasselas,* the eponymous hero begins in the happy valley, where "the blessings of nature were collected, and its evils extracted and excluded," but discovers that purity and perfection exclude meaningful life (*SJ*, 506). Existence oppresses by its monotony and insipidity, and those who have known no other life "sit stupid in the gloom of perpetual vacuity" (534). With the aid of Johnson's mouthpiece, Imlac, Rasselas and his sister escape to the world of imperfection and surprise. Possessing the singular advantage of entering life from outside with all means at their disposal, the prince and princess aspire to the perfect, or at least the best, "choice of life." They consult one wise person after another, but although many claim to know the answer, experience refutes them all.

The structure of each encounter repeats itself and shapes the plot. The title of one chapter, "The Prince Finds a Wise and Happy Man," paraphrases Rasselas's expectation, but Imlac advises caution with all eloquent teachers of morality: "They discourse like angels, but they live like men" (546). Sure enough, when the wise and happy man's daughter dies, his stoic morality proves useless. Rasselas advises him to apply his own precepts, but the supposed sage can only ask what comfort they can offer now that his daughter is gone forever. Rasselas leaves reflecting on "the inefficacy of polished periods and studied sentences" (547).

When prince and princess try the beauty of a pastoral life, they find that the shepherds, far from the elevated beings described by the poets, "are so rude and ignorant, so little able to compare the good with the evil of the occupation, and so indistinct in their narratives and descriptions," that they have grown spiteful as well. "Their hearts were cankered with discontent . . . [and they] looked up with stupid malevolence toward those that were placed above them" (547). When Rasselas and his sister visit a celebrated hermit, they arrive on the day he has renounced his way of living to return to society.

Each adventure affords the opportunity for prosaic apothegms:

Rasselas reproached himself . . . having not known, or not considered, how many useful hints are obtained by chance, and how often the mind, hurried by her own ardour to distant views, neglects the truths that lie open before her. (515)

Inconsistencies, answered Imlac, cannot be right, but, imputed to man, they may both be true. (522)

Even the virtuous fall sometimes to variance, when their virtues are of different kinds, and tending to extremes. (559)

Thus it is, said Nekayah, that philosophers are deceived. There are a thousand familiar disputes which reason can never decide; questions that elude investigation, and make logick ridiculous; cases where something must be done, and where little can be said. . . . Wretched would be the pair above all names of wretchedness, who should be doomed to adjust by reason every morning all the minute details of a domestick day. (566–67)

Every hour, answered the princess, confirms my prejudice in favour of the position so often uttered by the mouth of Imlac, "That nature sets her gifts on the right hand and on the left." Those conditions, which flatter hope and attract desire, are so constituted that, as we approach one, we recede from another. There are goods so opposed that we cannot seize both, but by too much prudence, may pass between them at too great a distance to reach either. (567)

The world perplexes with its variety and uncertainty, we must decide on the basis of imperfect knowledge, logic falls short before daily difficulties, one good choice precludes another, and even virtues may contend with each other. In our time, Isaiah Berlin offered the best-known version of this last point: "[T]he notion of the perfect whole, the ultimate solution, in which all good things coexist, seems to me to be not merely unattainable—that is a truism—but conceptually incoherent. . . . Some among the Great Goods cannot live together. . . . We are doomed to choose, and every choice may entail an irreparable loss."[6]

Tiny Alterations

Reproaching himself for missing the obvious, Rasselas reflects that "the mind, hurried by her own ardour to distant views, neglects the truths that lie open before her." Wittgenstein's constant advice—"Don't think, but look!"—also redirects our gaze to what seems so familiar that we do not consider it.

> The aspects of things that are most important for us are hidden because of their simplicity and familiarity. (One is unable to notice something—because it is always before one's eyes.) . . . And this means: we fail to be struck by what, once seen, is most striking and most powerful. (*PI*, 50e)

Among long genres, realist novels most consistently direct our attention to the quotidian world around us. Suspicious of theory's abstractions, they urge: "Don't think, but look!" To teach us to see the ordinary, they populate their stories with details and particularities other narrative genres avoid.

Although it stresses the importance of "the minute details of a domestick day," *Rasselas* does not describe minute details. Resembling Voltaire's *Candide* or Swift's *Gulliver's Travels* more than *Middlemarch* or *Anna Karenina*, *Rasselas* obeys the conventions of satire and assiduously avoids realist particularities. It follows Imlac's advice that a poet's business "is to examine, not the individual but the species; to remark general properties and large appearances; he does not number the streaks of the tulip, or describe the different shades of verdure of the forest" (*SJ*, 527). The realist novel does number the streaks of the tulip and—Turgenev takes this possibility literally—describes a forest's different shades of verdure.

Realist novels also describe individuals with attention to all that is particular to them. They show us the psychological specificities that make Elizabeth Bennet, Dorothea Brooke, or Anna Karenina different from all other women. They also illuminate each consciousness from within so we can sense how people "differ from themselves" from moment to moment. Readers trace the minutest alterations of self.

Tolstoy expressed the sense of life common to the prosaic apothegm and the realist novel:

> [The painter] Bryullov one day corrected a pupil's study. The pupil, having glanced at the altered drawing, exclaimed, "Why, you only touched it a tiny bit, but it is quite another thing." Bryullov replied: "Art begins where that *tiny bit* begins."
>
> That saying is strikingly true not only of art but of all life. One may say that true life begins where the tiny bit begins—where what seem to us minute and

infinitely small alterations take place. True life is not lived where great external changes take place—where people move about, clash, fight, and slay one another—it is lived only where these tiny, tiny infinitesimally small changes occur. (*TRE*, 81)

Tolstoy praises Dostoevsky for representing the hero of *Crime and Punishment*, Raskolnikov, by such tiny alterations. According to Tolstoy, Raskolnikov lived his true life, and made his decision to kill the old lady, neither when doing anything dramatic nor considering great philosophical questions—nor even thinking about the old lady at all. That decision was made when he was just lying on his couch thinking of nothing in particular, "when only his consciousness was active: and in that consciousness tiny, tiny alterations were taking place" (*TRE*, 82).

One reason realist novels in general, and Tolstoy's in particular, demand great length is that they trace the tiniest alterations of consciousness from moment to moment. However brief the prosaic apothegm may be, its inner logic generates a work as long as *War and Peace*.

Prosaic Values

All realist novels focus on the details of daily life. Some in addition represent the ordinary as the source of value. A good life is one lived right moment to moment.

In these "prosaic novels" (as we might call them), what matters most in moral life is our daily kindness or cruelty to the people nearest us.[7] We owe the greatest obligations not to Russia or to all mankind, as Levin discovers in *Anna Karenina*, but to one's family and neighbors. The real heroes—they are usually heroines—are to be found not on the battlefield but in the nursery. We do the most good when we make small changes that improve the texture of ordinary existence.

Tolstoy loved Benjamin Franklin, who caught this prosaic spirit when he argued that modest improvements do the most good: "Human felicity is produced not so much by great pieces of good fortune that seldom happen as by little advantages that happen every day."[8]

Middlemarch: A Process and an Unfolding

Middlemarch teaches both the importance and the value of the ordinary. Its interwoven plots concern the encounter of simple ideals with complex realities. It opposes idealizing genres, such as the epic or the saint's life, to the realist novel. And in the aphorisms it uses in profusion, it subjects wise sayings, dicta, and heroic pronouncements to the skeptical judgment of sardonic maxims and prosaic apothegms.

Dorothea aspires to live a life like Saint Theresa's, "who found her epos in the reform of a religious order," but was born to a different, more prosaic time and genre (*MM*, 7). She lives, we might say, as a sort of refugee from higher genres, and she keeps trying to view the real world in terms of them. And so she perceives in Mr. Casaubon manners and features that "made him resemble the portrait of Locke" (18); she imagines that marrying him would be like marrying Pascal; and she hears his bombastic pronouncements and banal dicta as the summons to a life above the ordinary. "Everything I see in him corresponds to his pamphlet on Biblical cosmology," she tells her sister Celia, who responds with appropriate dismay at Dorothea's astral vision and her blindness to obvious facts (22). To Celia, "notions and scruples were like spilt needles, making one afraid of treading, or sitting down, or even eating" (22). Eliot's epigraph to this chapter cites the passage where Don Quixote mistakes a barber's basin for the resplendent helmet of Mambrino.

Like Dorothea, other characters see themselves in terms of one or another high genre. Casaubon imagines he is an unappreciated scholarly genius capable of discovering "the key to all mysteries." Will Ladislaw detects in his own lack of discipline the breadth of true artistic genius. And Lydgate, who hopes to find the "primitive tissue," becomes entangled in daily snares. Each story examines, as the novel's first sentence suggests, "how the mysterious mixture [man] behaves under the varying experiments of Time" (7). Of such a complex mixture, different for each person, we can only say that it will surprise. To know exactly how, we must not think but look.

To teach us finer perception, the author draws, from specific incidents, morals in the form of prosaic apothegms:

> He [Lydgate] was at a starting point which makes many a man's career a fine subject for betting, if there were any gentlemen given to that amusement who could appreciate the complicated probabilities of an arduous purpose, with all the possible thwartings and furtherings of circumstance, all the niceties of inward balance, by which a man swims and makes his point or else is carried head-long. The risk would remain, even with close knowledge of Lydgate's character; for character too is a process and an unfolding. (144–45)

> Our vanities differ as our noses do; all conceit is not the same conceit, but varies in correspondence with the minute mental make in which one of us differs from another. (145)

Our passions do not live apart in locked chambers, but, dressed in their small wardrobe of notions, bring their provisions to a common table and mess together feeding out of the common store according to their appetite. (161)

Will was not without his intention to be generous, but our tongues are little triggers which have usually been pulled before general intentions have been brought to bear. (351)

A human being in this aged nation of ours is a very wonderful whole, the slow creation of long interchanging influences; and charm is a result of two such wholes, the one loving, and the other loved. (393)

"Oh, how cruel!" said Dorothea, clasping her hands. . . . "Besides, there is a man's character beforehand to speak for him."

"But, my dear Mrs. Casaubon," said Mr. Farebrother, smiling gently at her ardour, "character is not cut in marble—it is not something solid and unalterable. It is something living and changing, and may become diseased as our bodies do." (698–99)

One cannot foretell a man's destiny from his qualities, because what we call a single quality consists of many different ones. Each slight difference can make a big difference depending on all the contingencies, all the thwartings and furtherings, a person encounters. What is more, these qualities interact in strange ways and in innumerable combinations. Each person represents a process of countless historical pressures, the slow creation of long interchanging influences as well as of biographical layerings, which never cohere into a consistent self.

Each person is not only complex but also constantly evolving. Moment by moment, thought by thought, decision by decision, everyone alters in minute but cumulative ways. No one is cut in marble.

Like ourselves, our intentions at any given moment are also composite, reflecting several immediate desires and influences along with more general patterns and a patchwork of habits. It is hard to say what motivates our choices and, therefore, to judge them ethically. There are pale shades of good and ill that elude any simple description.

Wherever one might be tempted to generalize or formulate laws, Eliot directs us to the fine shadings we have overlooked. She allows us to contemplate how minutiae matter. Like the law as Holmes characterizes it, people as Eliot describes them have never quite integrated all their new habits or dispensed

with outmoded ones. We include unassimilated novelties and vestigial qualities. Even the smallest alterations and inconsistencies can lead to surprises.

The Fragment of a Life

Epilogues to novels presume a temporality different from the rest of the
work.[9] In epilogue time there are no surprises. After the main part of a novel
narrates complex events taking place in a relatively brief period, its epilogue
projects the rest of characters' lives in a few strokes. In epilogue time, characters do not live their lives but live out their lives. Nothing essential will change,
and so it is possible to draw straight lines. Epilogue time dispenses with the
prosaic vision.

For many novelists, this presumption of a change in temporality represents
a falsity, a mere concession to artistic convention, like a final double marriage.
Life is all middle. These authors may therefore avoid epilogues altogether. *Anna
Karenina* adds part 8 after the heroine's death, but it unfolds in the same temporality as the rest of the book. *War and Peace* includes two "epilogues," but
neither takes place in epilogue time. Alternatively, an author may use an epilogue but warn us against taking its temporality as true to life.

Eliot's epilogue begins with an apothegm warning against imagining that
life ever unfolds as it does in epilogues. "For the fragment of a life, however
typical, is not the sample of an even web; promises may not be kept, and an
ardent outset may be followed by declension; latent powers may find their
long-waited opportunity; a past error may urge a grand retrieval" (*MM*, 789).
All future moments will be, as all past moments were, just other presents, not
entirely derivable from predecessors and open to surprises. Prosaic time can
never be outrun.

Where God Is

Middlemarch stresses the supreme value of the ordinary. Other genres presume
that tragedy pertains to rare critical moments, but for Eliot an "element of tragedy . . . lies in the very fact of frequency. . . . If we had a keen vision and feeling
of all ordinary human life, it would be like hearing the grass grow and hearing
the squirrel's heart beat, and we should die of that roar which lies on the other
side of silence" (*MM*, 189). Dorothea learns that real goodness, as well as tragedy, lies in small deeds. And so "the effect of her being on those around her was
incalculably diffusive; for the growing good of the world is partly dependent
on unhistoric acts; and that things are not so ill with you and me as they might

have been, is half owing to the number who lived faithfully a hidden life, and rest in unvisited tombs" (795).

Pierre learns much the same lesson in *War and Peace*. All his life he has sought the meaningful in dramatic stories, critical moments, and obscure theories. He has seen life as epic heroism guided by the grand dictates of fate, while succumbing to the language of the summons, the dictum, and mystical obscurities. Until his captivity by the French, he sought a hidden God, but at last learns "not by words or reasoning, but by direct feeling, what his nurse had taught him long ago: that God is here and everywhere" (*W&P*, 1320).

Truth is not hidden, it is camouflaged. Cloaked in its ordinariness, it escapes detection. To discern it, we need, not the hermetic language of philosophers, but the ability to notice the world before us. When Pierre learns to see the richness of daily experience, he "felt like a man who, after straining his eyes to peer into the remote distance, finds what he was seeking at his very feet. All his life he had been looking over the heads of those around him, while he had only to look before him without straining his eyes" (1320).

As always in Tolstoy, one needs to focus one's attention more keenly. Previously, "in everything near and commonplace he [Pierre] had seen only what was limited, petty, commonplace and meaningless" (1320). Imagining truth to be remote, "he had equipped himself with a mental telescope and gazed into the distance. . . . Now, however, he had learned to see the great, the eternal, the infinite in everything, and therefore, in order to look at it, he had naturally discarded the telescope through which he had till then been gazing over the heads of men, and joyfully surveyed the ever-changing, eternally great, unfathomable, and infinite life around him. And the closer he looked, the happier and more serene he was" (1320).

Pierre looks more perceptively at other people, too, and appreciates the ways in which they differ from each other and from themselves. Previously, he had fallen into despair when he discovered "the infinite variety of men's minds, which prevents a truth from ever appearing the same to any two persons" (528). Now he finds the shades of difference fascinating. He draws closer to people by valuing their otherness. Above all, he acknowledges

> the possibility of every person thinking, feeling, and seeing things in his own way. This legitimate individuality of every man's views, which formerly troubled or irritated Pierre, now became the basis of the sympathy he felt for other people and the interest he took in them. The difference, sometimes the complete

contradiction, between men's opinions and their lives, and between one person and another, pleased him and drew from him a gentle, ironic smile. (1323–24)

It is the gentle smile with which one confides a prosaic apothegm.

Admitting Other Genres

The prosaic apothegm and the realist novel acknowledge the legitimate individuality of other genres. If the truth escapes all formulations of it, then no one genre can be sufficient.

At some moments we properly turn to the confident "hedgehog" genres—the wise saying, the dictum, and the summons—as well as to the more skeptical "fox" genres, the sardonic maxim and the two types of apothegm.[10]

Realist novels readily incorporate other genres—speeches, short stories, romances, satires—with varying degrees of approval or irony. They include many short genres as well. Even those genres most hostile to the novel's overall spirit may appear in a surprising range of tones, ranging from withering irony to qualified approval.

Dicta sometimes elicit our sympathy for the good intentions that make them appealing. Out of unselfish idealism, Turgenev's Bazarov insists that self-interest is the only human motivation. When Pierre believes he has discovered the key to history, we smile at his good-heartedness. It would be altogether too easy to dismiss these characters and their sayings. The best prosaic authors know that wisdom, no matter how capacious and conscious of complexity, may outwit itself. Sometimes hedgehogs out-think foxes, and true foxes know there are hedgehog moments.

The prosaic spirit can also accommodate wise sayings. By and large, prosaic apothegms regard proverbs as failing the test of experience. No providential order guarantees rewards for virtue or prudence. And yet, the faith that things are somehow ultimately right can make them so. As we have seen, William James, a fox given to outfoxing foxes, compares faith to trust: distrust of others tends to justify itself, but so does trust. Trust makes others more trustworthy. "The desire for a certain kind of truth here brings about that special truth's existence."[11]

So, too, a person's faith in the meaningfulness of things often makes them meaningful. "His faith acts on the powers above him as a claim, and creates its own verification. . . . *[F]aith in a fact can help create the fact*" (James, 24–25). James cites Pascal in this sense: "[T]he heart has its reasons that reason does not know" (21).

In *War and Peace*, Tolstoy treats proverbs in this tolerant spirit. In captivity, Pierre meets the wise peasant Platon Karataev, who teaches him, by example, to see the beauty in everyday events and the nearest people. Karataev's faith in the world justifies itself, not by freeing him from suffering, but by attuning him to all the small goodnesses existence offers.

Karataev speaks in proverbs, but his wisdom does not reside in what they say. Their content barely rises above banality. What gives these proverbs meaning is their use: Karataev applies just the right saying to illuminate the shifting quality of each moment. Their profundity lies in nothing that could be placed in an anthology—nothing textual, as we would say—but in the sensitivity that makes them just the right way to characterize a fleeting context.

"The proverbs that were prevalent in his speech," Tolstoy explains, "were . . . those folk sayings which taken out of context seem to have so little meaning, yet when aptly applied acquire the significance of profound wisdom" (*W&P*, 1163). Context is all. Karataev "would often say the exact opposite of what he had said on a previous occasion, yet both would be right" (1163). If wisdom resided in the text, contradiction would matter, but as Karataev applies proverbs, the apparent contradiction stems from the different qualities of each occasion. So sensitive is Karataev to context that if Pierre asks him to repeat a proverb, Karataev gives him a somewhat different one because the moment has subtly shifted. Karataev "did not understand, could not grasp the significance of the words apart from their context" (1163).

No one can perceive surroundings more keenly than Karataev. He discerns all the fine shadings and tiny alterations that others overlook. And what he sees in them is meaningfulness and beauty. "The chief charm of his talk lay in the fact that the most ordinary incidents—often those that Pierre himself had witnessed without taking notice of them—acquired a ceremonious beauty in his account of them" (1162). Karataev loves to listen to soldiers' stories about real life. "He smiled happily when listening to such stories, now and then putting in a word or asking a question, all aimed at bringing out for himself the moral beauty of what was related" (1162).

By including this character, Tolstoy acknowledges truths beyond realism, while allowing the spirit of the prosaic apothegm to adapt another's genre's wisdom.

CONCLUSION

The Great Conversation

The single adequate form for *verbally expressing* authentic human life is
the *open-ended dialogue*. . . . To live means to participate in . . . the world
symposium.   —Mikhail Bakhtin (*PDP*, 293)

The ancients paired opposing genres. Satyr plays accompanied tragedies,
epics provoked mock epics, satire answered philosophy.[1] Legend ascribed to
Homer not only the *Iliad* and the *Odyssey* but also their parody, *The Battle of
the Frogs and Mice*. In the dispute between philosophy and satire, Socrates and
Diogenes represented both.

At the end of the *Apology*, Socrates professes to be willing to die ten times
over if, as he imagines, he can meet the great thinkers and poets in the afterlife.
"Above all, I should like to spend my time there, as here, in examining and
searching people's minds, to find out who is really wise among them, and who
only thinks that he is."[2] Eternity would be endless dialogue. Ancient menippean
satires, such as Lucian's "Dialogues of the Dead," staged such otherworldly arguments. The shades of thinkers from different periods confronted each other
for endless debate. Readers arrived at no final answer.

Bakhtin saw such debates as expressing the idea that "truth is not born nor
is it to be found inside the head of an individual person, it is born *between
people* collectively searching for truth, in the process of their dialogic interaction" (*PDP*, 110). By the same token, no single philosophy or genre could ever
adequately represent the complexity of the world.

In setting short genres against each other, I have hinted at the same point.
No matter how many genres literature develops, we require more. Expand
knowledge, and learn to see the increased store as too small.

Experience exceeds any take on it. One reason to study the history of literature is to discover more understandings of life than we could otherwise imagine. With every genre we master, we acquire a new set of eyes on the world. By the same token, we escape the prison of familiar worldviews when we study other civilizations, so long as we let them speak in their own terms and not hurry to characterize them in ours. As we range over epochs and across cultures, we realize that, no matter how capacious our perspective, it is never large enough. Truth does not simplify, it ramifies.

The more genres one understands, the more readily one can develop their contrasting views. One can arrive at better answers by imagining old thinkers disputing new questions. Literature lives not as a mere succession of masterpieces but as a great symposium always enlivened by contact between past and present.

Of all the genres I have examined, only the prosaic apothegm clearly recognizes its inadequacy to the world's complexity. As it shows some overlooked oddity making nonsense of competing theories and genres, it readily applies that insight to itself. It knows its limits and acknowledges its need for outside wisdom. We rarely find proverbs, witticisms, or maxims in quest of alien truth, but they all find a comfortable home, and are treated with qualified respect, in realist novels reflecting the spirit of prosaic apothegms.

Middlemarch and *War and Peace* present a conversation among short genres and an open-ended competition of worldviews. Each genre plays a role and voices its values in the books' great dialogues, much as the experience of each person, seriously considered, offers something valuable. So Pierre learns when he wisely acknowledges "the possibility of every man thinking, feeling, and seeing things in his own way. This legitimate individuality of every man's views, which formerly troubled or irritated Pierre, now became the basis of the sympathy he felt for other people and the interest he took in them" (*W&P*, 1322). Developing the spirit of prosaic apothegms, prosaic novels teach us to expand our vision to include perspectives at odds with our own. Even dicta can be taken seriously if rephrased as perceptive exaggerations, and the great realist novels try to do so.

Whether mystic or prosaic, the apothegm neither affirms nor denies, but gives a sign. The sign points to the need for more apothegms and for more aphorisms of all sorts. The long and short of it is, no matter how many aphorisms we know, we are in want of more. If we follow the spirit of apothegms, we will set them against each other and allow their dialogues to develop in surprising ways. Above all, we will try to keep the conversation going.

NOTES

INTRODUCTION

1. The title of a first-century work remarkably popular in the Middle Ages, Valerius Maximus's *Memorable Deeds and Sayings*, captures the approach. A person *was* the deeds he performed and the things he said.

2. For a detailed account of Bakhtin's approach to genres, see *MBCP*, 271–305.

3. In my earlier articles on these genres, I used the term "aphorism" for the works I here call "apothegms." Likewise, I referred to the family of all short genres as "quotations." But because I use the term "quotations" in a quite different sense in my book *The Words of Others: From Quotations to Culture* (New Haven, CT: Yale University Press, 2011), I have chosen in the present study to refer to the family of all short genres as "aphorisms" and the ones discussed in Chapters 2 and 6 as "apothegms."

4. My thanks to R. Bracht Branham for showing me the significance of this passage.

CHAPTER 1

1. Charles Darwin, *On the Origin of Species: A Facsimile of the First Edition*, ed. Ernst Mayr (Cambridge, MA: Harvard University Press, 1981), 411–13.

2. See Tzvetan Todorov, *The Fantastic: A Structural Approach to a Literary Genre*, trans. Richard Howard (Ithaca, NY: Cornell University Press, 1975).

3. For a detailed exposition of Bakhtin's theory of genres, see *MBCP*, 271–305. I also draw on *BOG*.

4. On genre memory, see *MBCP*, 295–97.

5. Consider (as sentiment and prose) this Fullerism, frequently displayed on dorm-room posters:

Here is God's purpose—
for God, to me, it seems,
is a verb
not a noun. (*YBQ*, 296)

CHAPTER 2

1. As translated in Francis M. Dunn, *Tragedy's End: Innovation and Closure in Euripidean Drama* (New York: Oxford University Press, 1996), 17. The five plays ending this way are *Alcestis, Medea, Andromache, Helen,* and *The Bacchae.*

2. David Grene and Richmond Lattimore, eds., *The Complete Greek Tragedies*, vol. 5, *Euripides I* (Chicago: University of Chicago Press, 1956), 123. Dunn notes that in *Medea* the first line is different and gives it as: "Zeus in Olympus dispenses many things" (Dunn, 204).

3. David Grene and Richmond Lattimore, eds., *The Complete Greek Tragedies: Sophocles I* (Chicago: University of Chicago Press, 1965), 150–51.

4. In *Oedipus at Colonus*, Oedipus defends himself to others by asserting his blamelessness in any human terms:

Oedipus: The bloody deaths, the incest, the calamities
You speak so glibly of: I suffered them,
By fate, against my will! . . .
And tell me this: if there were prophecies
Repeated by the oracles of the gods,
That father's death should come through his own son,
How could you justly blame it on me?
On me, who was yet unborn, yet unconceived,
Nor yet existent for my father and mother.   (*Sophocles I*, 123–24)

Oedipus: If someone tried to kill you here and now,
You righteous gentleman, what would you do,
Inquire first if the stranger was your father?   (*Sophocles I*, 124)

5. Cited in Dunn, 4.

6. Elie Halévy, *The Growth of Philosophic Radicalism*, trans. Mary Morris (Boston: Beacon, 1955), 6.

7. G. K. Chesterton, *The Father Brown Omnibus* (New York: Dodd, Mead, 1951).

8. Jeremy Bentham, *An Introduction to the Principles of Morals and Legislation* (New York: Macmillan, 1984), 1–2 (opening paragraph).

9. B. F. Skinner, *Walden Two* (New York: Macmillan, 1962), 193–95.

10. Rene Descartes, *Meditations*, in *"Discourse on Method" and "Meditations,"* trans. Laurence J. Lafleur (Indianapolis, IN: Bobbs-Merrill, 1960), 82.

11. *The Leibniz-Clarke Correspondence*, ed. H. G. Alexander (Manchester, UK: Manchester University Press, 1965), 16.

12. Gottfried Wilhelm Leibniz, *Discourse on Metaphysics, Correspondence with Arnauld, Monadology*, trans. George Montgomery (La Salle, IL: Open Court, 1989), 19.

13. *Catechism of the Catholic Church* (Mahway, NJ: Paulist Press, n.d.), 13.

14. Among recent authors who advance all-encompassing explanations, Nobel prize winner Gary Becker faults Bentham for not going far enough: Bentham allegedly neglects the principle of stable preferences, thus ensnaring himself in tautologies. Properly understood, "the economic approach to human behavior" as Becker defines it explains all aspects of life. Among Becker's best-known dicta we find: "[H]uman behavior is not compartmentalized, sometimes based on maximizing, sometimes not, sometimes motivated by stable preferences, sometimes by volatile ones, sometimes resulting in an optimal accumulation of information, sometimes not. Rather, all human behavior can be viewed as involving participants who maximize their utility from a stable set of prefer-

ences and accumulate an optimal amount of information from a variety of markets." The economic approach suggests that "a useful theory of criminal behavior can dispense with special theories of anomie, psychological inadequacies, or inheritance of special traits and simply extend the economist's usual analysis of choice." Gary S. Becker, *The Economic Approach to Human Behavior* (Chicago: University of Chicago Press, 1978), 14, 40.

15. Benedict de Spinoza, "Ethics," in *The Chief Works of Benedict de Spinoza*, trans. R. H. M. Elwes, 2 vols. (New York: Dover, 1951), 2:68.

16. As cited in Stuart Hampshire, *Spinoza* (London: Faber and Faber, 1956), 83.

17. For a more detailed consideration of utopian literature, see *BOG*.

18. Edward Bellamy, *Looking Backward, 2000–1887* (New York: Signet, 1960), 90.

19. Sigmund Freud, "A Difficulty in the Path of Psycho-Analysis," in *The Standard Edition of the Complete Psychological Works of Sigmund Freud*, ed. James Strachey with Anna Freud, Alex Strachey, and Alan Tyson, vol. 17 (London: Hogarth Press, 1991), 152.

20. Arthur Schopenhauer, *Essays and Aphorisms*, ed. R. J. Hollingdale (London: Penguin, 1970), 31.

21. Darwin, *Origin of Species*, 1.

22. As cited in Rosalie L. Colie, *Paradoxia Epidemica: The Renaissance Tradition of Paradox* (Princeton, NJ: Princeton University Press, 1966), 24–25.

23. Nicholas of Cusa, "On Learned Ignorance," in *Selected Spiritual Writings*, trans. H. Lawrence Bond (New York: Paulist Press, 1997), 89–91.

24. Immanuel Kant, *Critique of Pure Reason*, trans. Norman Kemp Smith (New York: Modern Library, 1958), 3.

25. As cited in Marvin R. O'Connell, *Blaise Pascal: Reasons of the Heart* (Grand Rapids, MI: William B. Eerdmans, 1997), 96.

26. Wittgenstein's debt to Tolstoy is discussed extensively in Alan Janik and Stephen Toulmin, *Wittgenstein's Vienna* (New York: Simon and Schuster, 1973); and in Ray Monk, *Ludwig Wittgenstein: The Duty of Genius* (New York: Free Press, 1990). Monk also stresses Wittgenstein's debt to Dostoevsky.

27. See A. C. Graham, *Disputers of the Tao: Philosophical Arguments in Ancient China* (La Salle, IL: Open Court, 1993), 216–17. I am indebted to Graham in my discussion of Lao Tzu.

28. As cited in Monk, 178.

29. George Santayana, "Carnival," in *Theories of Comedy*, ed. Paul Lauter (Garden City, NY: Anchor, 1964), 420.

30. I cite the translation that serves as the epigraph to Rebecca West's novel *The Thinking Reed* (New York: Viking, 1936), facing title page.

31. "After all," as Thomas Nagel famously asked, "what would it be like to be a bat if one removed the viewpoint of the bat?" Thomas Nagel, "What Is It Like to Be a Bat?" in *The Mind's Eye: Fantasies and Reflections on Self and Soul*, ed. Douglas R. Hofstadter and Daniel C. Dennett (Toronto: Bantam, 1981), 398. The title of Nagel's essay has itself become a frequently repeated apothegm of our time, our version of an ancient paradox.

32. Desiderius Erasmus, *The Praise of Folly*, trans. Hoyt Hopewell Hudson (Princeton, NJ: Princeton University Press, 1974), 8.

33. Aeschylus, *Agamemnon*, in *Aeschylus I: Oresteia*, trans. Richmond Lattimore (Chicago: University of Chicago Press, 1953), 74–75.

34. William James, *The Will to Believe and Other Essays in Popular Philosophy* (New York: Dover, 1956), 62.

35. The famous passage reads: "The self-fulfilling prophecy is, in the beginning a *false* definition of the situation involving a new behavior which makes the originally false conception come *true*. The specious validity of the self-fulfilling prophecy perpetuates a reign of error. For the prophet will cite the actual course of events as proof that he was right from the outset." See Robert K. Merton, "The Self-Fulfilling Prophecy," in *Social Theory and Social Structure*, rev. ed. (Glencoe, IL: Free Press, 1963), 423.

36. *Dostoevsky: A Self-Portrait*, ed. Jesse Coulson (London: Oxford University Press, 1962), 72; italics mine.

37. For a superb account of this essay and Tolstoy's interest in Taoism, see Michael Denner, "Tolstoyan Nonaction: The Advantage of Doing Nothing," *Tolstoy Studies Journal* 13 (2001): 8–22.

38. Aldous Huxley, *Brave New World* (New York: Harper and Row, 1969), 163.

CHAPTER 3

1. Aristotle, *Rhetoric*, in *BWA*, 1405.

2. In Chapter 3 of *The Confessions of Jean Jacques Rousseau*, trans. J. M. Cohen (Harmondsworth, UK: Penguin, 1953), 113.

3. *Joubert: A Selection from His Thoughts*, ed. Katharine Lyttleton (London: Duckworth, 1912), 55.

4. Baldesar Castiglione, *The Book of the Courtier*, trans. Charles S. Singleton (Garden City, NY: Doubleday, 1959), 43.

5. In Disraeli's *Lothair* we read: "When a man fell into his anecdotage it was a sign for him to retire from the world" (cited in *BBA*, xiv).

6. And rather humorless "misquotation" debunkers conclude that the wit took the line from elsewhere.

7. For more on sports time, see *N&F*, 173–80.

8. Oscar Wilde, "The Critic as Artist," in *The Portable Oscar Wilde*, ed. Richard Aldington and Stanley Weintraub (New York: Penguin, 1981), 134.

9. Oscar Wilde, "A Few Maxims for the Instruction of the Over-Educated," in *The Major Works*, ed. Isobel Murray (Oxford: Oxford University Press, 2008), 570.

10. Perhaps the tortures of hell? Could the strange pleasure we get from Hieronymus Bosch derive in part from the wit, the sheer inventiveness, of his demonic imagination? Could this sort of wit, placed strangely in stories for children, explain the appeal of Roald Dahl?

11. Although, amazingly enough, Victor Hugo's novella *The Last Day of a Man Condemned* was one of Dostoevsky's favorite works even before his mock execution!

12. Herbert Lockyer, *All the Last Words of Saints and Sinners* (Grand Rapids, MI: Kregel, 1969), 152.

13. M. J. Cohen and John Major, *History in Quotations* (London: Cassell, 2000), 525.

14. Oscar Wilde, "Phrases and Philosophies for the Use of the Young," in Aldington and Weintraub, *Portable Wilde*, 739. Compare: "Mrs. Cheveley: 'A woman's first duty in life is to her dressmaker, isn't it? What the second duty is, no one has as yet discovered'" (from *An Ideal Husband* [Aldington and Weintraub, *Portable Wilde*, 738]); and "In all unimportant matters, style, not sincerity, is the essential. In all important matters, style, not sincerity, is the essential" ("Phrases and Philosophies for the Young" [Aldington and Weintraub, *Portable Wilde*, 739]).

15. "Cynic" derives from the Greek word for dog (*kunikos*, "doglike"); thus, his response is "I am Diogenes the Dog."

16. As elsewhere, I am indebted here to Robert Belknap.

17. Henri Bergson, "Laughter," in *Comedy* (Garden City, NY: Doubleday, 1856), 78.

18. George Orwell, "Politics and the English Language," in *The Collected Essays, Journalism and Letters of George Orwell: In Front of Your Nose, 1945–1950* (New York: Harcourt Brace, 1968), 134.

19. The best study of Turgenev's poetics and worldview is Elizabeth Cheresh Allen, *Beyond Realism: Turgenev's Poetics of Secular Salvation* (Stanford: Stanford University Press, 1992).

20. G. K. Chesterton, "The Scandal of Father Brown," in *The Father Brown Omnibus* (New York: Dodd, Mead, 1951), 543.

21. All quotations are drawn from *IBE*: (1) p. 254, (2) p. 259, (3) p. 260, (4) p. 270, (5) p. 273, (6) p. 304, and (7) p. 206.

22. The first is from *Lady Windemere's Fan*, as cited in *MDQ*, 611; the second is from *The Portrait of Dorian Gray* (*MDQ*, 612).

23. W. H. Auden, "An Improbable Life," in *Oscar Wilde: A Collection of Critical Essays*, ed. Richard Ellmann (Englewood Cliffs, NJ: Prentice Hall, 1969), 136.

24. Joel Chandler Harris, *The Complete Tales of Uncle Remus* (Boston: Houghton Mifflin, 1995), 8.

25. For a sampling of Native American trickster stories—about Coyote, Iktomi, Mink, Rabbit, and others—see *American Indian Trickster Tales*, ed. Richard Erdoes and Alfonso Ortiz (New York: Penguin, 1998). See also Paul Radin, *The Trickster: A Study in American Indian Mythology* (New York: Schocken, 1972). The late Dell Hymes first introduced me to Coyote stories.

26. I borrow this explanation from Sheila Murnaghan's superb introduction to the Lombardo translation: Homer, *Odyssey*, trans. Stanley Lombardo (Indianapolis, IN: Hackett, 2000), lxiii.

27. Homer, *The Odyssey: The Story of Odysseus*, trans. W. H. D. Rouse (New York: Signet, 1007), 3.

28. Fitzgerald gives: "formidable for guile." Homer, *The Odyssey*, trans. Robert Fitzgerald (New York: Vintage, 1990), 145.

29. I borrow the terms "surprisingness" and "eventful" (in this sense) from Bakhtin.

30. Mikhail Bulgakov, *The Master and Margarita*, trans. Diana Burgin and Katherine Tiernan O'Connor (New York: Random House, 1996), 8.

31. Lord Byron, *Don Juan*, ed. Leslie A. Marchand (Boston: Houghton Mifflin, 1958), vii.

32. Alexander Pope, *The Dunciad*, bk. 4, ll. 239–40 and 249–52, in *Selected Poetry and Prose*, ed. William K. Wimsatt, Jr. (New York: Holt, Rinehart and Winston, 1965), 435.

33. See the catalogue volume, Tom Stankowicz and Marie Jackson, *The Museum of Bad Art: Art Too Bad to Be Ignored* (Kansas City, MO: Andrews and McMeel, 1996).

34. See http://www.darwinawards.com/. For example: "(11 March 1978, France) The singer Claude Francois, whose stellar career can be compared to that of Elvis Presley, popularized rock and roll music in France. One evening, he returned to his Paris apartment from a busy touring schedule, and ran a bath. While standing in the filled tub, he noticed a light bulb that wasn't straight, tried to straighten it . . . and was electrocuted."

35. http://www.bulwer-lytton.com/.

36. Denis Dutton, "Language Crimes: A Lesson in How Not to Write, Courtesy of the Professoriate," *Wall Street Journal*, February 5, 2009, http://denisdutton.com/language_crimes.htm.

37. Cited by Dutton from Butler's "Further Reflections on the Conversations of Our Time," from *Diacritics* (1997), http://denisdutton.com/bad_writing.htm.

38. From *The Location of Culture* (Routledge, 1994), http://denisdutton.com/bad_writing.htm.

39. Sigmund Freud, *The Psychopathology of Everyday Life*, trans. Alan Tyson (New York: Norton, 1965), 6.

40. Don Atyeo and Jonathon Green, eds., *Don't Quote Me!* (London: Chancellor, 2002), vii.

41. On the fallacies of "backshadowing," see Michael André Bernstein, *Foregone Conclusions: Against Apocalyptic History* (Berkeley: University of California Press, 1994); and *N&F*.

42. Perhaps that is why headlines use the present tense to indicate past action: the sense is that the action has been accomplished so recently it might as well be present. Or perhaps it's more like a not-so-instant replay.

43. Christopher Lehmann-Haupt, "Of Cats and Music and Taste, All Passing in Time," review of *With My Trousers Rolled: Familiar Essays*, by Joseph Epstein, *New York Times*, May 18, 1995, http://www.nytimes.com/1995/05/18/books/books-of-the-times-of-cats-and-music-and-taste-all-passing-in-time.html?scp=2&sq=&st=nyt. "On the subject of terrible puns, he [Epstein] records the caption of the lucky journalist who wrote beneath a photograph of Aristotle Onassis looking at the home of Buster Keaton, which Onassis was thinking of buying, 'Aristotle contemplating the home of Buster.'"

44. I rely here on my own memory of the headline of a British newspaper in 1970, when Mia Farrow's twin boys were born.

45. Cited (as folklore) in a letter to the *New York Review of Books*, October 10, 1985. One can easily find allusions to this supposed headline (or close variations) by Googling it. So far as I can tell, all references reflect its status as a piece of folklore. I recently came across it again in Toby Young, "Status Anxiety," *Spectator*, August 23, 2008, http://www.spectator.co.uk/columnists/all/903171/status-anxiety.thtml.

46. Attributed to Yogi Berra, BrainyQuote.com, 2011, http://www.brainyquote.com/quotes/quotes/y/yogiberra141506.html.

47. Similar remarks have also been attributed to Addison and others. See *CHQ*, 588.

48. The first of these comes from Twain's first book, *The Innocents Abroad*. The other three are all "attributed," that is, they are less than adequately validated and vary in wording. But whether or not they were said by Mark Twain, they belong, like so many quotations, to that semimythic figure "Mark Twain." Or as I prefer to say, they belong to the "second speaker" Mark Twain. I discuss this aspect of quotations in *The Words of Others: From Quotations to Culture* (New Haven, CT: Yale University Press, 2011).

Versions of the weather comment are given in *YBQ*, 782. "Wagner's music" can be found in *The Wit and Wisdom of Mark Twain*, ed. Aaron John Loeb (New York: Barnes and Noble, 1996), 56. Versions of "The reports of my death" can be found in *YBQ*, 781, and *ODQ*, 803. The smoking comment is in Loeb, *Wit and Wisdom*, 75, and *MDQ*, 582 (often given as "a thousand times").

49. *The Complete Humorous Sketches and Tales of Mark Twain*, ed. Charles Neider (Garden City, NY: Doubleday, 1961), 261.

50. Believe it or not, that has been the practice and claim of Richard Pevear and Larissa Volokhonsky in their many celebrated versions of the Russian classics—translations praised in the *New Yorker* and the *New York Review of Books* and which won a PEN translation award. As Pevear explains, they strive to reproduce the original syntax to show the author's style; but how is a reader to tell an author's stylistic innovation from an ordinary Russian syntactical construction or simple idiom? I discuss what is wrong with their renditions in "The Pevearsion of Russian Literature," *Commentary* 130, no. 1 (July/August 2010), 92–98.

51. Given in *YBQ* as "Common looking people are the best in the world; that is the reason the Lord makes so many of them" (464), with the version I have cited traced to the *New York Tribune*, December 20, 1903.

52. Richard Brinsley Sheridan, *Six Plays*, ed. Louis Kronenberger (New York: Hill and Wang, 1966), 47. Malapropisms were of course already well known from Shakespeare. For example, Elbow speaks in them in *Measure for Measure* ("two notorious benefactors"; "void of all profanation in the world that good Christians ought to have"; "my wife, sir, whom I detest before heaven" [act 2, sc. 1]). *The Yale Shakespeare*, ed. Wilbur L. Cross and Tucker Brooke (New York: Barnes and Noble, 1993), 409.

53. *The Complete Short Stories of Mark Twain*, ed. Charles Neider (Garden City, NY: Doubleday, 1957), 49.

54. *DI*, 404; I have amended the translation.

55. From Chapter 5 of *Through the Looking Glass* (*AIW*, 150).

CHAPTER 4

1. See J. D. Ray, "Egyptian Wisdom Literature," in *Wisdom in Ancient Israel: Essays in Honor of J. A. Emerton*, ed. John Day, Robert P. Gordon, and H. G. M. Williamson (Cambridge: Cambridge University Press, 1998), 19. R. B. Y. Scott's introduction to *ABPE* dates this work to 2600–2175 BC.

2. *Sayings of the Fathers, or Pirke Aboth,* ed. and trans. Joseph H. Hertz (n.p.: Behrman House, 1945), 35. Hertz comments: "[T]hey who resort to violence become victims of violence. Hillel, and the Rabbis after him, clung to the Biblical belief of retributive justice," which could be forestalled only by repentance (34).

3. *BOP,* 3 (commentary to Psalm 1).

4. "Some interpreters discern anticipation of reward and punishment beyond the grave here: v. 3 may refer to the tree as 'transplanted' beyond the present condition of earth; v. 5 employs a definite article with judgment, possibly foreseeing a final reckoning. Early Christian writers interpreted the tree as the cross and the life-giving water as baptism" (*HBC,* 434).

5. Homer, *Odyssey,* trans. Stanley Lombardo (Indianapolis: Hackett, 2000), 132. But this calculus is far from certain. Before this passage, Nausicaa has said to Odysseus: "Zeus himself, the Olympian god, / Sends happiness to good men and bad men both, / To each as he wills" (bk. 6, ll. 192–94).

6. *SCT,* 31. One of the Five Confucian Classics, the *Classic of Documents* "consists of announcements, counsels, speeches, or similar oral reports said to have been made by various rulers and their ministers from the time of the sage rulers Yao and Shun down to the early Zhou period" (*SCT,* 25).

7. *ODQ,* 620–25. "Fools rush in," "A little learning," and "To err is human" are from the *Essay on Criticism;* "Hope springs eternal" from the *Essay on Man.*

8. *ODQ,* 604, from the *Essay on Criticism.*

9. Psalms 23:5. Alter gives: "You set out a table before me in the face of my foes" (Alter, 79).

10. In the *Rhetoric,* Aristotle uses the term "enthymeme" to mean, not a logical syllogism with an unstated part, but a "rhetorical syllogism" that is merely "probable": "The propositions forming the basis of Enthymemes, though some of them may be 'necessary,' will most of them be only usually true" (*BWA,* 1352). Aristotle explains that "some proverbs are also maxims" (1416).

11. Erasmus seems well aware of Aristotle's purely instrumental view of wise sayings; see *AE,* 14.

12. For numerous examples, see the entry "Modern Proverbs" (*YBQ,* 526–30).

13. Unless otherwise identified, the proverbs in this discussion may be found under the headings "Modern Proverbs" and "Proverbs" in *YBQ,* 525–30 and 607–22.

14. *YBQ,* 483, from Chapter 15 of *The Prince.*

15. *The Sayings of the Desert Fathers: The Alphabetical Collection,* trans. Benedicta Ward (Kalamazoo, MI: Cistercian Publications, 1975), 75–76.

16. *The Wisdom of the Desert: Sayings from the Desert Fathers of the Fourth Century,* trans. Thomas Merton (Boston: Shambhala, 2004), 45.

17. William Blake, "The Marriage of Heaven and Hell," in *Complete Writings, with Variant Readings,* ed. Geoffrey Keynes (Oxford: Oxford University Press, 1969), 150–52.

18. Arthur Schopenhauer, *Essays and Aphorisms,* ed. and trans. R. J. Hollingdale (London: Penguin, 1970), 41. Schopenhauer called his collection *Parerga and Paralipomena* (1851).

19. "Eloi, Eloi, lama sabachtani? which is, being interpreted, My God, my God, why hast thou forsaken me?" is the version of Jesus's last words given in Mark 15:34; the almost identical verse occurs in Matthew 27:46.

20. Or we could consider the work an essay reporting a conversation. The "I" who reports it, presumably Plutarch, is also a participant. See Plutarch, "On God's Slowness to Punish," *Essays*, trans. Robin Waterfield (London: Penguin, 1992), 250–93, and the editor's introduction, 239–49.

21. Plutarch, *Essays*, 253. Olympichus alludes to the proverb, which the editor supplies in full as it is quoted by Sextus Empiricus.

22. Tobit 4:6–7. Citations from Tobit are from *The New Oxford Annotated Bible, with the Apocryphal/Deuterocanonical Books*, 3rd ed., ed. Michael D. Coogan et al. (Oxford: Oxford University Press, 2001).

23. Walter Benjamin, "The Storyteller: Reflections on the Work of Nikolai Leskov," in *Illuminations: Essays and Reflections*, ed. Hannah Arendt (New York: Harcourt Brace, 1968), 108.

24. *Aesop's Fables*, trans. Laura Gibbs (Oxford: Oxford University Press, 2002). The first written collection of the fables was apparently done by Demetrius of Phalerum, whose collection titled *Aesopica* is now lost. The Roman poet Phaedrus did a Latin version and Barius a Greek version, both in verse, in the first century AD. Gibbs also draws on Aphthonius, fourth century, and points out that he states in his *Progymnasmata* that Aesop was the best of all the writers of fables, thus showing we are dealing with a generic tradition. Some fables are attributed to Avianus (fifth century) and others to "Syntipas" (Michael Andreopulus). Gibbs also includes fables by the ninth-century Byzantine Ignatius Diaconus, from an expanding tradition ascribed to "Romulus" dating from the tenth century; by the monk Ademar of Chabannes (eleventh century); and by Odo of Cheriton (thirteenth century). See her excellent introduction, pp. ix–xli.

25. See Robert Temple's introduction to Aesop, *The Complete Fables*, trans. Olivia and Robert Temple (London: Penguin, 1998), xii.

26. Sam Pickering cites Locke in his introduction to *Aesop's Fables*, ed. Jack Zipes (New York: Signet, 2004), 4–5.

27. Cited from a letter of September 27, 1749, in *AE*, xxvi.

28. From a letter to Lucia Joyce, April 27, 1935, as reprinted in *Leo Tolstoy: A Critical Anthology*, ed. Henry Gifford (Harmondsworth, UK: Penguin, 1971), 200–201.

29. Excerpted from "The Russian Point of View," in Gifford, *Leo Tolstoy*, 189–90.

30. This is not the only case of Tolstoy choosing a misleading title. "The Death of Ivan Ilych" turns out to be about not his death but his dying. "Master and Man" (*Khozyain I rabotnik*) is not about a master and his worker but about the disappearance of that distinction when we understand life as love.

31. Tolstoy, "God Sees the Truth, but Waits to Tell," in *The Short Stories of Leo Tolstoy*, trans. Arthur Mendel and Barbara Makanowitzky (New York: Bantam, 1960), 207.

32. The obvious example is "The Death of Ivan Ilych." I have argued that the same is true of *Anna Karenina* in *"Anna Karenina" in Our Time: Seeing More Wisely* (New Haven, CT: Yale University Press, 2007).

33. Harold Rosenberg, "The Herd of Independent Minds," in *Discovering the Present: Three Decades in Art, Culture, and Politics* (Chicago: University of Chicago Press, 1973), 15–28.

34. The quotation from Tocqueville is from Joseph Epstein, *Alexis de Tocqueville: Democracy's Guide* (New York: HarperCollins, 2006), 4. The line from Goethe is cited in R. Bracht Branham, "Satire," in *The Oxford Handbook of Philosophy and Literature* (Oxford: Oxford University Press, 1009), 152. The other citations are from the section "Fools and Folly" in *PDE*, 125–27.

35. Robert Alter has been kind enough to lend me the manuscript of his translation of Qohelet (Ecclesiastes). I cite intermittently his version and the King James Version on the following basis: wherever I cite Alter's commentary on a passage, I also cite his translation. I also cite it whenever his version corrects the meaning of the King James Version. Where there is no significant difference, and the King James Version is familiar, I cite it. References to "Qohelet" followed by chapter and verse (e.g., "Qohelet 6:19") are to the Alter translation; references to "Ecclesiastes" are to the King James Version. When I am citing Alter's commentary, I indicate "Qohelet" followed by page numbers of the manuscript, e.g., "Qohelet, 42–43."

36. Alter gives several examples of proverbs followed by refutations. For example, he reads the two sentences of 5:9—"He who loves money will not be sated with money, and he who loves wealth will have no crop. This, too, is mere breath"—as a traditional proverb, followed by Qohelet's dismissal.

37. Alter gives "a time of mishap will befall them all," instead of "time and chance happeneth to them all," and he interprets "time of mishap" as "probably" meaning not chance but death. In that case the verse does not say that the outcome of the race is not necessarily to the swiftest but that death levels all victories. Even so, the King James version of the line has remained perhaps the best-known expression in English of unpredictability.

38. Alter: "It is possible that Qohelet's uncompromising insistence on death as a realm of utter extinction is a polemic response to the new doctrine of an afterlife that was beginning to emerge toward the end of the biblical period" (Qohelet, 59).

39. I largely agree with Robert Pippin's view of Nietzsche in a book that appeared after this manuscript was completed: Robert B. Pippin, *Nietzsche, Psychology, and First Philosophy* (Chicago: University of Chicago Press, 2010). Pippin shrewdly observes: "Nietzsche is much better understood not as a great German metaphysician, or as the last metaphysician of the West, or as the destroyer or culminator of metaphysics, or as very interested in metaphysics, or a new theory of nature at all, but as one of the great 'French moralists.' . . . The questions are clear: what *sort* of psychologist is a 'moraliste'?" (9). Pippin points out how often Nietzsche cites La Rochefoucauld, Pascal, and Montaigne.

As a maximist, Nietzsche is above all a psychologist, which is why, I suppose, he also observes: "Dostoyevsky is of importance—Dostoyevsky, the only psychologist, by the way, from whom I had anything to learn: he is one of the happiest accidents of my life, even more so than my discovery of Stendhal" (*TI*, 110).

40. As cited in Joseph Epstein, "La Rochefoucauld: Maximum Maximist," in *Life Sentences: Literary Essays* (New York: Norton, 1997), 207.

41. Francesco Guicciardini, *Maxims and Reflections (Ricordi)*, trans. Mario Domandi (Philadelphia: University of Pennsylvania Press, 1965), 47.

42. See Joseph Epstein, *Envy: The Seven Deadly Sins* (Oxford: Oxford University Press, 2003).

43. Benjamin Franklin, "Autobiography," in *Autobiography and Other Writings*, ed. Russel B. Nye (Boston: Houghton Mifflin, 1958), 32.

44. *HATH*, 40. Nietzsche continues: "La Rochefoucauld and those other French masters of soul searching . . . are like accurately aimed arrows, which hit the mark again and again, the black mark of men's nature" (40–41).

45. See Thomas Szasz, *Anti-Freud: Karl Kraus's Criticism of Psychoanalysis and Psychiatry* (Syracuse, NY: Syracuse University Press, 1990), 24, 103 (two distinct versions are given).

46. David Hume, *Principal Writings on Religion including "Dialogues Concerning Natural Religion" and "The Natural History of Religion,"* ed. J. C. A. Gaskin (Oxford: Oxford University Press, 1993).

47. "Mr. Hume, in the Natural History of Religion, sagaciously remarks that the most refined and philosophical sects are consistently the most intolerant" (*DAF*, 159).

48. This line, which has now become a maxim used as if it were an anonymous saying, appears in Georg Büchner's *Danton's Death* (1835; *YBQ*, 112). It reworks a more awkward statement by the French revolutionary Pierre Vergniaud made at his trial in 1793: "There is reason to fear that the Revolution may, like Saturn, devour each of her children one by one" (*YBQ*, 788).

49. I am especially indebted here to Joseph Epstein's description of "aphorisms" in two essays: "Chamfort, Artist of Truth," in *Pertinent Players* (New York: Norton, 1993), 160–78; and "La Rochefoucauld: Maximum Maximist," 205–23).

50. The three maxims are from La Rochefoucauld (*LaR*, 104, 104, 91).

51. Cited from Epstein, "Chamfort," 174. Epstein observes: "Here we have the *donné* for nearly all aphorists. Ah, if only man had the simple good sense to be content in solitude" (174).

52. The concluding couplet of "The Vanity of Human Wishes," in *SJ*, 58.

53. *The Portable Swift*, ed. Carl Van Doren (New York: Viking, 1963), 434–35.

54. Thomas Malthus, *An Essay on the Principle of Population*, ed. Geoffrey Gilbert (Oxford: Oxford University Press, 2008), 9.

55. Or as he also puts the point: "[T]o one [historian] it is the majesty of the Roman, the Spanish, or the French state; to another it is freedom, equality, and a certain kind of civilization that prevails in a little corner of the world known as Europe" (*W&P*, 1413).

56. C. Northcote Parkinson, *Parkinson's Law and Other Studies in Administration* (Cutchogue, NY: Buccaneer, 1957), 2.

57. Laurence J. Peter and Raymond Hull, *The Peter Principle* (New York: HarperCollins, 2009), 15.

58. Theodore Dalrymple, *Life at the Bottom: The Worldview That Makes the Underclass* (Chicago: Ivan R. Dee, 2003), 132–33.

59. Stephen Potter, *The Theory and Practice of Gamesmanship, or The Art of Winning without Actually Cheating* (n.p.: BN Publishing, 2009), 20.

60. Robert K. Merton, *Social Theory and Social Structure* (Glencoe, IL: Free Press, 1963), 423.

61. Swift, 479. The difference, of course, is that the physicians Gulliver describes "know how to approve their sagacity to the world by a seasonable dose" (479), whereas Merton is speaking of *unwitting* self-fulfillment. But those who call in a physician for a sick patient do resemble Merton's prophets because, once they believe his prognosis, they unwittingly ensure he will be proven correct. For if he should be proven incorrect, his reputation will suffer in the eyes of the world. And so their confidence in the lugubrious outcome is generally warranted.

62. Robert K. Merton, *On the Shoulders of Giants: A Shandean Postscript* (New York: Harcourt Brace, 1985), 174.

63. Szasz, *Anti-Freud*, 127, 119.

64. See Merton, "Manifest and Latent Functions," in *Social Theory and Social Structure*, 19–84.

65. Ambrose Bierce, *The Devil's Dictionary* (Garden City, NY: Dolphin, n.d.), 97, 87, 52.

66. As cited in Epstein, "Chamfort," 178.

67. *Boswell's Life of Johnson*, ed. Anne H. Ehrenpreis and Irvin Ehrenpreis (New York: Washington Square Press, 1965), 67.

68. Gustave Flaubert, *The Dictionary of Received Ideas*, trans. Geoffrey Wall (London: Penguin, 1994), 2, 2, 49, 1.

69. Lucian, "Timon," in *Selected Satires of Lucian*, ed. and trans. Lionel Casson (New York: Norton, 1968), 250–51.

70. I have in mind the magnificent stories of Vsevolod Garshin, such as "Reminiscences of Private Ivanov" and "Artists," as well as the still more complex story cycle by Isaac Babel, *Red Cavalry*.

71. *BK*, 777. The saying is often used as if it were an anonymous Latin proverb, but in fact it belongs to Terence.

CHAPTER 5

1. *The Landmark Thucydides*, trans. Richard Crowley and Robert B. Strassler, ed. Robert B. Strassler (New York: Free Press, 1996), 114.

2. From Kafka's diaries (*MDQ*, 151).

3. The remark is "attributed" and constitutes a quotation that has arisen from what the *Oxford Dictionary of Quotations* calls "oral tradition" (*ODQ*, 828).

4. From Dryden's "Alexander's Feast" (*ODQ*, 287).

5. William Shakespeare, *Henry IV, Part I*, ed. Roma Gill (Oxford: Oxford University Press, 1966), act 5, sc. 1.

6. As cited in R. F. Christian, *Tolstoy's "War and Peace": A Study* (Oxford: Oxford University Press, 1962), 64.

7. The phrase serves as the title of one of Havel's essays. See Václav Havel et al., *The Power of the Powerless: Citizens against the State in Central-Eastern Europe* (Armonk, NY: M. E. Sharpe, 1985), 23.

8. Alexander Solzhenitsyn, *Nobel Lecture* (New York: Farrar, Straus and Giroux, 1972), 33–34.

9. Joseph Addison, *"Cato: A Tragedy" and Selected Essays*, ed. Christine Dunn Henderson (Indianapolis, IN: Liberty Fund, 2004), 68.

10. Valerius Maximus, *Memorable Deeds and Sayings: One Thousand Tales from Ancient Rome*, trans. Henry John Walker (Indianapolis, IN: Hackett, 2004), 1. The introduction cited below is also Walker's.

11. William Shakespeare, *Henry V*, ed. Roma Gill (Oxford: Oxford University Press, 2000), act 4, sc. 3.

12. John Milton, *Paradise Lost: A Poem in Twelve Books*, ed. Merritt Y. Hughes (New York: Odyssey, 1962), bk. 1, ll. 663–69.

13. *Beowulf*, trans. Seamus Heaney (New York: Farrar, Straus and Giroux, 2000), ll. 2860–63.

14. Laurence Sterne, *The Life and Opinions of Tristram Shandy, Gentleman*, ed. James Aiken Work (New York: Odyssey, 1940), 64.

15. Aristotle, *Rhetoric*, in *CWA2*, 2248.

16. See *The Great Thoughts*, comp. George Seldes (New York: Ballantine, 1996). The history of the work's creation can be found in the introductions by Seldes, Henry Steele Commager, and David Laskin, each written for one of the book's editions and all included in the 1996 version.

17. Georg Christoph Lichtenberg, *The Waste Books*, trans. R. J. Hollingdale (New York: New York Review Books, 2000), 62.

18. In his introduction Hollingdale notes: "The attentive reader will notice that one or two aphorisms appear more than once, in slightly different wording, and he will understand why they do" (Lichtenberg, xxv). What is more, variations of the same idea occur in *very* different wordings as the idea is approached from different directions.

19. Charles Dickens, *Christmas Books* (Oxford: Oxford University Press, 1987), 69–70.

20. As cited in *Virtual History: Alternatives and Counterfactuals*, ed. Niall Ferguson (New York: Basic Books, 1999), 1.

21. *Roads Not Taken: Tales of Alternative History*, ed. Gardner Dozois and Stanley Schmidt (New York: Ballantine, 1998); *What If? The World's Foremost Military Historians Imagine What Might Have Been*, ed. Robert Cowley (New York: Berkeley Books, 1999); *What Might Have Been: Leading Historians on Twelve "What Ifs" of History*, ed. Andrew Roberts (London: Phoenix, 2005).

22. Jorge Luis Borges, *Labyrinths: Selected Stories and Other Writings*, ed. Donald A. Yates (New York: New Directions, 1964), 28.

CHAPTER 6

1. In *Victorian Poetry: Clough to Kipling*, ed. Arthur J. Carr (New York: Holt, Rinehart and Winston, 1966), 240–41.

2. I am indebted to correspondence with Walter Jost and conversations with the late Stephen Toulmin for my understanding of Wittgenstein's writing.

3. Obviously apocryphal; a parody for which I cannot locate a source.

4. Carl von Clausewitz, *On War*, ed. and trans. Michael Howard and Peter Paret (Princeton, NJ: Princeton University Press, 1984), 119.

5. Quotations from Lorenz as given on Michael Cross's Caltech website "The Butterfly Effect," http://crossgroup.caltech.edu/chaos_new/Lorenz.html.

6. Isaiah Berlin, *The Crooked Timber of Humanity: Chapters in the History of Ideas*, ed. Henry Hardy (New York: Knopf, 1991), 13. The title of this volume alludes to a well-known prosaic apothegm of Immanuel Kant which also serves as the book's epigraph: "From the crooked timber of humanity no straight thing can ever be made" (*ODQ*, 441).

7. The tradition includes, at a minimum, Jane Austen, Anthony Trollope, George Eliot, Leo Tolstoy, and (in drama and story) Anton Chekhov. Among more recent novels we might add George Orwell's *Keep the Aspidistra Flying* and Barbara Pym's *Excellent Women*.

8. Benjamin Franklin, "Autobiography," in *Autobiography and Other Writings*, ed. Russel B. Nye (Boston: Houghton Mifflin, 1958), 119.

9. For more on epilogue time, see *N&F*, 190–93.

10. I allude, of course, to Isaiah Berlin's famous distinction between two types of thinkers. Hedgehogs "relate everything to a single central vision . . . a single, universal organizing principle," while foxes "pursue many ends, often unrelated and even contradictory" and think in a variety of ways. Foxes "lead lives, perform acts, and entertain ideas that are centrifugal rather than centripetal[;] their thought is scattered or diffused, moving on many levels, seizing upon the essence of a vast variety of experiences and objects for what they are in themselves, without, consciously or unconsciously, seeking to fit them into . . . one unchanging, all-embracing . . . unitary inner vision." Isaiah Berlin, "The Hedgehog and the Fox," in *Russian Thinkers*, ed. Henry Hardy and Aileen Kelly (Harmondsworth, UK: Penguin, 1979), 22.

11. William James, "The Will to Believe," in *"The Will to Believe and Other Essays in Popular Philosophy" and "Human Immortality: Two Supposed Objections to the Doctrine"* (New York: Dover, 1956), 24.

CONCLUSION

1. On the pairing of ancient genres, and on satire as an answer to philosophy, see R. Bracht Branham, "Satire," in *The Oxford Handbook of Philosophy and Literature*, ed. Richard Eldridge (Oxford: Oxford University Press, 2009), 139–61.

2. Plato, *Socrates' Defense (Apology)*, in *The Collected Dialogues of Plato, including the Letters*, ed. Edith Hamilton and Huntington Cairns (Princeton, NJ: Princeton University Press, 1989), 25.

INDEX

Cited aphorisms and other quotations have often been shortened.

191–94, 230; prosaic, 193–94, 230, 233–34; in *W&P*, 192–94, 234–35

"Heroes have the whole earth for their tomb," 175, 183

Heroines of the nursery, 17

Herz, Joseph H., 246n2

Heywood, John (*Dialogue of Proverbs*), 127

"Hidden because of their familiarity" (Wittgenstein), 229

"Hideous, ghastly mistake" (Bellamy), 37

Hierarchology, 164

"Higher and higher platitudes" (Daley), 97

Hillel, Rabbi, 114–15, 246n2

Hinge of time, 180

Hippocrates, 4, 124, 221

History: and historians, 13, 116, 122, 131, 188; and progress, 161; virtual, 209–10

History in Quotations, 81

"Hitherto concealed" (Engels), 37

Hitler, Adolf, 124, 179, 185

Hollingdale, R. J., 251n18

Holmes, Oliver Wendell, Jr., 215–16, 220, 232

Holy Ghost, 38–39

"Holy rage" (Bernard of Chartres), 175–76

Homer: *Battle of the Frogs and Mice*, 237; *Iliad*, 91, 237; *Odyssey*, 91–92, 237, 246n5

Homo sum (Terence), 170, 250n71

Honor, 181–93

"Hope springs eternal" (Pope), 120

Horace, 218

Horticulture comment, 70, 64

"Hour of maximum danger" (Kennedy), 177, 179, 184

"House divided" (Mark and Lincoln), 119

"How": "many divisions has the Pope?" (Stalin), 124; "many natures" (Pascal), 202, 204; "things did not happen," 209

"How Mr. Rabbit" (Harris), 90–91

"How Much Land?" (Tolstoy), 133–34

Howlers, 96

Hugo, Victor, 98; *Last Day of a Man Condemned*, 242n11

Huizinga, Johan, 210

Human, All Too Human (Nietzsche), 142, 198–99, 204–5

Hume, David: *Dialogues Concerning Natural Religion*, 151; and Hume's law, 153–54, 162; *Natural History of Religion*, 151–52, 153–54, 227, 249n47

Humiliation, 148–49

"Hunger of imagination" (Samuel Johnson), 44

Hustings, 17

Huxley, Aldous, *Brave New World*, 65

Hymes, Dell, 243n25

Hymn to Shumash, 112

Hypocrisy, 168; and belief, 150–54; a tribute of vice to virtue, 143–44, 148

Hypothesis, 6, 39–41, 47, 164–65

Hypothetical, 205

"I": "had the radio on" (Monroe), 109; "returned and saw under the sun" (Ecclesiastes), 140; "should wish to be Diogenes" (Alexander); "shoulda said," 68; "think, therefore I am" (Descartes), 30; "transmit but do not create" (Confucius), 119

Icaromenippus (Lucian), 110

Ickes, Harold, 178

Identification with characters, 145

Identity, cultural, 173–74, 178

Ideology, 15, 35, 154, 187

Idiot (Dostoevsky), 20, 42, 45, 65, 78–79

Idiota da mente (Nicholas of Cusa), 45

If: "God himself has stood ready" (Kepler), 39; not now, when?; "there were no God" (Voltaire and D); "you can't beat 'em, join 'em," 123; "you were my wife" (Churchill), 74–75

Iktomi, 243n25

Iliad (Homer), 91, 237

"Image that has no image" (Dostoevsky), 45

"Imaginary lines on the ocean" (Tolstoy), 213

Imagination vs. dicta, 35

Imperative, 122

Imperfection, 40–41, 220, 227–28

Importance of Being Ernest, The (Wilde), 9, 86–87, 89–90

Improvisation, 68, 73, 83, 93–95

Impunity, 165

Impurity, 216, 217–18

"In": "all things faith" (George), 181; "every practical matter" (Tolstoy), 221

In-betweenness, , 201, 204

Inappropriate, 53

"Incalculably diffuse" (George Eliot), 223

"Include me out" (Goldwyn), 105

Incompleteness or unfinishedness, 196, 198–200, 201–2, 209–10

Incomprehension, 106, 109, 111

Inconsistency, 202–4, 217–18, 220, 228

"Incredulous are most credulous" (Pascal), 23

"Indispensable minus" (Dostoevsky), 92

"Inefficacy of polished periods" (Samuel Johnson), 227

Inertia vs. soul, 84
Inevitability, 179, 200, 207. *See also*
　Determinism and indeterminism
"Inferior watchmaker" (Leibniz), 32
Infinite: "heavens" (Tolstoy), 45; regress, 35;
　"variety of men's minds" (Tolstoy), 234
"Infinitely small alterations" (Tolstoy), 230
Infinity of space, 203
Innocents Abroad, The (Twain), 106, 109,
　245n48; and innocent persona, 106–11
Insane asylums, 33
Inspector General, The (Gogol), 101
Inspired innocence, 7
Instant ancestry, 188
Instantaneous: creation, 41; games, 73–76
Instruction and instructions, 96, 121–22
Instructions for King Meri-ka-re, 112, 115;
　Instructions of 'Onchsheshonqy, 115;
　Instructions of Amem-em-ope, 112–13;
　Instructions of Ptah-hotep, 3, 112–13
"Insufficiency of human enjoyments (Samuel
　Johnson), 43
Insult, 74–76, 80–81, 91, 168; "to the beasts"
　(Dostoevsky), 169; and insultee, 73
Intellectuals, 97, 157, 182, 213; Tolstoy, Orwell,
　or Flaubert on, 137, 150, 166 maxims on,
　137–38, 150, 165, 168
Intelligence, 23, 119, 123, 141, 224
Intentions, 232. *See also* Will
Interim, 126–31
"Into a space unseen" (Sophocles), 22
Introduction to the Principles of Morals
　(Bentham), 28
Inverse: detective stories, 26–28; providence,
　140
Iron laws of history, 32
Irony of origins: of beliefs, 150–51, 161–62, 170;
　of feelings, 148–50; and irony of outcomes,
　170; and La Rochefoucauld, 149–50
It's a Wonderful Life (film), 208
"Its own negation," 29, 32
Iwo Jima, 181

Jackson, Holbrook, and G. K. Chesterton,
　Platitudes Undone, 157
James, William, "Will to Believe," 58–60, 235
Jefferson, Thomas, 174
Jeremiah, Book of, 113
Jewish origin, 75
Job, Book of, 7, 128–29; and Job comforters, 128
John, Gospel of, 117–18
Johnson, Samuel, 2–3, 71, 72–73, 81, 165;

Rasselas, 2, 43–44, 64, 167, 222, 227–29;
　"Vanity of Human Wishes," 2, 158–59
Jokes, 17, 93, 102, 131; and jokebooks, 89–90
Jones, John Paul, 174
Joubert, Joseph, 3, 69, 148–49, 156
Joyce, James, 133–34
Judo, mental, 74
Jumping Frog essay (Twain), 107
Justice, 116, 121, 149–53 passim, 158, 178; and
　interim, 127–31; and Tolstoy's moral tales,
　134–36
Juvenal, 159

Kant, Immanuel, 217; *Critique of Pure Reason*,
　44, 55; "crooked timber," 252n6
Karma, 116
Keaton, Buster, 104, 244n43
Keats, John, 98
Keep the Aspidistra Flying (Orwell), 252n7
Kennedy, John F., 1, 177, 179, 184–85, 209
Kepler, Johannes, 30, 39
"Key to all mysteries" (George Eliot), 231
Kierkegaard, Søren, 60
King James Bible, 116, 138–41
King, Martin Luther, Jr., 174
Kings 1 and 2, 112, 118
Kisewetter's Logic, 54
"Kissing in the basket" (Danton), 80–81
Kitsch, 99
Kleos, 183
"Know the whole cloth" (Flaubert), 138
"Know thyself," 125
Knowing about vs. from within, 53
Knowledge, 6, 55–58
Kraus, Karl, 3, 7, 151, 162, 164–65
Krylov, Ivan, 131
Kutuzov, General 62, 87, 88–89, 189

La Bruyère, Jean de, 3, 10, 158
La Fontaine, Jean de, 131
La Rochefoucauld, François de, 3–10 passim,
　140, 142, 146–50 passim, 154–59 passim,
　163–68 passim, 218; and Nietzsche, 248n39;
　on wit, 86
Lady Windemere's Fan (Wilde), 243n22
Lamoral, Charles-Joseph, 137
Language: Spinoza and, 34; W and, 214
Lao Tzu, *Tao Te Ching*) 10, 21, 41, 46–48, 211;
　and nonaction, 61–62
Laskin, David, 251n16
Last Day of a Man Condemned, The (Hugo),
　242n11